The Valuation of Information Technology

Lisa,
I hope you enjoy
the book!

Cheers,

Wiley Financial Management Series

Business Portfolio Management: Valuation, Risk Assessment, and EVA™ Strategies, by Michael S. Allen, Strategic Decisions Group

The Valuation of Information Technology: A Guide for Strategy Development, Valuation, and Financial Planning, by Christopher Gardner

The Valuation of Information Technology

A GUIDE FOR STRATEGY DEVELOPMENT, VALUATION, AND FINANCIAL PLANNING

Christopher Gardner

JOHN WILEY & SONS, INC.

New York ➤ Chichester ➤ Weinheim ➤ Brisbane ➤ Singapore ➤ Toronto

Published by John Wiley & Sons, Inc.

Published simultaneously in Canada.

This publication is designed to provide accurate and authoritative information in regard to the subject matter covered. It is sold with the understanding that neither the author or the publisher is engaged in rendering legal, accounting, or other professional services. If legal advice or other expert assistance is required, the services of a competent professional person should be sought.

Library of Congress Cataloging-in-Publication Data:

Gardner, Christopher, 1957–
    The valuation of information technology : a guide for strategy development, valuation, and financial planning / Christopher Gardner.
        p.   cm. — (Wiley financial management series)
    Includes bibliographical references and index.
    ISBN 0-471-37831-3 (cloth : alk. paper)
    1. Information technology—Management. I. Title.
II. Series.
HD30.2.G37   2000
658.4'038—dc21   99-046349

Printed in the United States of America.
10 9 8 7 6 5 4 3 2 1

To the NICU kids . . .

. . . , their families, and the medical
professionals in charge of their care.

Contents

Acknowledgments

Writing a book involves both your professional and personal life. The ideas in this book come from experience gained throughout a career that has been focused on technology strategy development and an academic background in technology and finance. In this regard, I am indebted to the many clients, colleagues, friends, and teachers with whom I have worked.

Special thanks within this group go to the reviewers who labored through early drafts of the manuscript and provided many helpful comments. To impose some quality control, the following experts read the chapters noted: Jim Szafranski, a marketing manager at Tut Systems, Chapters 2, 3, and 4 along with Paul Hase, a partner at Hase-Schannen Research, who reviewed the questionnaire in Chapter 3; Dr. Khasha Mohammadi, a member of the technical staff at Bell Labs and now president of e-networks, Chapter 5; Larry Heyl, a principal engineer at Apple Computer, Chapters 6 and 7; and Jens Jorgensen, an associate partner at Andersen Consulting, Chapter 8. Dr. Rainer Famulla, a partner at Andersen Consulting, and Steve Bonner, former president of the Construction Information Group at McGraw-Hill, provided input on the overall book. An additional contribution was made by Dr. Gagan Choudhury of AT&T Laboratories.

I have been privileged to have Professor Mel Schwartz of the physics department at Stanford and Columbia Universities (now retired) provide valuable advice at crucial junctures in my career over a 20-year period. His influence has been direct, substantial, and positive, setting me forth on my journey to combine science with industry. Professor Merton Miller taught me corporate finance at the University of Chicago and instilled in me the belief that there was some hope for applying quantitative methods to business. Professor Robert S. Hamada, dean of the University of Chicago Graduate School of Business, provided crucial support for the book's publication.

I am indebted to four individuals for relaying some of the lessons they have learned from publishing: Tom Davenport, who has authored *Working Knowledge, Process Engineering, and Information Ecology*; Geoffrey Huck, a senior editor at the University of Chicago Press; Frank Ostroff, who is the author of *The Horizontal Organization*; and Professor Edward Tufte of Yale University, who founded Graphics Press.

My partners at PricewaterhouseCoopers LLP have offered encouragement and expressed unselfish support for the book. Their dedication to fairness and accuracy makes the fact that they cared meaningful. They have my respect and appreciation.

My editor, Jeanne Glasser, has been a true professional and a joy to work with throughout the publication process. She has been ably assisted by Linda Indig, managing editor. The entire team at John Wiley & Sons of marketing, sales, production, distribution, and service personnel have my thanks.

The staff of Phoenix Technical Publications have done a wonderful job of producing the illustrations. They are leaders in developing accurate and readable technical manuals for Silicon Valley. Final preparation of the manuscript was skillfully done by Nancy Marcus Land and her staff at Publications Development Company. Companies that have graciously provided material and illustrations for the book are CACI, Chrislin, IBM, Palo Alto Cable Coop, RAND, Seagate, Sun Microsystems, and Toshiba. My thanks here to Ron Kirkeeng, Ron Seese, Leland Johnson, and David Reed.

The emotional drive that enabled me to complete the book can be traced to family and friends who provided support for what became a more than one-year effort. My gratitude goes to my wife, Magdalen, and my son, George; my parents, Joseph and Ida; my brothers and sisters, Tony, Nancy, John, Margo, James, Julie, Grandy, Martha, Maria, Andy, Georgia, and Tasos; and to my longtime friend Skip Bean.

The involvement of all these individuals not only improved the text, it helped sustain me while writing it. Without them there simply would be no book. Their support has been strong enough that I could convince myself to write another!

C.G.

Introduction

Information technology does not come with instructions on how to use it. The success stories in information technology are widely known: America Online, @Home, Windows 95, the Macintosh, Sabre. The truth, however, is there has also been an unnecessarily high number of failures. To list just a few representing several hundred million dollars in write-offs: Qube, Indax, Teleaction, Topview, OS/2, DR-DOS, Professional PC, PCjr, the Newton. For the companies involved, these were simply great planning disasters.

The reason for this mediocre record is that the effect of information technology on a company's shareholder value has been largely unpredictable. Companies have found they must choose among a bewildering number of possible alternatives for using information technology. Without a method for analyzing these alternatives, choices have had to be made on the basis of fragmentary data, guesswork, and plain luck. Under these circumstances, a change in personnel, perspective, or even mood can lead to the choice of a different alternative. This is chaos—a small change in initial conditions can lead to a large difference in the future outcome.

To cut through the chaos, people are needed who know how to measure the shareholder value created by an information technology system *before it is built*. Measurement can answer the critical questions: What contribution will an information technology system make to a company's shareholder value? How can an information technology system be constructed to create shareholder value? In other words, not just determine the effect of a system on shareholder value but guide the activities involved in its construction in the first place.

The growth in the use of information technology has created strong demand in industry for people skilled in measuring shareholder value, who can answer these questions. This book lays out a method for measuring the effect on shareholder value of information technology systems, so that readers may develop this skill themselves.

The techniques developed in the book reflect nearly 20 years of research and experience in the high-technology industry and management consulting, as well as the latest academic thinking in technology and finance. They have been tested and put into practice at companies such as AT&T, Compaq, and McGraw-Hill. Their application has led to, and explains, major developments in industry such as AT&T's acquisition of the cable television giant Tele-Communications, Inc.

■ THEMES AND CONCLUSIONS

This book is a *tool* for creating shareholder value with information technology. Five themes have shaped the writing:

1. *A shareholder value perspective.* The responsibility of management is to generate sustained high returns for their shareholders. This objective is infused throughout the book.

2. *A focus on getting answers.* The book explains step-by-step how to estimate the shareholder value created by an information system. The answer arrived at is in the form of a share price, which is the most practical, relevant, and understandable form for management.

3. *A real-world connection.* Intertwined throughout the text are examples that show how the analytical methods described are applied in practice. These examples are timely, dealing with opportunities such as home banking, cable modems, PBXs, the AT&T/Tele-Communications merger, and a Time Warner/@Home joint venture.

4. *An emphasis on ease of use.* Liberal use of pictures, direct language, and an intuitive organization make the text clear and accessible. It is written at the undergraduate level. Solutions are provided for the problem sets that conclude each chapter. A glossary, bibliography, and index are provided. A downloadable file of the three spreadsheets illustrated in the text is available as supplemental material at christophergardner.com.

5. *A widely applicable approach.* Any information system that can be specified in a quantitative way can be analyzed using the techniques in the book. The entire range of computer system structures from large-scale networks to small-scale palmtops, as well as analog system structures, such as television, the phonograph, and microfilm, can be analyzed successfully. The information system does not need to be built to be analyzed.

After concluding the book, readers will have sufficient knowledge to tackle many kinds of practical problems. They will have the skill to apply an analytical approach that lays bare how to assess whether the economics of an information technology system are attractive. This will make corporate decision making more rational and the results repeatable. The long-term benefit for companies will be more productive use of capital and labor because fewer investment mistakes will be made in applying information technology in their organizations.

■ INTENDED READERSHIP

This book is intended for management consultants, business executives, technology professionals, financial analysts, venture capitalists, and anyone else with an interest in information systems development. The book can be used as a *management* tool that lays out the questions that need to be addressed in developing an information system, and as an *analytical* tool that lays out how to get the answers. This results in three types of audiences who will benefit from this book: (1) consultants will use the book for both purposes to provide a complete solution to the problem of developing an information system; (2) business executives will use it as a management tool to structure the work involved in developing an information system; and (3) technology professionals will use the book as an analytical tool to conduct this work on behalf of management.

Readers can come from any industry. The book, if it serves its purpose, should become dog-eared from use especially by those in information-intensive industries such as media (entertainment and publishing), telecommunications (telephone, broadcasting, and cable), financial services (banking and insurance), and high technology (computing, software, storage, and networking).

■ SIMILAR BOOKS

There is nothing in the current literature on business and technology, of which the author is aware, that addresses the subject of this book in a *quantitative* way. This book starts with an initial information system concept and carries it all the way through to a quantitative determination of *the actual effect the information system has on the share price of a company*. It integrates techniques from three disciplines— market research, computer science, and corporate finance— to show how to maximize the chances for an economic success in applying information technology. It is a disciplined, rigorous book, not a casual read. It is hoped that some will view it as a standard reference.

A major flaw of most books on the management of technology is that they do not treat their subject in a multidisciplinary and quantitative fashion. The focus is usually on one aspect of the management of technology—such as marketing, finance, manufacturing, or research and development—which is discussed in a prolix style. The result is a book that provides a partial view of the problem and does not get specific about economic impact. The books that do provide a quantitative approach do not focus on information systems. Yet business executives and technical professionals are expected to judge the impact their information system decisions have on a company's share price. Today, they must rely on their experience and intuition to sort through this problem, which is often faulty as their track record shows, since they lack a proper tool at this time.

■ ORGANIZATION OF THE BOOK

The structure of the book is intuitive. Chapter 1 describes the overarching framework and the limits of its applicability. Chapter 2 shows how to identify an opportunity worth capitalizing on. Chapters 3 and 4 focus on listening to the "voice of the customer," translating it into a demand assessment. Chapters 5 and 6 cover the construction of a system, dealing in turn with information flows and capacity requirements, and system design alternatives. Chapter 7 begins the assessment of system economics by describing the process of cost estimation. Chapter 8 shows how the results from the previous chapters can be integrated into an economic model for decision making.

The book is written in a deductive style. The conclusion logically derives from the sequence of points made previously. This means the last chapter is just as important as the first. Though some chapters may be skipped if the reader is already familiar with the material, the argument of the book depends heavily on following the steps described chapter-by-chapter in sequence.

■ A WORD OF CAUTION

Shareholder interests are relentlessly pursued and upheld in this book. The reader should maintain a broad perspective when deciding whether to move forward with an investment in an information technology system. The shareholder's standpoint is not the only one worth considering. From an ethical standpoint, the issue of whether the information system provides a social good must be resolved. The shareholder's standpoint is represented by a large body of management literature such as *Competitive Advantage, In Search of Excellence,* and *The Economic Way of Thinking.* This book belongs to this genre. The ethical standpoint represents a rich topic that has been explored in works of art like *Fail-Safe, Jurassic Park, The Truman Show,* and *1984.* This book is about as far removed from these works as can be imagined.

Depending on the context, sometimes the word *product* or *service* is used in the text. These words should be thought of as interchangeable. The selection of one over the other in a passage is purely stylistic.

A book such as this probably contains some errors, though every effort has been made to eliminate them. Comments, factual or otherwise, are welcome and can be sent to the author by visiting christophergardner.com. Corrections will be incorporated into future printings of the book.

Part I

Framework

Chapter 1

Overarching Framework

But come, you suitors, since here is a prize set out before you; for I shall bring you the great bow of godlike Odysseus. And the one who takes the bow in his hand, strings it with the greatest ease, and sends an arrow clean through all the twelve axes, shall be the one I go away with ...

—Penelope promising marriage to the best archer
The Odyssey of Homer XXI, 73–77
(translated by R. Lattimore)

We begin by describing the overarching framework for analyzing the economics of information technology systems, around which this book is structured. The starting point is to develop a clear understanding of the objective used to distinguish attractive systems from those that are not.

■ 1.1 OBJECTIVE

The objective of information technology systems development in business is to increase the wealth of shareholders by adding to the growth premium of their stock. Ideally, the increase achieved should be the maximum obtainable. Maximizing shareholder wealth consists of maximizing the value of the cash flow stream generated by operations, specifically those cash flows that are generated by a future investment in an information technology system (see Figure 1.1). This is

3

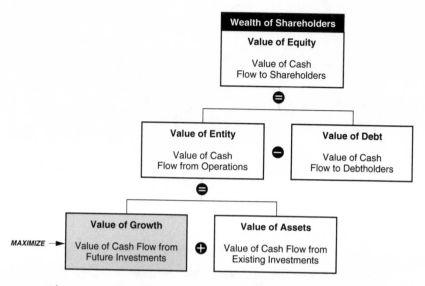

Figure 1.1 Strategic Objective: Maximize Value of Growth.

the objective that is used here as the basis for determining whether an information technology system has attractive economics.

■ 1.2 ANALYTICAL FRAMEWORK

Conceptually, the framework for analyzing the economics of information technology systems is simple. The first step is to identify the target customer opportunity. The second step is to align the information technology system to cost-effectively provide the features customers want. The third and final step is to accurately measure the economic value that can be captured (see Figure 1.2). An analogy can be drawn between this process and archery: picking the target, aiming the bow and arrow at the most vital point, and gauging the spoils before shooting.

The practical application of this analytical framework, however, is complex. It requires taking a quantitative approach

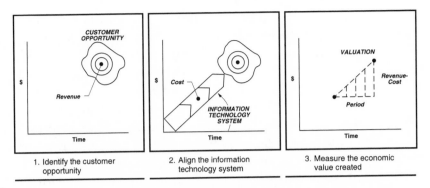

Figure 1.2 Analytical Framework.

at each step, with the level of accuracy obtained proportional to the amount of rigor in the analysis. The result is the quantification of the shareholder value created by an information technology system.

Often a first analysis will show that what customers desire is not technically achievable or economically attractive. Multiple iterations of an analysis may be required to resolve the tension between segment-specific desires and time-dependent technology and economics. As in archery, a target may be beyond the reach of the bow and arrow (not technically achievable) or a target may not be worth expending an arrow on (not economically attractive). In this way, wild ideas can be separated from those that truly have promise, based on their bottom line impact.

■ 1.3 SCOPE

To avoid possible confusion, the range of information technology systems encompassed and the limits of applicability of the framework need to be spelled out.

An information technology system is defined as a means for automating data, voice, video, or multimedia information flows. This definition is broader than the classical datacentric view to reflect that a digital signal of adequate bandwidth can carry any of these types of information, leading to the convergence of industries that once separately handled data, voice, and video. Simultaneously, it includes the traditional analog approaches of the past that are still with us today. *Data,* as used here, includes all alphanumeric and graphical information (e.g., text, spreadsheets, graphics). *Voice* includes all audio information (e.g., speech and music). *Video* includes all image information (e.g., still-frame and full-motion). *Multimedia* is any combination of the preceding.

➤ Range of Systems Encompassed

Any information system that can be specified in a quantitative way can be analyzed with this framework. The range of systems encompassed is, therefore, quite general. Essentially, any "black box" where information is input, processed, and output falls within our capability for analysis. The information system does not need to be built to be analyzed.

To illustrate (see Figure 1.3), at the highest level the *information* represented can be video, voice, and data separately or in combination. The signal used to represent the information can be digital or analog. The *system* can be networked or stand-alone. If networked, communication can be one-to-one (switched) or one-to-many (broadcast). Transmission can be interactive (2-way) or passive (1-way). Additional choices of distance (e.g., local or long-distance), medium (e.g., wired or wireless), and detailed implementation approach can be made. Thus, the entire range of computer system structures, from large-scale networks to small-scale palmtops, can be analyzed successfully. In addition, analog system structures, such as television, the phonograph, and microfilm can be analyzed.

➤ Limits of Applicability

The output of the analysis is a valuation of the cash flow stream generated by an information technology system. The

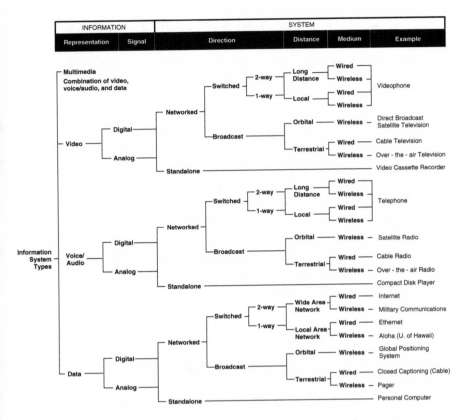

Figure 1.3 Range of Systems Encompassed.

limits of its applicability emerge, therefore, under those circumstances in which a well-defined valuation cannot be calculated. The circumstances that characterize this danger zone are:

➤ The use of the system cannot be clearly described or understood by customers. This can make it extremely difficult to assess the revenues from new services or estimate the cost savings that can be achieved.

➤ The capacity and performance requirements of the system cannot be determined. This can create a situation where the type of system that should be built is unknown.

➤ The system design has technical problems that have never been solved before, creating large uncertainties in function, performance, schedule, and cost estimates.

➤ Costs are not well understood. For example, potential cost variations are large and unpredictable. This can create a situation where establishing a reasonable cost estimate is prone to substantial error.

These circumstances often arise when one is dealing with "bleeding" edge technology, highly complex projects, and far-out time horizons. In the 1950s, estimating the demand for computers was difficult because potential customers (or vendors for that matter) could not envisage its uses. In the early years of computer networking, nobody knew whether the traffic would consist of mostly short or long, frequent or infrequent messages—a consideration with major implications for network capacity and performance. The developers of supercomputers planned to use revolutionary wafer-scale integrated circuits, until they encountered insurmountable heat dissipation problems. Last, improperly sized application software development efforts have often led to large, unpredicted cost overruns.

Two approaches for handling the analysis can provide useful results (see Figure 1.4), should you find yourself in this danger zone. The first applies when the accuracy of the valuation falls just below the minimum acceptable level (see Figure 1.5) and involves performing a "scenario assessment." In this case, scenarios should be developed that can be translated into variations of inputs, and a range of valuations obtained to bracket the results and gauge the amount of uncertainty and risk. The second approach applies when the error in the valuation is extreme, and can be used to set system development targets. Here, a domain of valuations should be obtained by parameterizing the inputs and deriving the combinations of input levels that yield acceptable valuations. These input level combinations can then be set as system development targets.

The *minimum acceptable accuracy level* is a function of the magnitude of the financial impact and the degree to which the business case either for or against is compelling (see Figure 1.5). The magnitude of the financial impact can

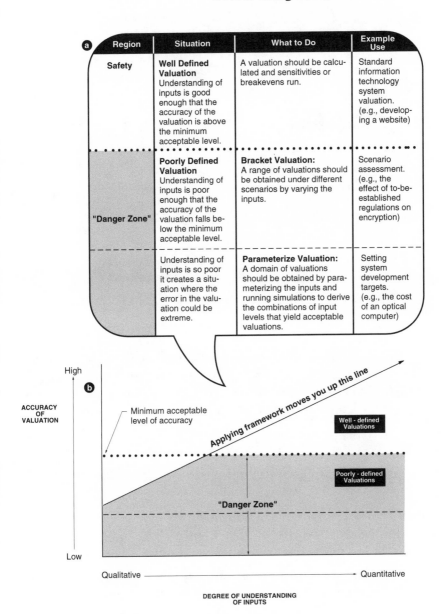

Figure 1.4 Limits of Applicability.

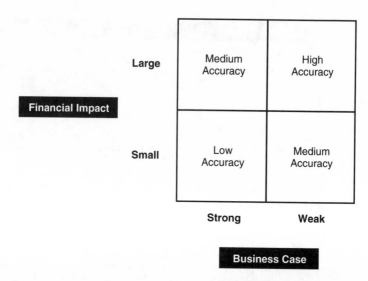

Figure 1.5   Minimum Acceptable Level of Accuracy of Valuation.

be assessed against capital budgets and income projections. The business case can be viewed as strong if the valuation is found to be large in either a positive (for) or negative (against) direction. It is weak if the valuation is close to zero.

■ PROBLEMS AND SOLUTIONS

Problem 1.1:   Under what conditions is maximizing shareholder wealth (equity value) identical to maximizing the value of the cash flow stream generated by a system?

Solution: The value of equity equals the value of operations less the value of debt. The value of operations and debt is equal to the cash flow from operations and the cash flow to debtholders, respectively, discounted at the appropriate risk-adjusted rates. So the required conditions are the cash flow to debtholders must be held constant and the system project does not change the risk profile.

Problem 1.2: What are some ways the analytical framework could result in a finding that the economics of a system are unattractive?

Solution: The customer opportunity could be of insufficient size; the cost to address the opportunity may be too high; the window of opportunity may be too narrow or too distant in time; and the risk of failure may be too high.

Problem 1.3: What are some examples that fit the definition of an information technology system other than those listed in Figure 1.3?

Solution: High-definition television, amateur radio, and stereo systems.

Problem 1.4: Give some additional real-world examples of cases that fall outside the limit of applicability of the analytical framework.

Solution: Massively parallel processors, josephson junctions, optical computers (as of 1999).

Part II

Customer Opportunity

Chapter 2

Directing Attention

They sought it with thimbles, they sought it with care;
    They pursued it with forks and hope;
They threatened its life with a railway-share;
    They charmed it with smiles and soap.

And the Banker, inspired with a courage so new
    It was matter for general remark,
Rushed madly ahead and was lost to their view,
    In his zeal to discover the Snark.

—Lewis Carroll, *The Hunting of the Snark:*
An Agony in Eight Fits

Identifying a customer opportunity worth capitalizing on—and developing a clear understanding of it—is necessary for guiding the design of an information technology system and assessing the demand for the services it will provide. This is relatively hard to do if the customer opportunity is based on speculation about the future, which is the case when developing new or enhanced services. It is easy if the customer opportunity has an extensive historical record, which is the case when information technology is applied to reduce the cost of providing existing services.

Directing attention toward either of these types of promising opportunities involves surveying each of the sources of shareholder value. The amount of value delivered to and received from customers must be measured to assess the overall level of demand (the size of the pie). The amount of value that can be captured from shareholder rivals must be measured to assess the relative advantage of the company to satisfy the demand (how the pie is sliced). For existing service cost reduction opportunities, the overall level of demand can often be assumed to be unchanged, greatly simplifying the work.

■ 2.1 VALUE DELIVERED TO AND RECEIVED FROM CUSTOMERS

To identify promising customer opportunities requires broadly knowing the customer segment to target, the information requirements of the activities performed, and where value can be added.

Customers can be either consumers or businesses. Consumers can be segmented in a variety of ways, using their physical, mental, behavioral, experiential, financial, and relational characteristics to describe them. Similar characteristics apply to businesses. One or more segments can be served simultaneously (see Figure 2.1).

There are three important tests of a segmentation. First, the customers within it should have common wants so a consistent strategy can be put in place to serve them. Second, a segmentation needs to be "actionable," which means there must be a way to efficiently reach customers falling within it. Today, specialized databases and mailing lists are typically used for this purpose (e.g., Dun & Bradstreet). In the future, customers may post this information on the Internet themselves. Third, there must be a promising business opportunity associated with the segment. To determine this, the investigator must examine the information requirements of the activities performed by each segment.

Information requirements span news, entertainment, advertising, communications, transactions, analysis, and so on. Activities performed by *consumers* can be described as how they spend their time at home, work, and commuting or traveling.[1]

Consumer Characteristics		
Physical	**Mental**	**Behavioral**
• Age	• Education	• Usage
• Size	• Religion	• Occupation
• Sex	• Language	• Habits
• Health	• Skills	• Travel
• Location	• Disposition	• Hobbies
Experiential	**Financial**	**Relational**
• Life-Stage Event	• Income	• Family
• Occasion	• Assets	• Work
• Act-of-God	• Liabilities	• Community
• Promotion	• Profitability	• Military
• Legal Action	• Risk	• Political
Business Characteristics		
Physical	**Organizational**	**Behavioral**
• Age	• Culture	• Usage of Inputs
• Size	• Strategy	• Product Output
• Growth	• Skills	• Processing Method
• Safety	• Values	• Efficiency
• Location	• Systems	• Motives
Developmental	**Financial**	**Relational**
• Lifecycle Stage	• Income	• Customer
• Inflection Point	• Assets	• Supplier
• External Shock	• Liabilities	• Competitor
• Expansion	• Capital	• Investor
• Merger	• Risk	• Regulator

Figure 2.1   Customer Segments—Examples.

Combining possible information requirements with each consumer activity reveals promising new opportunities to serve consumers. For example, bank transactions are frequently conducted while consumers are commuting or traveling but can also be conducted while consumers are at home. Applying an age-based segmentation, children as well as adults could be potential users of an electronic branch-in-the-home, creating an opportunity to build a *bank-for-kids,* not just home banking for adults. Further fractal-like examination will reveal a rich set of information requirements to support the banking activities of children, such as transactions to transfer funds between accounts of a parent and child.

Activities performed by *businesses* can be categorized under functions such as research and development, manufacturing, sales, service, and administration. An alternative categorization is to use processes such as product development, manufacturing workflow, logistics, customer communications, and service and repair. *Combining possible information requirements with each business activity reveals promising new opportunities to serve businesses.* For example, insurance policy purchase transactions may be normally handled by the sales function but could also be cross-sold by policy service. These combinations can include providing several types of information for a single activity. Advertising could be coupled with a purchase transaction so that demand stimulation and fulfillment occur simultaneously, and music could be added to reinforce the brand.

Sharing information between segments, and across or within activities, increases the universe of opportunities and must also be considered (see Figure 2.2). This can be examined by tracing how information flows among consumers or businesses. For example, in the construction industry CAD files of blueprints could be shared by the architect, contractor, inspector, and owner segments; an exchange for rapidly allocating technical resources in a computer company would involve sharing information on equipment and technical personnel across the activities of engineering, manufacturing, and service; lastly, software can be used to integrate news, analysis, communications, and transactions to improve the investment performance of a Wall Street trader.

Factors that affect the value delivered to customers must also be noted as part of the information requirements of an activity. A description should be developed of the content, format, timeliness, and correctness of the information to be provided.[2] Sometimes an opportunity can be based solely on improving one of these factors, such as offering foreign-language formats of magazines, speeding up the analysis of

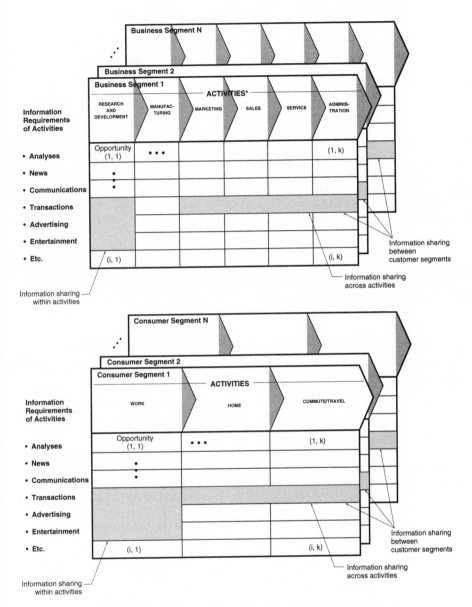

* These can be shown as functions (used here), or as core processes, organizational units, etc.

Figure 2.2 Framework for Identifying Promising Customer Opportunities.

1. Introduction

A. Courtesies

Make introductions and thank interviewee for agreeing to participate.

B. Research Objectives

Relay that the point of the interview is to understand what information would be most valuable to interviewees so that they may be better served. This will require understanding:
The activities they perform and any trends/changes.
The associated information requirements.
The potential value to them of this information.

C. Guidelines

Discuss how the results will be treated. Usually it is helpful to state that they will not be asked for any proprietary or confidential information and will not be quoted without permission.

Provide a brief overview of the questions you plan to ask and how long the discussion should last. Get confirmation that they are comfortable with this and ask if there are any questions.

2. Questions to Ask

Before asking the following questions, the interviewer should develop hypotheses on the answers to test specific ideas on possible opportunities and to keep the discussion focused.

A. Activities Performed

What activities do you perform in a typical day?
What sequence do these activities follow?
What is the objective of each activity?
When are these activities performed?
Who else is involved in each activity and what is their role?
Where are these activities performed?
How are these activities performed?
What trends/changes do you foresee?

B. Information Required

What information would you like to have to perform these activities?
How should this information be organized—content/format/timeliness/
correctness
How could the information that you do have be improved?
How could information be shared?
Between segments.
Across or within activities.
We have several ideas on new information opportunities. Do you think these information services would be useful to you?

C. Potential Value

Which activities take the most money or time to complete?
How much do you spend on these activities?
Which activities are the most important in terms of value leveraged?
How much economic leverage do they have?

Figure 2.3 Customer Opportunity Interview Guide.

What gains can you realize in wages, revenue, or investment income if you had the information you want?

What information substitutes are available?

How much are you spending on this substitute information?

Will the information you want reduce your risk? How much?

Would the ideas we described earlier deliver significant value to you? How much?

If you had the choice between spending your money on the new information we could provide versus spending it on your other alternatives, which would you choose? What are these alternatives?

3. Wrap-Up

A. Background

Capture any relevant information on the background of the interviewee such as:

Role and responsibility.

Experience.

Name, address, phone number.

B. Closing

Thank the interviewee for his/her time. Ask for referrals and permission to follow up if needed.

Provide an honorarium as needed.

Figure 2.3 *(Continued)*

pricing movements in the stock market, and improving the security of financial transactions.

To narrow down the opportunities that have been identified at this point, the evaluator must interview customers to determine what information requirements are most valuable to them (see Figure 2.3). The potential value can be gauged by the gains that can be realized in customer wages, revenue, or investment income; the amount of customer spending on substitute information; the reduction of assumed risks; and opportunity costs. In the case of an electronic bank-for-kids, the value to consumers is in such things as the interest earned on deposits, the tax benefits of sheltering interest income in a child's bank account, the amount saved by parents avoiding trips to the bank, the benefits of teaching children good financial habits, and the reduced risk of loss of funds due to the safety and security offered by a bank (see Figure 2.4). This value must outweigh the value of any alternative opportunities that a consumer sacrifices to sign up for an electronic bank-for-kids.

	Annual Value to Consumers	Assumptions
Interest Earned by Child on Deposits	$5 per child	Child places $200 in gifts and allowances on deposit earning 5% interest. This, however, does not apply to the 50% of children with a previous bank account who already earn this interest.
Taxes Avoided by Sheltering Interest Income	$90 per child	Parents transfer $5,000 into child's account which generates $250 interest income that is taxed at the child's rate of 0% rather than the parents' rate of 36%. Convenience of electronic transfers between accounts makes this tax shelter attractive even if children have a previous bank account.
Savings from Eliminating Trips to the Bank	$25 per household	Each trip to the bank takes half an hour; 6 trips are made per year by the 50% of children who have bank accounts already (this savings only applies to them); the average wage of parent accompanying the child is $17 per hour.
Benefits of Teaching Kids Good Financial Habits	$25 per child	Estimate savings at 12% of child's deposits each year. Greater interaction with an electronic bank causes this benefit to carry over to children who have bank accounts already.
Reduced Risk of Loss of Funds Due to Safety & Security of Bank Account	$5 per child	Estimate loss reduction at 5% of child's deposits each year. This value is already received by the 50% of children with a previous bank account.
Subtotal	$150 per year for 1 child	
Total	About $300 per year for 2.2 children (average married couple with children)	

Figure 2.4 Value to Consumers of an Electronic Bank-for-Kids.

A market profile that details the size of each customer segment must be developed so that opportunities can be scaled to reflect the number of potential customers.[3] In the case of a bank-for-kids, data that shows the size of the children's segment by age, family income, and households with computers would be useful. This can be found using resources like the U.S. Bureau of the Census, the "Sports Illustrated for Kids Omnibus Study," the book *Kids as Customers: A Handbook of Marketing to Children* (New York, Lexington Books), the U.S. National Center for Education Statistics, and Dataquest reports (see Figure 2.5). After examining the data provided by these resources, it is apparent that the "family income of $50,000 and over" segment is the most

Money Income of Families with Children under 18 Years Old Living with One or Both Parents—1995

Family Income	Number of Households with Children Under 18 Living with:		
	Both Parents	Mother Only	Father Only
$50,000 and over	10,054,000	370,000	123,000
$40,000 to $49,999	3,030,000	258,000	56,000
$30,000 to $39,999	3,194,000	484,000	105,000
$25,000 to $29,999	1,409,000	302,000	58,000
$15,000 to $24,999	2,535,000	926,000	173,000
$10,000 to $14,999	1,002,000	772,000	103,000
$5,000 to $9,999	632,000	1,133,000	73,000
under $5,000	289,000	764,000	45,000

Source. U.S. Bureau of the Census; Analysis.

Children Using Computers at Home—1993

Family Income	Prekindergarten and Kindergarten %	Grades 1–8 %	Grades 9–12 %
$75,000 and over	38	62	61
$50,000 to $74,999	26	45	46
$40,000 to $49,999	22	33	34
$35,000 to $39,999	13	26	28
$30,000 to $34,999	19	21	29
$25,000 to $29,999	12	19	22
$20,000 to $24,999	7	13	18
$15,000 to $19,999	7	11	14
$10,000 to $14,999	5	6	9
$5,000 to $9,999	1	5	5
under $5,000	1	4	7

Source. U.S. National Center for Education Statistics, "Digest of Education Statistics."

Figure 2.5 Market Profile of Bank-for-Kids Segments.

likely segment to sign up for an electronic bank-for-kids as well as the most attractive to serve.

If we focus our initial offering at the "family income of $50,000 and over" segment, 10.5 million households can be targeted, of which about 50% have children already using computers at home. This means that there are about 5.25 million households that could receive about $300 per year in value from this service, and another 5.25 million households waiting in the wings as computers penetrate the home more fully. These numbers are significant when compared with the retail customer base of the largest U.S. banks. Approximately $1.5 to $3 billion in value would be generated for this particular customer segment by a bank-for-kids.[4]

At this point we now know very crudely the potential value to customers and the size of each customer segment. The resulting estimate of the magnitude of the customer opportunity provides perspective on how much value there is to go around among the shareholder rivals that will lay claims on it. A company's *shareholders* must vie with *customers* who would like to pay as low a price as they can for the value they receive; *competitors* will try to divert as many customers toward themselves as possible; *suppliers* will try to keep the cost of purchased items as high as possible; *employees* will try to maximize their compensation levels; and the *government* will impose taxes and regulations (see Figure 2.6).

Just how much value can be retained by shareholders is a function of the relative advantage of the company. A quick assessment of whether a company is significantly vulnerable to one of these rivals should be made to see if there are any showstoppers that would argue against pursuing the opportunity further. If there are none, the techniques laid out in the remainder of this book will show how to quantify the shareholder value that could be generated. Generally speaking, if the magnitude of the customer opportunity is large, it is more likely that there will be enough value to go around for all rivals. Of course, the more customers, suppliers, and employees—and the fewer the competitors, taxes,

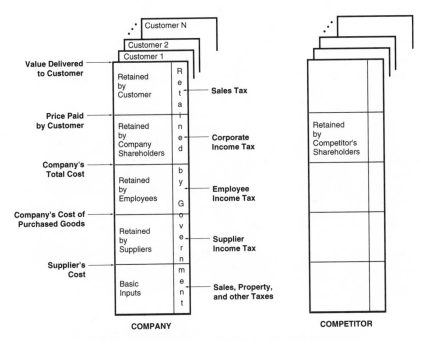

Figure 2.6 Value Captured by Shareholder Rivals.

and regulations—the better for the shareholder. The most promising opportunities, then, are those providing the greatest value to the largest number of customers and where the competitive advantage is high.

Returning to the bank-for-kids example, the value received by a bank from these customers could be substantial, if we assume the tax advantages draw in more deposits from the parents, the market share of the bank increases, and the household retention rate improves (see Figure 2.7). These are quite possible, for an electronic bank could be designed to manage deposits to maximize tax benefits, and a strategic partnership with a key player in the kids market such as The Walt Disney Company or Time Warner could create a sustained competitive advantage. A bank offering an electronic bank-for-kids does not appear to be significantly vulnerable to its other rivals—employees, suppliers, and the government. A rough estimate of the opportunity for banks is then $175 per year per household multiplied by the size of the

	Annual Value to Bank	Assumptions
Interest Income on Child's Deposits	$4 per child	4% spread on $200. Applies to the 50% of children without a previous bank account.
Fee Revenue	$6 per child	$1 per month for special requests. Applies to the 50% of children without a previous bank account.
Increase in Parent's Deposits Drawn in by Tax Advantages	$40 per child	Additional $1,000 in deposits at 4% spread. Applies to children with and without a previous bank account.
Increase in Market Share	$25 per household	5% of households are new to the bank. Each household generates $10,000 in deposits at 4% spread and $10 per month in fees ($520 x 5%).
Savings from Use of Electronic Distribution	$5 per child	Teller transaction costs $1.50 more than PC transaction. Savings are realized on 6 transactions per year. Applies to the 50% of children with a previous bank account.
Increased Retention of Household Banking Relationship:		Annual household attrition rate drops from 15% to 10%. Average household generates $520 per year in revenue. Cost to acquire a new household is $100.
Revenue gained	$25 per household	
Expense saved	$5 per household	
Increase in Loans	$0	No effect.
Subtotal	$110 per year for 1 child	
Total	About $175 per year for 2.2 children (average married couple with children)	

Figure 2.7 Value Received by Bank Offering an Electronic Bank-for-Kids.

target segment, or nearly $1 to 2 billion per year. This customer opportunity has promise, and a decision by a bank to direct attention to it would be sensible. The next step is to replace the many assumptions and leaps of faith made up to this point with hard data (see Chapter 3).

■ 2.2 VALUE CAPTURED FROM RIVALS

An information technology system can strengthen the relative advantage of a company, enabling it to capture value away from its rivals. This means the information technology system will result in reductions in (1) the bargaining power of customers, (2) the market share of competitors, (3) expenditures on suppliers, (4) employee payrolls, or (5) government taxes and regulation.

It is also possible for an information technology system to improve the asset utilization of a company, enabling shareholders to increase the return on invested capital and capture value from debtholders. This means the information technology system will result in reductions in (6) the amount of invested capital. An example is a just-in-time inventory system that reduces inventory levels, and therefore working capital requirements.

Each of these six types of reductions can be large enough to provide justification for investing in an information technology system, independent of any new or enhanced services that may be provided to customers. For example, automated teller machines were justifiable on the basis of reductions in teller payrolls alone.

Information technology systems will typically result in incremental reductions in one or more of the six areas previously listed. It is also common for imitation by competitors to render these advantages temporary. But bold and lasting reductions can be achieved. One of the most important ways this occurs is through the formation of new business models.

Let's examine some business models for the media industry which have broad relevance as a result of the increasing information intensity of business. One could argue that a media business is lurking in every company. If you doubt this, note that automobile companies now manufacture cars with more semiconductor content than steel (e.g., Lexus); airlines develop large-scale transaction processing systems (e.g., Sabre), and utilities lay fiber-optic lines alongside pipelines during construction (e.g., Houston Industries). Our discussion of these business models is limited to highlighting just one of the ways relative advantage among rivals is shifted.

➤ Example 1. Reduction of Competitor Market Share

A simple business system for an electronic media company is shown in Figure 2.8. It applies to over-the-air broadcasters, cable operators, online service providers, and Internet site administrators. In the 1950s, over-the-air broadcast technology for television was just able to provide a few channels economically, and the pioneering companies competed

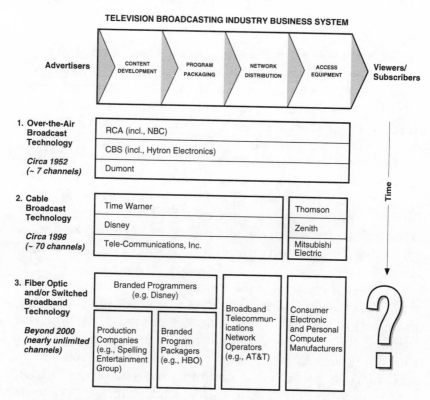

Figure 2.8 Television Broadcasting Industry Structure.

against each other as vertically integrated businesses in the effort to create an end-to-end communications system. RCA, in particular, viewed programming as a way to stimulate sales of their television receivers.

In time, broadcast standards necessary to prevent station interference and to promote industry development allowed the manufacture of television sets to break away into a separate consumer electronics industry with Thomson, Zenith, and Mitsubishi now commanding the largest U.S. market share. Cable television operators, in addition, increased the supply of channels, taking industry leadership away from most of the over-the-air competition. Continued limits on the availability of channels, even with cable television technology, have kept the remaining business system as of 1999 populated by vertically integrated players who need to make sure there is an outlet for their content and, conversely, content for their outlet.

Sometime in the 2000s, however, one can predict that channels will become abundant with the deployment of fiber-optic transmission lines and switched broadband technology. To prevent broadband network owners from having an unfair advantage, the regulatory environment is likely to co-evolve to provide for owners of content to have equal access to channel capacity, breaking down the economic linkages between the content and network components of the business system. When this occurs, controlling channel capacity will no longer be strategic and the network distribution part of the business system will break away into a separate broadband network industry. The need for a consistent brand among program packagers, and the difficulties in fostering a creative culture in a captive environment, will make the program packaging and content development parts of the business system a mixed bag of integrated and independent companies.

The end result is a divided business system where integrated system competitors have ceded market share to component competitors. Similar industry evolutions have occurred in computers (triggered once personal computer standards were established) and in banking (with the securitization of credit). Industries tend to divide as they expand, as comparative advantages among competitors become more economically significant.

➤ Example 2. Reduction of Employee Payroll

The traditional business model for a media company that serves to bring consumers and businesses together is based on subscription/usage and advertising money flowing to the media company (see Figure 2.9).

Applying information technology to these established business models can improve the productivity of employees. Tools now exist for automating the editorial process, automatically inserting advertisements into programming, managing network operations, and performing remote diagnostics on access equipment. The end result is a reengineered business system where more work can be done with fewer people.

➤ Example 3. Reduction in Customer Bargaining Power

Money flowing between a media company and its customers can be redirected in unconventional ways. A unidirectional flow creates a polarized business system that acts as a customer advocate rather than as a forum for bringing consumers and businesses together (see Figure 2.10).

The consumer advocate media company represents consumers to businesses. This is a media company oriented toward purchasing. A major effort is expended in gathering information on businesses, inducing them to provide discounts, and trying to make them responsive. The end result is a reduction in the bargaining power of businesses and an increase in the bargaining power of consumers.

The business advocate media company represents businesses to consumers. This is a media company oriented toward solicitation. A major effort is expended on gathering

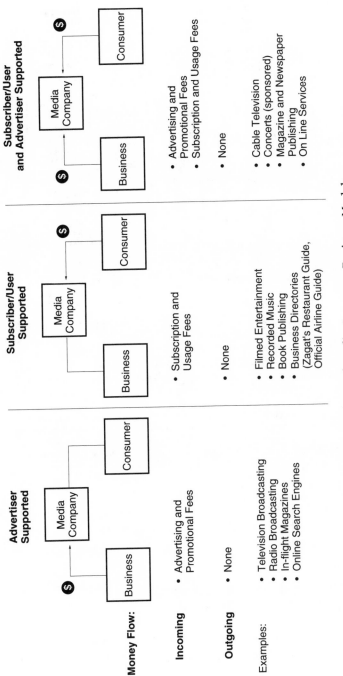

Figure 2.9 Traditional Media Company Business Models.

Subscriber/User and Advertiser Supported

Money Flow: Business → Media Company ← Consumer

Incoming
- Advertising and Promotional Fees
- Subscription and Usage Fees

Outgoing
- None

Examples:
- Cable Television
- Concerts (sponsored)
- Magazine and Newspaper Publishing
- On Line Services

Subscriber/User Supported

Money Flow: Business → Media Company → Consumer

Incoming
- Subscription and Usage Fees

Outgoing
- None

Examples:
- Filmed Entertainment
- Recorded Music
- Book Publishing
- Business Directories (Zagat's Restaurant Guide, Official Airline Guide)

Advertiser Supported

Money Flow: Business → Media Company → Consumer

Incoming
- Advertising and Promotional Fees

Outgoing
- None

Examples:
- Television Broadcasting
- Radio Broadcasting
- In-flight Magazines
- Online Search Engines

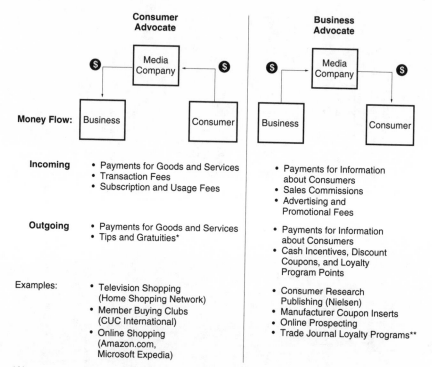

Figure 2.10   Customer Advocate Media Company Business Models.

information on consumers, inducing them to make purchases, and trying to make them loyal. The end result is a reduction in the bargaining power of consumers and an increase in the bargaining power of businesses.

➤ Example 4. Reduction in Supplier Expenditures

Another possibility is that money flows directly between consumers and businesses, creating a direct purchase and direct advertising business system (see Figure 2.11).

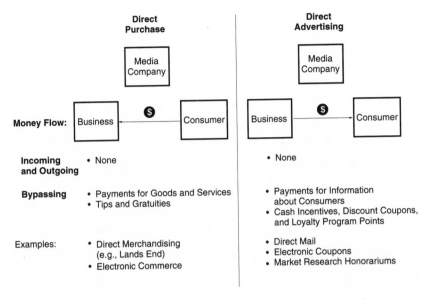

Figure 2.11 Bypassed Media Company Business Models.

In this situation, consumers find businesses and businesses find consumers on their own. Consumers, for a price, might make information about themselves available to companies. Similarly, businesses might make information about themselves available to consumers so they can purchase goods and services directly. The end result is the media company is bypassed completely, no longer acting as a supplier to either consumers or businesses.

➤ Example 5. Reduction in Taxes Paid

Media company business models can connect consumers to businesses in remote locations (see Figure 2.12). Global communications networks provided by AT&T, Motorola, Sky Broadcasting, and others are extending this ability. Businesses can locate in areas with favorable tax laws, and customers can purchase goods by mail order and avoid sales tax. An example is the Home Shopping Network. It sells Gateway personal computers by mail order, so customers avoid sales

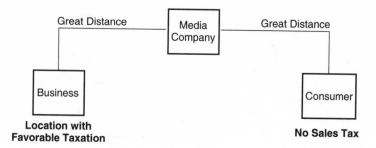

Figure 2.12 Borderless Media Company Business Model.

tax on a product from a manufacturer located in South Dakota where there is no individual or corporate state income tax. The end result is a reduction in taxes paid to the government.

➤ Example 6. Reduction in Invested Capital

The Internet enables any personal computer to act as a window into a worldwide network of computers belonging to millions of businesses, organizations, and individuals. For media companies, whose primary product is nothing but information, the Internet can act as a global 24-hour distribution network whose costs are widely shared. Media companies with large physical plants dedicated to producing and distributing media such as newspapers (with their printing presses and truck fleets), music publishers (with their compact disc factories and record stores), and movie studios (with their film production factories, theaters, and video rental stores) may find they can cut back on their invested capital in these areas by using the Internet. *The New York Times,* Thorn EMI (EMI Music and HMV superstores) and Viacom (Paramount Studios, National Amusements theatres, and Blockbuster video stores) are representative of the kinds of companies for whom this applies. ATM networks have already enabled a similar development to occur in banking. The role of the traditional bank branch has been usurped to a great degree by ATMs that require far less investment in property, plant, and equipment. Electronic home banking will carry this even further. If you consider that a bank is in many respects like a media company, except that it primarily handles transactions rather than news or entertainment, the probability that a similar development will occur for media companies appears high.

You now know the ways information technology systems can provide value to shareholders. The focus of Chapter 3 is on assessing customer demand (i.e., the value received from customers) since this is the primary question for new or enhanced services and the most difficult to answer. The other sources of value however, should not be forgotten in building the business case for an information technology system.

■ PROBLEMS AND SOLUTIONS

Problem 2.1: What are the fundamental characteristics of a customer segmentation? What are some additional examples of ways to segment customers?

Solution: A customer segmentation should be made up of subsets of customers whose intersection is the null set, and whose union is the universe of all customers. Additional ways to segment customers include size of household, marital status, nationality, usage level.

Problem 2.2: What is an example of an existing and a future customer opportunity?

Solution: For the segment of consumers who are located in cars during the day, to provide them with telephone service. For the segment of businesses involved in providing health care to patients at home, to offer a videophone service for remote diagnosis and monitoring ("housecalls").

Problem 2.3: What are some sources of data that could be useful in constructing a market profile that describes the size of each customer segment?

Solution: Dun & Bradstreet, U.S. Bureau of the Census, Simmons Market Research Bureau.

■ NOTES

1. Based on Maslow's theory of human motivation, human behavior is dominated and organized only by unsatisfied needs. Consumers are generally striving to satisfy physiological (e.g., hunger), safety (avoidance of harm), love (affection), self-esteem (respect), and self-actualization (fulfillment) needs, in this order of importance (A.H. Maslow, "A Theory of Human Motivation," *Psychological Review 50* (1943) 370–396).

2. See Section 5.1 for definitions.

3. See Section 3.6.

4. The reference material for developing a market profile will inform you that 50% of children already have a bank account, which is good news and bad news. Although there is a large market for a bank-for-kids offering, it will have to be structured with direct appeal to kids and parents to switch the 50% who already have accounts. Considering how poorly children are served by banks, this is probably not hard.

Chapter 3

Voice of the Customer

What we do not understand we do not possess.

—Goethe

Once we have identified a new or enhanced service, we need to develop a more precise understanding of it. This means replacing assumptions with facts that establish the customers who are to be served, the features they value, the amount they are willing to pay, and their likelihood to purchase the service. The work discussed in Chapter 2 provides some answers to these questions, but a more thorough verification by customers is necessary to raise our level of confidence in the attractiveness of the opportunity.

To resolve these issues requires careful market research be performed, and the voice of the customer relied on to provide the answers. In designing the research, (1) an appropriate method must be chosen for listening to customers, (2) a clear set of questions developed to address the issues, (3) the product requirements customers value most discerned from the answers, and (4) the results translated into an assessment of demand. Each aspect is discussed in turn.

■ 3.1 METHODS OF LISTENING

Several methods for listening to customers can be used: interviews, focus groups, surveys, conjoint analyses, market tests, and product introductions, in order of qualitative to quantitative measurement. Quantitative demand data is required if the economics of an information technology system hinge on the demand for new or enhanced services and the investment cost is high. Qualitative demand data is adequate if the economics can be justified on cost savings alone or if only a small investment is required.

Interviews are conversations with individual customers, where probing of their responses to the preceding issues is possible. *Focus groups* are moderator-led discussions with a group of customers (typically about 10), where multiple perspectives on the issues can be obtained. *Surveys* are formal

	Method for Listening to Customer					
	Interview	**Focus Group**	**Survey**	**Conjoint Analysis**	**Market Test**	**Product Introduction**
Best Suited For:	Qualitatively identifying: • customer segments • product features and gauging: • willingness to pay • likelihood to purchase	Qualitatively revealing the range of: • customer segments • product features and assessing the variations in: • willingness to pay • likelihood to purchase	Quantifying by customer segment: • value of individual product features • willingness to pay • likelihood to purchase	Quantifying by customer segment: • value of combinations of product features • willingness to pay • likelihood to purchase	Measuring actual demand under controlled conditions	Measuring actual demand under uncontrolled conditions
Sample Size*	1	10	100's	100's	100's	100's
Normalized Cost* (interview=1)	1	10	100	1000	10,000+	100,000+
Time Required*	1 hour	1 week	1 month	4 months	1+ year	2 to 3+ years

————— **Complexity** —————————————————▶

▲

* Order of magnitude for typical case.

Typically represents point where major resource commitment must be made

Figure 3.1 Primary Research Methods for Assessing Demand for New Products or Services.

questionnaires administered to a large number of customers to obtain a statistically valid distribution of responses to the issues. *Conjoint analyses* combine interview and survey techniques to obtain in-depth, statistically valid distributions of responses to the issues, where combinations of features are assessed. *Market tests* are trial-and-error experiments that provide observations of customer responses to the issues under controlled conditions. *Product introductions* are trial-and-error experiments that provide observations of customer responses to the issues under uncontrolled conditions (see Figure 3.1). All these methods can be applied to resolve issues other than those addressed here.

The predictive accuracy of these methods progressively increases due to a reduction in the sources of error (see Figure 3.2). Selection of a particular method depends on the predictive accuracy desired, the number of customers in the target market, budget constraints, and schedule requirements. A perfectly sensible approach in many cases is to apply each method in succession, applying the learning from the previous stage to the next, in a process of refinement that leads to intense product/market focus.

The complexity of the methods increases in proportion to the level of predictive accuracy obtained. The interview

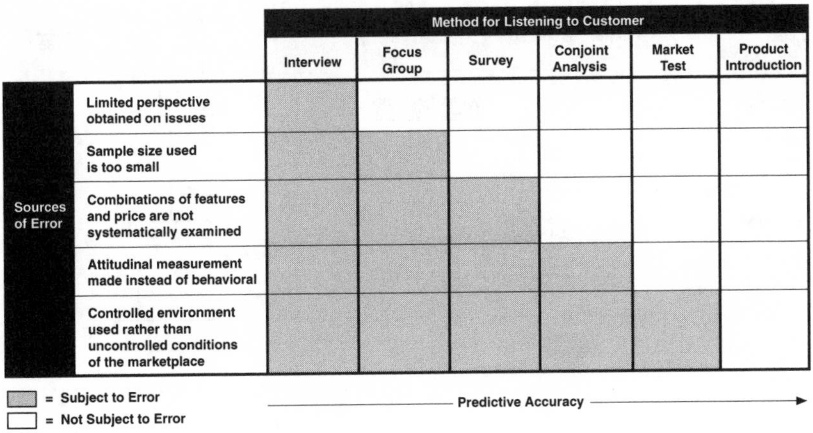

		Method for Listening to Customer					
		Interview	Focus Group	Survey	Conjoint Analysis	Market Test	Product Introduction
Sources of Error	Limited perspective obtained on issues	▦					
	Sample size used is too small	▦	▦				
	Combinations of features and price are not systematically examined	▦	▦	▦			
	Attitudinal measurement made instead of behavioral	▦	▦	▦	▦		
	Controlled environment used rather than uncontrolled conditions of the marketplace	▦	▦	▦	▦	▦	

▦ = Subject to Error
☐ = Not Subject to Error

Predictive Accuracy ⟶

Figure 3.2 Sources of Error.

method is the most simple. It consists of six steps: (1) Describe the information product, (2) select the interviewees, (3) plan the discussion, (4) organize the logistics, (5) conduct the interviews, and (6) derive the product requirements, as well as the demand levels (see Appendix A, Figure A.1).

The focus group method adds the complications associated with conducting group interviews of customers. The need for a trained moderator dictates retaining a market research firm. In addition, some adjustments to the key activities in each step of the interview method are necessary (see Appendix A, Figure A.2).

The survey method involves careful sample and research design, as well as the use of analytical tools to create, tabulate, and sort the responses in a database (see Appendix A, Figure A.3).

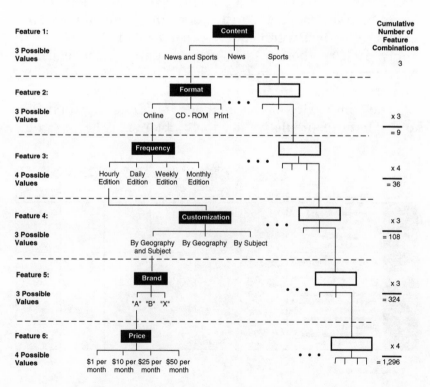

Figure 3.3a Possible Feature Combinations.

The conjoint analysis method represents a significant increase in complexity, as the name suggests. It involves having customers rate different combinations of features and price by sorting through cards or computer screens that have a unique service description (i.e., combination of features, one of which is price) written on them (see Figure 3.3). This reveals the value customers place on different product

	Card 1	Card 2		Card 15 to 20
Content	News & Sports	News		Sports
Format	Online	CD - ROM		Print
Frequency	Hourly Edition	Daily Edition	• • •	Weekly Edition
Customization	By Geography & Subject	By Geography		By Subject
Brand	"A" Company	"B" Company		"X" Company
Price	$50 per month	$10 per month		$1 per month

Note: Price can be considered a feature

Figure 3.3b   Feature Combinations Tested.

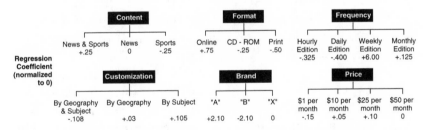

Figure 3.3c   Feature Contribution to Likelihood to Purchase Rating.

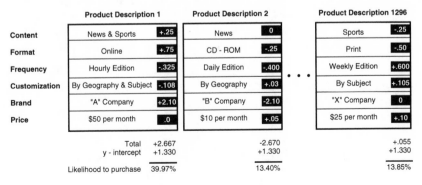

Figure 3.3d   Calculation of Likelihood to Purchase Rating.

descriptions and the trade-off they are willing to make between features and price. Computer modeling allows simulating all combinations of features and price if a proper sample of possibilities is chosen. A total of eight steps are required: (1) Describe the information product, (2) retain a market research firm, (3) select the participants, (4) design the conjoint research, (5) organize the logistics, (6) conduct the conjoint fieldwork, (7) derive the product requirements, and (8) derive the demand levels (see Appendix A, Figure A.4).

The market test method provides behavioral, rather than attitudinal, data on customers. It involves creating a physical version of the information product in sample quantities, for actual use and purchase by a selected group of test subjects and locations, under controlled conditions. The investment cost and time requirement can be substantial. Seven steps are required: (1) Develop a sample quantity of the information product, (2) retain a market research firm, (3) select the test subjects/locations, (4) plan the measurements, (5) organize the logistics, (6) conduct the market test, and (7) derive the product requirements, as well as the demand levels (see Appendix A, Figure A.5).

The product introduction method involves creating production quantities of the information product for actual use and purchase by any customer in a selected target market, under uncontrolled conditions. Exit cost must now be considered, in addition to investment cost and time requirement. Again, seven steps are required: (1) Develop production quantities of the information product, (2) retain a market research firm (optional), (3) select the target market, (4) plan the measurements, (5) organize the logistics, (6) launch the product, and (7) derive the product requirements, as well as the demand levels (see Appendix A, Figure A.6).

■ 3.2 CHOOSING WHO TO LISTEN TO

The choice of method for listening to customers' opinions has to take into account some practical considerations. Generally,

OVERVIEW OF CONJOINT ANALYSIS

Conjoint analysis is an important tool that is not widely understood. Consider an information service opportunity with the possible features shown in Figure 3.3a. A total of 1,296 possible feature combinations exist. A specific subset of these possibilities is chosen, called an "orthogonal array"* that allows estimating all 1,296 possibilities without having to test each one. This subset is constrained to number between 15 and 20 possibilities to limit the complexity of the research for the participants. This typically restricts the number of features to 6 or 7, assuming each feature can have 2 to 4 different values. Each of the 15 to 20 feature combinations represents a unique service description that is written on a card or computer screen (see Figure 3.3b). Participants in the conjoint research are asked to rate these service descriptions on a scale, usually from 0 to 10 where "0" indicates a zero likelihood to purchase and "10" indicates a certain likelihood to purchase. A multiple regression is then performed to calculate the contribution each feature value makes to the likelihood to purchase rating. This contribution is the regression coefficient, also known as the "part-worth" or "utility" (see Figure 3.3c). By adding together the contributions of all the feature values in a service description and adding in the y-intercept term, an estimate of the likelihood to purchase is obtained. In this way, not only can the respondents' ratings of the 15 to 20 service descriptions be recreated, to a good approximation, but ratings for all 1,296 possible feature combinations can be estimated (see Figure 3.3d). Analysis of a group of respondents' ratings can be used to identify patterns among customer segments. Examination of the spread between the contributions of a feature's values can reveal the relative importance of a feature, with large spreads indicating high importance, and low spreads indicating low importance.

* See P.E. Green, "On the Design of Choice Experiments Involving Multifactor Alternatives," *Journal of Consumer Research, 1* (September 1974), 61–68.

a sample of customers is sought that is both representative of the population and adequate in size to provide statistically valid results. Compromises abound, however, as you transverse the spectrum of methods. Interviews and focus groups rarely provide statistically valid data unless the number of customers in the target market is small (e.g., the number of customers for commercial satellites). When a company has a large number of customers, it can't involve many of them individually in the design process. Instead, it must try either to create a cross-section of participants that is representative of the whole, or to focus more narrowly on participants from a segment to reveal the full spectrum of views, which are weighted accordingly. Surveys and conjoint analysis, on the other hand, provide statistically valid data. Surveys often overkill in the number of responses received from a representative population because the incremental cost of an additional survey completion is low. Conjoint analysis involves the careful setting of sample quotas to ensure no wasteful responses are received in the representative segments because the incremental cost of an additional conjoint interview is high. The size of the sample is adequate when its relevant characteristics are stable. If there is a wide range in characteristics, a larger sample is needed to reach stability. Market tests and product introductions are typically run until a large enough sample of representative customers has been involved to judge whether success has been achieved.

■ 3.3 DESCRIBING THE INFORMATION PRODUCT

To obtain an accurate measure of the customer opportunity, the information product must be described as clearly as possible. This can be done (in order of increasing precision) verbally, in written form, through a videotaped demonstration, using a prototype/sample, or by showing the actual

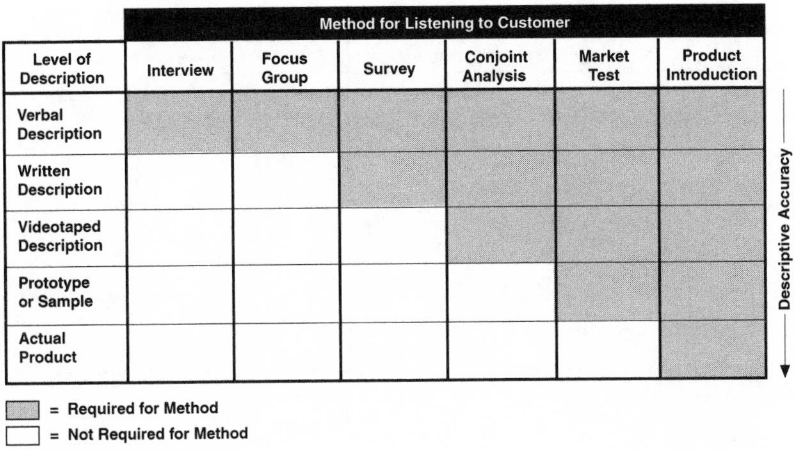

Level of Description	Method for Listening to Customer						Descriptive Accuracy
	Interview	Focus Group	Survey	Conjoint Analysis	Market Test	Product Introduction	
Verbal Description	▓	▓	▓	▓	▓	▓	
Written Description			▓	▓	▓	▓	
Videotaped Description				▓	▓	▓	
Prototype or Sample					▓	▓	
Actual Product						▓	

▓ = Required for Method
☐ = Not Required for Method

Figure 3.4 Minimum Level of Description Required.

product. A minimum level of description is required, depending on the method used for listening to customers (see Figure 3.4). The descriptions should be factual in content, stating the product uses, features, and performance; and neutral in tone, avoiding salesmanship as much as possible.

■ 3.4 FORMULATING THE QUESTIONS TO ASK

For any of the methods for listening to customers, the research should be designed to obtain data in two areas: background of the respondent and features, price, and purchase likelihood (see Figure 3.5).

➤ Background Questions

Background questions provide data for segmenting respondents to establish the specific customers that should be served. The questions generally fall into the categories of segmentation characteristics discussed earlier: physical,

Question Categories	
Background on the Respondent	**Features, Price, and Purchase Likelihood**
Purpose: Used to search for customer segments.	Used to determine what features customers value, how much they are willing to pay, and their likelihood to purchase.
Description: A detailed description of the type of customer the respondent represents by identifiable characteristics: - Physical - Mental/Organizational - Behavioral - Experiential/Developmental - Financial - Relational	Actual data on the respondent's preferences and attitudes.

Figure 3.5 Research Design Structure.

mental/organizational, behavioral, experiential/developmental, financial, and relational.

Answers to an initial set of questions are needed to first separate potential participants into those who are suitable for the market research and those who are not. (Note: this does not apply to product introductions.) The instrument for conducting this is called a *prescreening questionnaire.* Typically, it focuses on determining:

➤ Whether the potential participant would actually find the information product of some benefit.

➤ Whether the potential participant is responsible for making the purchase decision for the information product, or influences the decision, or is a user of the information product.

➤ Which segment the potential participant falls in and whether there is an adequate number already.

➤ Whether the potential participant is willing to cooperate in the research.

Once qualified, the participant is scheduled to take part in the market research. Additional detailed background data can be obtained at that time.

The detailed background data sought differs based on whether potential buyers of the information product are consumers or businesses. Hypotheses on what might be important characteristics that underlie cause and effect (e.g., how an age group responds to a product feature that affects purchase intention) determine the specific background questions. Careful thinking is required since the number of potential background questions is large, while typically the important ones are few in number (see Figure 3.6).

As a result of these background questions, we can map customer characteristics against product features to identify how sets of characteristics (i.e., customer segments) correspond with sets of features (i.e., products) (see Figure 3.7).

➤ Features, Price, and Purchase Likelihood

A customer's inherent likelihood to purchase an information product is determined by the attractiveness of the

CONSUMER CHARACTERISTICS		
Physical	Mental	Behavioral
• What is your age? • What is your address? • What is your sex? • What is your state of health?	• What is your level of education? • What religious group do you belong to? • What language do you speak at home? • Do you know how to use a computer?	• How often do you read a newspaper? • What is your occupation? • How do you spend your leisure time? • How often do you travel?
Experiential	Financial	Relational
• When do you plan to retire? • When is your wedding anniversary? • Have you been in an auto accident? • Have you been promoted in the past year?	• What is your income? • Do you own your home? • How much is your average credit card balance? • Are you invested in stocks which involve a high degree of risk?	• How many are in your family? • Are you involved in any community charities? • Have you served in the military? • Are you a Democrat or a Republican?

Figure 3.6 Consumer Background Questions.

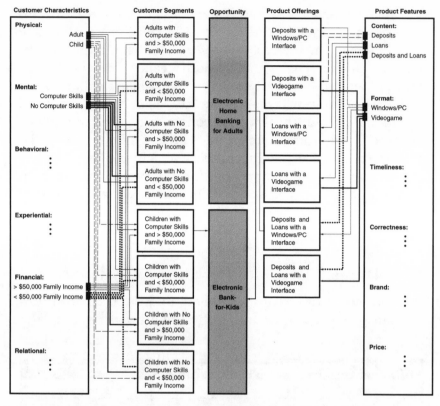

Figure 3.7 Mapping Customer Segments to Product Offerings.

features offered and the price that has to be paid for them. The questions of what features do customers value most, how much are they willing to pay, and what is their likelihood to purchase are, therefore, inseparable. They must be answered in unison.

A complication is that there are myriad product designs for which these questions could be asked. For the simple case of six features, each of which could assume three values (e.g., a feature such as content could have three values—news, sports, or news and sports) and one price, there are $3^6 \times 1 = 729$ possible feature combinations, or equivalently, separate product designs.

In general,

$$\text{Number of Product Designs} = V_1 \times V_2 \times \ldots \times V_F \times V_p$$

where V_f = Number of possible values of feature $f(1 \le f \le F)$,

$\quad V_p$ = Number of possible prices,

$\quad F$ = Total number of features

It is not practical to have customers evaluate their likelihood to purchase for each of these designs, unless V_f, V_p, and F are small. Customers have limited capacity to sort through a large number of complex choices, which forces narrowing the design possibilities for evaluation to a small subset, typically numbering no more than about 15 to 20. For interviews, focus groups, and surveys, this subset is chosen to be those designs with the most market promise. In the case of conjoint analysis, this subset is an "orthogonal array" (see description in box, earlier in this chapter) that allows modeling the entire range of design possibilities to determine the optimal design for reaching the market. In the case of market tests and product introductions, this subset is simply what is believed to be the optimal design.

Once a design has been described to a customer in terms of its features and price, the customer receives instructions that simultaneously ask what is their likelihood to purchase and explain how to answer that question.

To determine the likelihood to purchase a *new* information product, the instructions are of the form:

Apply a rating scale where 0 indicates there is no chance you would ever purchase the information product and 10 indicates you are certain you would purchase the information product. For each information product design, decide which number on this scale best describes how likely you would be to purchase this information product.

To determine the effect of the new information product on purchases of an *existing* information product:

Here is your highest rated design of the proposed new information product. If you were to purchase it, decide which number on the rating scale best describes how likely you would be

to not continue *purchasing the existing information product. Similarly, show how likely you would be to* make additional *purchases of the existing information product (a specific purchase quantity should be obtained).*

A more complete set of instructions for a conjoint analysis—which can be modified as needed for interviews, focus groups, or survey research—is shown in Figure 3.8.

For customers participating in a market test or product introduction, the questions are implied and the answers take the form of actual purchasing behavior, as measured by invoices.

Several additional questions are worth asking to help identify what combinations of features and price resonate with customers. To get a sense of their overall priorities, importance ratings can be obtained:

Please determine the relative importance of the following features and price by allocating 100 points among them, with the most important receiving the most points.

How can the product be changed to increase the likelihood to purchase to near certainty?

The answers to these questions will be directional and must be treated with caution. The tendency among customers will be to ask for as much as possible while paying as little as possible. The previous questions on likelihood to purchase reflect customers' trade-offs between prespecified features and price, which avoids this problem.

Investigators must try to ensure customers understand and focus on the purchase decision in the market research. This is done by creating a product demonstration, clearly communicating the features offered and price, removing participants from distractions, obtaining a time commitment from them of typically one hour, and paying them for their time. The investigator's significant effort to educate customers helps achieve an accurate measure of their likelihood to purchase. The ability to examine the actual product

1. Hello, I am <name>. I'd like to thank you for participating in the market research we are conducting. As you know, we are interested in your attitudes and opinions about the features of a proposed information service. As you consider this proposed service, keep in mind the information services you are currently using. The new service could substitute for, or complement, your existing services.

2. This booklet describes the proposed information service. Please take a few moments to read the service description on <page>.

3. Now that you have read the service description, we are going to show you a video to demonstrate how the various features of the proposed information service work.

4. With this as background, I'd now like to know what is the likelihood you would purchase the proposed information service. I am going to give you 16 cards. <hand participant cards arranged in random order> Each card contains a distinct set of features the proposed information service can have. Please take a few moments to look over these cards. Pick out those cards that represent a version of the information service you would be interested in. We can allow as much time as you need for this.

5. When you are done, could you please hand the cards you have selected back to me so I can record the identification numbers.

6. Now we are going to ask you to rate each of the versions of the information service you would be interested in. On a 0-10 scale, where 0 indicates there is no chance you would ever purchase and 10 indicates you are certain you would purchase, please rate each card you selected. Assume only the one version of the information service represented by a card is available. A rating can be used as many times as you like. <hand participant cards one at a time, arranged in random order, and record the results as you go>

7. If you wish, you may review your ratings and change them if you like. <record any changes>

8. There are existing information services available which are similar to the proposed service you have been considering <explain>. Do you purchase any of these existing services? If so, which ones? <if one or more, go to question 9, otherwise go to question 10>

9. Please rate how likely you would be to continue to purchase the existing information service(s) you use if you were to purchase the version of the proposed information service to which you gave the highest rating. <show this card> A lower rating. <show cards with the second and third highest ratings in succession> <go to question 11>

10. Please rate how likely you would be to purchase, in addition, an existing information service <specify>, if you were to purchase the version of the proposed information service to which you gave the highest rating. <show this card> A lower rating. <show cards with the second and third highest ratings in succession>

11. Now I'd like to ask you some background questions so we can segment the responses of the participants...Thank you very much for your cooperation.

Note: This is one of several possible research designs that could be used.

Adapted with permission from Hase-Schannen Research Associates.

Figure 3.8 Features, Price, and Purchase Likelihood Questionnaire.

in the case of market tests and product introductions simplifies this task.

Sometimes a new information product will undergo rapid enhancement so that later versions are much more attractive than initial versions. A product demonstration that shows the kinds of improvements that are expected and the dates they are anticipated allows this dynamic to be incorporated into the research results.

■ 3.5 DISCERNING PRODUCT REQUIREMENTS

Discerning product requirements differs depending on the research method.

➤ Interviews, Focus Groups, and Surveys

The result of interviews, focus groups, and survey research methods is a statement from the participants of the likelihood to purchase at a given price for each of the designs evaluated. When broken out by segment, we have:

$$\text{Likelihood to Purchase Design by Segment (\%)} = \frac{\text{Penetration of Segment (units)}}{\text{Market Segment Size (units)}}$$

To estimate the revenue potential of a design, we need to multiply the likelihood to purchase of a segment by price, then weight the result by the size of the market segment and sum over all segments:

$$\text{Revenue Potential of a Design} = \sum_{\substack{\text{Market} \\ \text{Segments}}} \left(\text{Market Segment Size} \times \frac{\text{Likelihood to Purchase}}{\text{Design by Segment}} \times \frac{\text{Price of}}{\text{Design}} \right)$$

All the data needed to evaluate this expression have been developed from the preceding work. The only variable remaining in this expression is price, since the market segment sizes are fixed, the designs have been prechosen, and the research results determine how the likelihood to purchase depends on the other variables. By varying price, we can see at what point the revenue potential of a design is maximized. The most attractive design is the one with the maximum revenue potential. The product requirements are simply the features and price this design represents. Figure 3.9 illustrates these relationships.

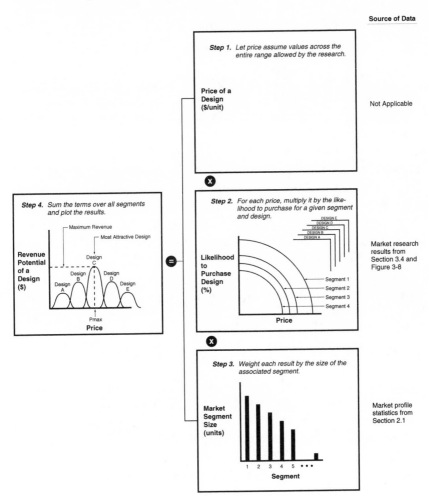

Figure 3.9   Relationships Used to Identify Most Attractive Design.

The approach described here to identify the most attractive design uses a basic objective of maximizing "revenue potential." This is one of several simplifications that result in finding a good approximation to the optimum design, but not necessarily the absolute optimum. For example, a more accurate, but far more complicated approach, is to maximize net present value.

Other designs may be attractive to market segments that are poorly served by the most attractive design. In this case, it may make sense to offer these products in addition to the most attractive product since they are complementary.

➤ Conjoint Analysis

The approach described earlier for discerning product requirements applies to conjoint analysis as well. Conjoint analysis improves the result by allowing many design possibilities to be modeled to determine the optimum design, rather than a prechosen subset. Since not all design possibilities can usually be examined, due to the effort this would take, heuristics are applied to guide the search. The first step is to calculate the contribution to the likelihood to purchase of each feature's possible values. This is done by the conjoint analysis software provided by the market research firm.[1] After weighting the contributions to reflect market segment size, the market-weighted contributions can be used to identify the designs that are likely to have the greatest market penetration. These designs are determined by picking the feature values that make the largest positive contribution to likelihood to purchase.

Often, the greatest market penetration occurs at the lowest price, and may not, therefore, represent the point of maximum revenue potential. To find this point, the price (of the designs with the greatest market penetration) is varied until the peak revenue potential is reached. The most attractive design is the one with the maximum revenue potential. The product requirements are the features and price this design represents.

The comments on complementary designs and alternative objectives from the preceding section apply as well. The extreme case where a large number of complementary designs are offered is essentially "mass customization" where customers design or tailor a product to suit their needs rather than having to accept the design offered to them. This allows a high degree of price discrimination by offering different versions of a product to different customers. The variables in a conjoint analysis can actually be viewed as the parameters around which customers design their own product. A conjoint analysis would be used in this case to link particular designs with customer segments and identify the design center (i.e., highest volume design).

➤ Market Tests and Product Introductions

An "optimum" design is chosen in advance for these research methods and, therefore, the product requirements are established ad initium. Once the research is completed, however, debriefing sessions with customers may provide feedback on how to improve the design.

■ 3.6 TRANSLATION INTO A DEMAND ESTIMATE

Assessing the annual revenue for a new product requires understanding how many customers will purchase it, when they will make their purchases, and the price they are willing to pay. If more than one new product is involved, a sum across the new products must be performed. We will assume only one new product in the following discussion.

➤ Equation of Demand

The equation of demand used to estimate the revenue opportunity is simply:

$$\text{Annual Revenue (\$)} = \sum_{\substack{\text{Market} \\ \text{Segments}}} \left(\begin{array}{c} \text{Annual Market} \\ \text{Segment Size (units)} \end{array} \right.$$

$$\left. \times \begin{array}{c} \text{Annual Likelihood} \\ \text{to Purchase (\%)} \end{array} \times \begin{array}{c} \text{Annual Price} \\ \text{(\$ / unit)} \end{array} \right)$$

This is the same as the earlier expression for revenue potential, except the terms are now time-dependent, and *we no longer need to consider any design other than the most attractive one identified in the previous section.* The additional data required to evaluate this expression is modest. The annual market segment size can be derived from segment growth trends such as population changes. The annual likelihood to purchase can be derived from the organizational constraints that affect the likely timing of purchase or by applying a simple S-curve which has been found to describe well the growth rate of new products. The annual price can be derived from an inflation rate and industry pricing trends. The relationships used to calculate the annual revenue opportunity are shown in Figure 3.10.

➤ Market Segment Size

Sizing the potential market segments has been discussed in Chapter 2 in the context of identifying attractive opportunities. As a term in the equation of demand it is used to weight the data obtained from samples of customers to accurately project research results across the market. To obtain an accurate demand estimate, it is important to pick the right units to measure market segment size. This requires understanding the fundamental purchasing unit. This could be number of individuals or households for consumer products, or number of desktops, departments, branches, divisions, or companies for business products. The size of a market segment is also time-dependent, which is why we must think of the annual market segment size. For example, the number of kids who could subscribe to an electronic banking service is a function of the size of the installed base

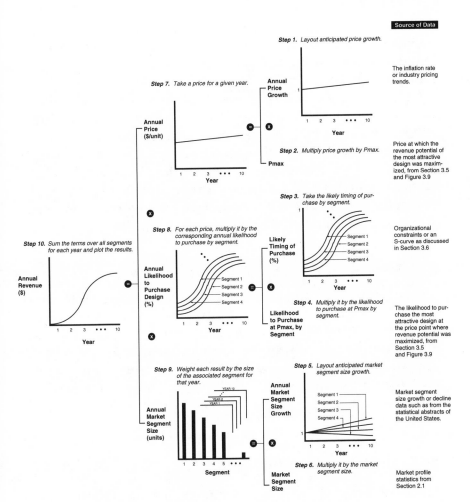

Figure 3.10   Relationships Used for a Demand Estimate.

of networked computers in the home, which will vary significantly with time up to the point where the technology reaches maturity. Two additional time-dependent cases must be considered: subscriptions and one-time purchases. For subscription sales, market segment size is unaffected by prior year sales. For one-time purchases, the cumulative number of customers from the time the product is introduced to the year in question must be subtracted from the market segment size.

To develop a profile of market segment size, one must gather segment sizing data in a way that allows it to be broken down to correspond to the segmentation scheme. For example, if industry focus is chosen as the segmentation scheme for business customers, a database such as Dun & Bradstreet that contains Standard Industrial Classification (SIC) codes is valuable. Once this is done, the segment sizing data needs to be verified by comparing counts with other sources and resolving issues such as double counting, unclassified entries, and data entry errors. Trends must then be incorporated into the data to reflect how market segment size may grow or decline on an annual basis.

➤ Price

The price used to calculate demand is the price at which the revenue potential of the most attractive design was maximized, P_{max} (defined earlier in this chapter). Price is time-dependent which is why we must transform P_{max} into an annual price. This can be done by multiplying P_{max} by anticipated price growth. Industry price trend data and the inflation rate determine the rate of price growth or decline on an annual basis.

➤ Likelihood to Purchase

Likelihood to purchase is the customers' rating of their probability of purchase on a scale of 0 to 10, where 0 means no chance of purchase and 10 means certain purchase. Obviously, to turn this rating into a probability, it must be transformed into a 0 to 100 scale. This rating condenses, into a single variable, the key results of the customer research.

The likelihood to purchase used for calculating demand is that of the most attractive design at the price point where revenue potential was maximized, P_{max}. Likelihood to purchase is time-dependent, however. To transform the likelihood to purchase of the most attractive design at Pmax into an annual amount, we can apply the organizational constraints that affect the likely timing of purchase. This is done by segment, as shown in Figure 3.10, and is less complicated than it sounds.

Organizational constraints can be found in development, manufacturing, distribution, marketing, sales, and service. For example, a sales representative may only be capable of closing one sale per day; if there are 1,000 sales representatives in the sales force, a limit of 1,000 sales per day can be made. Similarly, a development group may require 2 to 3 years to create a product and no demand can be filled during this period. These examples show how organizational constraints can be applied to determine the likely timing of purchase. Generally, each functional group's abilities must be gauged and the annual demand estimate must reflect these constraints. These constraints should also be considered in the context of the organizational ability to support switching from, or buying more of, existing products and a competitor's executional abilities.

An alternative to applying organizational constraints to determine the likely timing of purchase is to use a curve that commonly describes the growth rate of new products. We are going to derive this curve to expose the degree of generality that it holds.

➤ S-Curves

Let N be the number of individuals (or households, departments, companies, etc.) that are expected to purchase a product in the long run. This is just the market segment size, times the likelihood to purchase in the long-run.

At any given time, some number of these individuals will have purchased the product, say N_p, and some number will not have, say N_n. Clearly $N_p + N_n = N$, which we can write as

$$p + n = 1$$

where $p = \dfrac{N_p}{N}$ is the percent penetrated, and

$n = \dfrac{N_n}{N}$ is the percent not penetrated.

If the growth of p were allowed to proceed unchecked, an exponential law should apply, since this law is based on the reasonable assumption that the rate of growth is proportional to the size of the population penetrated, $dp/dt \propto p$. This can be thought of as an initial tendency toward increasing returns. Similarly, there are fewer and fewer individuals left to penetrate as p grows, so we should expect a counterforce to develop that will decelerate growth in proportion to the size of the population not penetrated, $dp/dt \propto n$. This can be thought of as a long-run tendency toward diminishing returns. Combining these, we have,

$$\frac{dp}{dt} = pn$$
$$= p(1 - p)$$

The curve that satisfies this differential equation is

$$p = \frac{e^t}{1 + e^t}$$

To set the rate at which the clock turns and the time the clock starts, we substitute

$$t \rightarrow at + b$$

where a is a scale parameter and b is a shift. This gives

$$p = \frac{e^{at+b}}{1 + e^{at+b}}$$

A plot of this function shows that its shape resembles an "S," which is why it is called an *S-curve* (see Figure 3.11).

S-curves have been used extensively as a demand trend line, and have been shown to describe well the growth of industries as diverse as telephones, autos, railroads, steel, cement, and agriculture.[2] The historical growth curves for a number of information technology products show this same S-shape, and the data can be fitted to an S-curve well. A plot

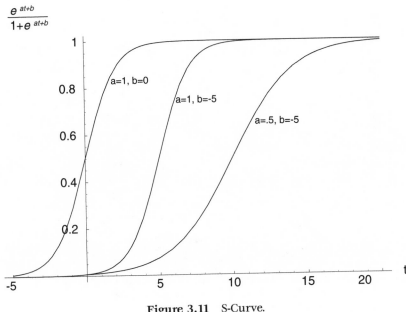

$$\frac{e^{\,at+b}}{1+e^{\,at+b}}$$

Figure 3.11 S-Curve.

of the U.S. household penetration of telephones, televisions, and personal computers from 1920 to 2000 confirms this, with only the Great Depression and World War II inducing a pause (see Figure 3.12).

➤ Refinements

Three important refinements can be made to improve the accuracy of the demand forecast:

1. To take into account the effect of entry by competitors.
2. To factor in the effect on current customer demand for existing products.
3. To correct for the difference between expressed attitudes and demonstrated customer behavior.

The effect of entry by competitors on revenue can be taken into account if brand is one of the features used to describe the product. Comparing the likelihood to purchase of

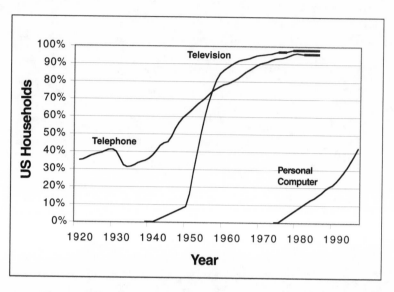

Figure 3.12   Historical Growth Rates for the Telephone, Television, and Personal Computer.

one brand against another will show which is preferred. The respondent is assumed to choose the product with the highest likelihood to purchase. This also allows modeling shifts in market share based on possible competitive moves.

The effect on current customer demand for existing products can be taken into account by tabulating the results from questions 8, 9, and 10 of the market research questionnaire (Figure 3.8). A complementary effect occurs if the new product stimulates additional purchases of an existing product. A substitution effect occurs if the new product is purchased in place of an existing product. This allows calculating the *incremental* demand generated by the new product which is important to making a sound economic decision.

A major systematic error that occurs with interviews, focus groups, surveys, and conjoint analyses is the difference between expressed attitudes and demonstrated behavior. This error is created because we are using surrogate information to estimate demand, that is, substitute information is used as a proxy for the actual information desired. Careful design cannot reduce this error entirely and

MOORE'S LAW

As an interesting and useful aside, S-curves apply to a wide range of other phenomena in the fields of business, biology, physics, and chemistry. An example is "Moore's Law" which states that the number of transistors per semiconductor chip doubles every 18 to 24 months. This represents a growth rate of 40% to 60% per year. Using the figure of 40% per year, Moore's Law can be written as

$$\frac{\text{Number of Transistors}}{\text{Number of Transistors in Year } t_0} = 1.4^{t-t_0}$$

$$= e^{(t-t_0)\log 1.4}$$

$$= e^{at+b}$$

where $a = \log 1.4$ and

$b = -t_0 \log 1.4$

So you can see, Moore's Law has a form that is similar to an S-curve when t is small.

We have used the figure of 40% per year because in remarks aimed at updating Moore's Law,[*] Intel Chairman Emeritus Gordon Moore has stated that minimum feature size is cut by $\frac{1}{2}$ every 6 years and that chip surface area increases by about 12% per year. This gives $4^{1/6} \times 1.12 = 1.41$, which is a growth rate of about 41% per year.

The results of a least squares fit applied to Intel's microprocessor history are in good agreement, yielding a growth rate of 42% per year.[**] Growth rates closer to 60% are observed for DRAMs and in the early period of the microprocessor revolution.

---

[*]Moore, G., "An Update to Moore's Law," *Intel Developer Forum*, September 30, 1997.
[**]The least squares fit to e^{at+b} resulted in $a = \log 1.42$ and $b = -1950 \log 1.42$. The data points used were {Model, Year, Number of Transistors}: {None, 1961, 4}, {4004, 1971, 2300}, {8008, 1972, 3500}, {8080, 1974, 6000}, {8086, 1978, 29000}, {80286, 1982, 134000}, {386, 1985, 275000}, {486, 1989, 1200000}, {Pentium, 1993, 3100000}, {Pentium Pro, 1995, 5500000}, {PentiumII, 1997, 7500000}, {M2012, 2012, 1000000000}.

(continued)

(Continued)

A clear problem with Moore's Law is that it goes on forever, with chips always increasing in density. Alternatively, if we think of a semiconductor chip as simply a surface with a maximum area that is populated by transistors and transistor "holes," then an S-curve relationship should apply. To follow this approach, we need to know the maximum transistor density that can be attained based on the limits imposed by physical laws. Intel has projected that at current growth rates, this limit will occur around the year 2017 when gates approach less than 10 atoms thick, which implies a transistor count of about 8.4 billion. A least squares fit of an S-curve to Intel's microprocessor history using this limit figure is in good agreement with Moore's Law,* as shown in Figure 3.13. It yields a growth rate of 40% per year that is pretty much constant until around 2010 when it starts to diverge from Moore's Law. The remarkable thing is how quickly the divergence becomes complete. In about ten years, growth flattens for the S-curve which, after a 50-year period of exponential growth in the microprocessor industry, is likely to feel like hitting a wall. Perhaps developments such as multistate transistors, die stacking, and wafer-scale integration will help circumvent the sudden deceleration of growth in transistor density that appears to lie ahead.

---

*The least square's fit to $\dfrac{e^{at+b}}{1+e^{at+b}}$ results in $a = \log 1.40$ and $b = -2017 \log 1.40$.

an estimate is the only way to correct for its impact. In our demand estimate equation, the likelihood to purchase, acquired through attitudinal research, is surrogate information for purchase behavior. A rule-of-thumb estimate, based on empirical studies, to correct for the impact of this error is to square the likelihood estimate. This scales back customers' tendency to be optimistic in their purchasing attitudes compared with their behavior. Other sources of "nonsampling" error in the market research that is systematic in nature are: the research instrument or interviewer may influence the result obtained; the respondent may give

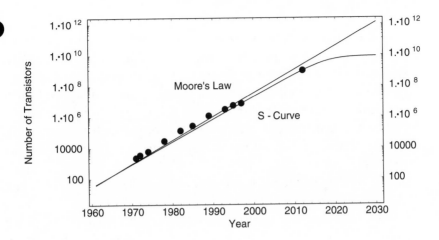

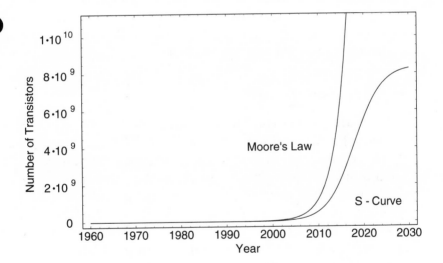

Figure 3.13 An S-Curve Version of Moore's Law:
(a) Logarithmic Scale (b) Linear Scale.

incorrect information; the processing, editing, coding, analysis, or interpretation of the data may be faulty; more accessible or agreeable respondents may be chosen to participate in the research who don't represent the general population; and the means for accounting for all the members of a population may not be entirely accurate, such as using a 10-year-old database for a rapidly changing customer base. Each of these non-sampling errors can be minimized through careful design of the research.

Sampling error occurs when the results derived from the sample do not represent the population accurately, as a result of random fluctuations in choosing a sample. Sampling error is affected by the homogeneity of the population being studied and by the size of the sample. In general, the more homogeneous the population and larger the sample, the smaller the sampling error. Sampling errors can occur in all market research except those that involve a complete enumeration of the population (census). It is a fundamental component of error in the research.

➤ Checking Results

It is worthwhile to compare the results of the demand estimate with other information sources to see the degree to which there is corroboration. A check against experienced managers' judgments about the size of the opportunity should be made. A comparison of historical sales against the demand estimate is another good test of realism. An examination of industry analysts' market projections and trends will provide further perspective. These provide independent estimates of the revenue potential that can help triangulate on an answer.

■ 3.7 OBTAINING FEEDBACK

No market research is foolproof, and therefore plans should be made for obtaining customer feedback on an ongoing basis if a decision is made to bring a new product to market.

There are a few ways to do this. First, customers can be interviewed after they have tried the product to learn what kind of experience they have had with it. This approach can also be extended to customers who have so far avoided purchases to explore the reasons why. Second, a system for logging in and evaluating customer service requests, suggestions, and complaints can be constructed. This database can be analyzed to find patterns, set priorities, and provide benchmarks for measuring progress. Third, actual sales levels can be tracked and analyzed to identify best practices and deficiencies within the organization. These methods create a feedback loop that provides the basis for a series of product and organizational improvements to be made. To make this feedback loop as direct as possible, it is often a good idea to have management, sales, engineering, and other functions man the phones occasionally, and to pass on the cost of customer service to the product group whose product the call was logged against.

■ PROBLEMS AND SOLUTIONS

Problem 3.1: Could the likelihood to purchase a design be transformed into an annual amount by including a question on the likely timing of purchase in the market research?

Solution: Yes, but this approach is not recommended. Obtaining customer opinions on the subject of their likely timing of purchase usually adds more uncertainty to an analysis than the alternatives of either applying organizational constraints that affect the likely timing of purchase or an S-curve describing the growth rate.

Problem 3.2: What products can you name where the growth rate is described well by an S-curve. Where it isn't.

Solution: Cellular phones, VCRs, microwaves, and radios are described well by an S-curve. Products that are failures (e.g., LISP machines), regulated (e.g., military-grade encryption), one-of-a-kind (e.g., computer art), or recalled (e.g., floating point processors that are found to generate errors) do not follow an S-curve.

Problem 3.3: How do you know when a sample size is large enough?

Solution: This is a deep question, and the reader is referred to the literature on statistical analysis for a full discussion (see, e.g., D.L. Harnett, *Introduction to Statistical Methods*, Reading, MA: Addison-Wesley, 1975, Chapter 6). Briefly, the population of interest is a single customer segment and we want to know how large must the sample be so that its relevant characteristics are stable (unaffected by increasing the population). The central limit theorem of statistics states that the shape of the sampling distribution (i.e., the probability distribution of mean values for all possible samples of size n) approaches a Gaussian distribution, as n gets large, no matter what the distribution of the population may be, with a mean equal to that of the population and a variance equal to $1/n$ of that of the population. In addition, the variance of the sample becomes a good approximation to the variance of the population, when n gets large. An empirical examination shows that the sampling distribution becomes Gaussian when the sample size is 30, even if the population distribution is substantially skewed. Larger values of n simply improve the approximation of the sample to the population.

■ NOTES

1. The contribution is the regression coefficient, mentioned earlier, that is obtained from an ordinary multiple regression program using variables that have a value of 0 or 1. Sawtooth Software, Bretton-Clark, and SPSS offer conjoint analysis software packages.

2. See, for example, Harold T. Davis, *The Analysis of Economic Time Series*, Boston: The Principia Press, 1941.

Chapter 4

When Customers Can't Express Themselves

There was a disturbance in my heart, a voice that spoke there and said, *I want, I want, I want!* It happened every afternoon, and when I tried to suppress it, it got even stronger . . . It never said a thing except *I want, I want, I want!*

— Saul Bellow, *Henderson the Rain King*

It sometimes happens that customers are not able to express their likelihood to purchase a new information product. They are uncertain what they need or how their needs could be satisfied. This can occur if the customer does not yet feel the needs fulfilled by the information product, or if the use of the information product requires knowledge that is lacking but will be acquired at some later point. The action embodied in the expression of a "likelihood to purchase" must be preceded first by motivation in the form of a felt need and, second, by an understanding of how the information product would actually meet this need. Ignorance on either count will result in customers not being able to express themselves accurately about their purchase intent.

Typically, this ignorance is most pronounced with major innovations. Customers may have adapted so well to life without this innovation they do not feel an immediate need for it; or understanding its uses may be beyond the imagination or skill of most. Yet there is an underlying attraction. Examples are readily found in information technology: mainframe computers in the 1950s, minicomputers in the 1960s, personal computers in the 1970s, and Internet-working in the 1980s. For each of these, the common phrase was that the product was "ahead of its time." There was latent demand; it just hadn't had time to develop fully.

In Chapter 3, it was assumed that customers can grasp the relevance of a new information service when market research is conducted. However, motivation and understanding increase over time in progressive societies, and the likelihood-to-purchase estimates recorded by market research represent only a snapshot in time. You may have your answer as to the near-term demand for the information product, but you could be way off for the long term (see Figure 4.1).

Four paths can be followed when customers cannot express themselves:

1. Redirect attention to a different customer segment or information product.
2. Stimulate a response to the information product.
3. Listen to the leading customers who foreshadow the needs of the entire segment.
4. Trust your instincts and go beyond what customer research can provide as input, but plan on reacting quickly.

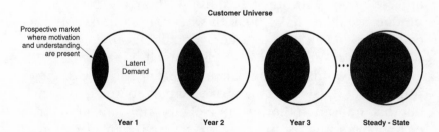

Figure 4.1 Dynamics of Latent Demand.

Issue   Action

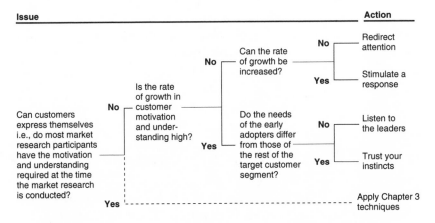

Figure 4.2 What to Do When Customers Can't Express Themselves.

Which path should be followed depends on the situation, as laid out in Figure 4.2.

■ 4.1 REDIRECTING ATTENTION

The problem of increasing levels of motivation and understanding does not always resolve itself quickly. A metamorphosis of sorts is required among customers. Time frames can be as lengthy as waiting for generational change, as with computer literacy. If the near-term demand is low even after taking steps to accelerate this metamorphosis, shifting the product focus to a different customer segment may provide a solution. You may not be talking to the right customers. The appropriate segment may fall outside the main market sector and comprise early adopters, technologists, or the well educated. In the early years of the personal computer, for example, Apple® found success with the Apple II® when it focused on the technology enthusiast and K–12 grade education segments. Similarly, it may make sense to redefine the product to improve its appeal to the original target customer segment. Perhaps a more incremental approach to its design will improve its accessibility to customers, or narrow the focus to a particular application niche. Apple Computer took the latter action to increase demand for the Macintosh among corporate customers when it focused on desktop publishing.

■ 4.2 STIMULATING A RESPONSE

To accelerate the process of increasing levels of motivation and understanding, measures can be taken to persuade, induce, or coerce customers. These measures can be incorporated into the market research to draw out their purchase intent. Doing this assumes similar measures will be taken in the marketplace.

Persuading customers involves communicating the value of the information product. Advertising and promotion practices suggest the form the communication can take. Words designed to define, explain, demonstrate, argue, appeal, compare, and contrast products are appropriate. Words alone may not be enough, however. Evidence may be necessary to back up claims, such as specifications, demonstrations, benchmarks, reviews, testimonials, or endorsements. Steve Jobs of Apple Computer is widely regarded as a master of customer persuasion, using an evangelical approach to product promotion.

Inducing customers involves overcoming motivational and skill barriers. Paying customers for their time while they learn about a product can help, and is standard practice to get respondents to participate in market research. Training programs can be offered. Companies like Intel fund a staff of "applications engineers" whose job it is to show customers how to adapt a product for their own use, which is an effective means to transfer knowledge and skills. Money-back guarantees, warranties, and free trials can be incorporated if there is confidence that product returns and service cancellations will be small. Additionally, if the information product is part of a larger whole, efforts can be made to ensure all the pieces are in place for a customer to realize the full value of the information product. Cable companies have done this by investing in cable programming (e.g., Home Shopping Network, CNN) and cable-based Internet access (e.g., @Home).

Coercing customers involves taking threatening actions to motivate and instill understanding. As competition intensifies, coercive measures are more frequently taken despite their diabolical nature. It is not uncommon for a company to enter the business of one of its customers to force more rapid adoption of a new product. Microsoft's entry into electronic banking and Intel's distribution of free software for placing calls over the Internet are examples of this. Another action is for a computer vendor to develop a system for one company in an industry at a reduced price, which forces the company's competitors to build systems that match its capability. This approach was adopted by IBM in creating the American Airlines Sabre online reservation system and the USAA insurance claim imaging system. Both of these systems put pressure on the other airline and insurance companies to have IBM build something similar for them. Controlling the degree of compatibility among software applications is another means for coercing customers; Microsoft used this technique to help its Excel spreadsheet software overtake Lotus 1,2,3. Sometimes the threatening action only needs to be implied to accomplish its intended propose. Dropping hints about legal, regulatory, security, and quality concerns falls into this category.

A word of caution—each of these measures is intended to artificially stimulate customers to increase their level of motivation and understanding of a new product. As with other stimulants, the effect of these measures may wear off quickly or generate a negative reaction. Efforts to persuade customers may be quickly forgotten, while efforts to coerce may cause resentment and drive customers away.

■ 4.3 LISTENING TO THE LEADERS

Some customers are at the forefront of their segment and in a position to speak for it. These customers foreshadow the needs of the entire segment because they are familiar with conditions that other customers will encounter later and respond to similarly. By confining participants in the market research to this group, we can get answers that are representative of the long-term potential of a new information product. To estimate annual demand, we need to have a sense of when the remaining members of the segment are likely to encounter similar conditions.

In the beginning of the personal computer industry, few consumers had experience with a personal computer and, therefore, were not in a position to express a likelihood to purchase PC add-ons (e.g., memory expansion boards) and application software (e.g., word processors). However, a small number at the forefront of their segment had purchased a personal computer. They were familiar with the capabilities of the PC and could readily express a likelihood to purchase PC add-ons and application software. If one assumed that the needs of these leading customers were the same as those to follow, the answers from the leading customers would represent the long-term potential of the entire segment. To complete an estimate of the annual demand for PC add-ons and application software, PC sales growth rates could be used to show how many consumers would join the segment leaders as owners of PCs.

The leading customers often differ in significant ways from those that follow them. The assumption that their needs are similar should therefore be considered carefully.

■ 4.4 TRUSTING YOUR INSTINCTS

There are cases where one has to go beyond market research results and develop an information product based on trusting your instincts. This last path applies if the majority of customers for an information product can't express their purchase intention accurately, while the minority who can do not speak for the entire segment. The Internet in its early years is an example. The majority of consumers had no experience with the Internet at this point in time and could not grasp the relevance of commercial Internet information services, while the early adopters were researchers and academics who did not represent the market for commercial Internet services. Developers of commercial Internet services such as Motley Fool, Sportsline, and Soap Opera Digest Online have had to rely on their instincts during these early years of the Internet, since market research could not provide much guidance on their prospects.

The quality of one's instincts improves with information and, therefore, the absence of guidance from customers places a premium on finding alternative sources of input. There are other sources of industry leadership to consult and rely on in making intuitive judgments about whether to pursue or abandon an opportunity. Internally, a company's engineers, sales representatives, service personnel, marketing specialists, and management are usually highly tuned to prospects and possibilities in the marketplace. They are often capable of putting themselves in customers' shoes and anticipating what they will want. It is common for them to be customers themselves (e.g., computer engineers are heavy users of computers). Externally, a company's suppliers, distributors, and competitors are in a similar position to provide useful guidance. The input from internal and external experts can be gathered through group discussion, individual polling, role playing, random contacts, and trend analysis. The intuitive judgment must be supplied by management.

Intuitive judgments are often wrong and preparations should be made for this possibility. Taking steps to maximize flexibility to change direction, including exiting, is critical. Commitment to a course must be accompanied by vigilance toward unforeseen obstacles.

■ PROBLEMS AND SOLUTIONS

Problem 4.1: What are some additional examples of situations where customers can't express themselves and what corresponding action should be taken?

Solution: Digital cameras have struggled with low levels of motivation and understanding among consumers for a long time, so redirecting attention to the high end professional segment, which can clearly benefit from digital editing, appears appropriate. Computer security remains an afterthought for many computer users, but extensive publicity about meaningful break-ins could stimulate a stronger response. Few have enough experience with telemedicine to have confidence in it, but listening to the leading customers is likely to provide insight into the broader market. Global positioning systems have been mostly used by the military, which provides little guidance on consumer purchase intentions, leaving one to trust one's instincts.

Problem 4.2: What action should be taken after making an attempt to stimulate a response from customers?

Solution: A second pass through the issues in Figure 4.2 is required, which will lead to one of four possible outcomes. If the stimulus was unsuccessful, then the action is to redirect attention. If the stimulus leads to a high rate of growth in customer motivation and understanding, but not a widespread ability for customers to express themselves, then the action is to listen to the leaders or trust your instincts. If the stimulus was successful, then the action is to apply the techniques of Chapter 3.

Problem 4.3: How does listening to the leaders differ from the techniques of Chapter 3?

Solution: Listening to the leaders is very similar to the process of targeting a segment, listening to its members, and factoring in segment growth trends described in

Chapter 3. The difference is that the leading customers in a segment are a surrogate for the other segment members. This introduces an additional source of error into the research results.

Problem 4.4: What is an example of an information product where trusting instincts proved to be wrong?

Solution: Go's pen computer, Apple's Lisa®, Thinking Machines' Connection Machine®, interactive television.

Part III

Information
Technology System

Chapter 5

Information Flows
and Capacity

In this final period of the twentieth century, we Americans have a more fluid system of power than ever before in our history. Quite literally, power floats ...

—Hedrick Smith, *The Power Game*

Knowledge is power.

—Francis Bacon, *Meditationes Sacrae*, 1597. De Haeresibus

Aligning an information technology system with a customer opportunity is accomplished by constructing an information technology system architecture.[1] The term *information technology system architecture* is defined as the organization of information technology resources to accomplish a business purpose. As the name suggests, an information technology system architecture can be broken down into an information architecture and a technology architecture. Conceptually, they can be thought of as two aspects of the same system: one being the *logical* organization of information flows and the other being the *physical* organization of the technical equipment and staff (see Figure 5.1). A fundamental principle governs the relationship between these two aspects of a system: *the information load must be in balance with the technology capacity*. Familiar examples that illustrate this balance principle and the dualism of logical-physical are transactions and

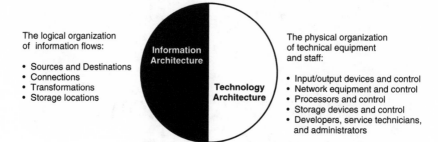

Figure 5.1 Information Technology System Architecture Framework.

point-of-sale machines; conversations and the telephone network; broadcasts and television networks; analyses and personal computers.

In this chapter, we will focus on the information architecture and in Chapter 6, the technology architecture. The point of an information architecture is to describe what information goes where and how much information needs to be handled. Simply put, it describes the information flows and capacity (load) requirements of the system.

■ 5.1 SOURCES & DESTINATIONS, CONNECTIONS, TRANSFORMATIONS, AND STORAGE LOCATIONS

The building blocks of an information architecture are sources & destinations, connections, transformations, and storage locations.

Sources & destinations are the information creators and users, respectively, and can be either human beings or equipment. They determine the beginning and end states of the information. These *states* are defined by the information structure and flux as seen by the creator or user.

The information *structure, $\psi(t)$,* is generally described by a combination of:

➤ Format—the arrangement of the data so as to be recognizable and useful.

➤ Timeliness—the time at which the data is sent and received.

➤ Correctness—the degree to which the data contains errors.

The information *flux*, $\phi(t)$ (also called traffic intensity) represents the rate of flow of information (see Figure 5.2). It is defined by the product of:

➤ Information Rate, $\lambda(t)$ *or* $\gamma(t)$—the number of messages (e.g., calls, packets) per unit time.

➤ Information Length, $L(t)$—the length of the messages, measured in units of time (e.g., seconds) or binary digits (e.g., bits).

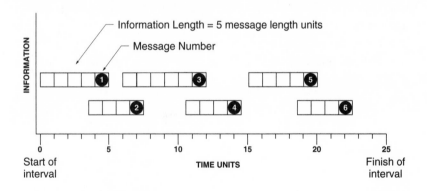

$$\text{Information Flux} = \text{Information Rate} \times \text{Information Length}$$

$$= \left[\left(\frac{6}{25} \right) \right] \times \left[\frac{(3 \times 4) + (2 \times 5) + (1 \times 6)}{6} \right]$$

$$= 1.12 \text{ message length units per unit time}$$

Figure 5.2   Information Intensity.

The information rate and length are often independent of one another, following separate processes and, therefore, have different descriptions. For example, the number of telephone calls is independent of their length. The underlying processes that give rise to information rates and lengths can be deterministic or probabilistic. In a *deterministic* process, a measurement of information rate or length can be predicted to have a specific value with certainty. It may be fixed or variable, so long as the time-dependency is known. A *probabilistic* process is one in which a measurement of information rate or length can only be predicted to have a range of possible values that differ in their relative frequency of occurrence.

Information flows fall into four categories, based on the behavior of the components of the information flux (see Figure 5.3). Deterministic information flows (Category A) are analyzed using a *fluid* model in which information is treated like a smooth continuous fluid. This model applies to analog systems, such as television, and overload or transient conditions in many digital systems where so much data has built up that nondeterministic flows are masked by the accumulated data. Probabilistic information flows (Categories B, C, D) are analyzed using a *queuing* model in which information is treated like a series of discrete intermittent blocks

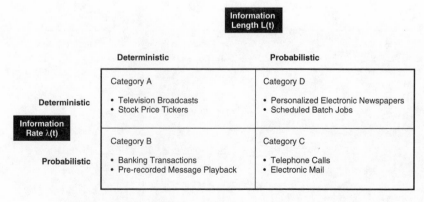

Figure 5.3   Information Flow Categories and Examples.

that can vary in length. This model applies to most digital systems, such as Ethernet networks, and some analog systems, such as plain old telephone service.

The information rate is called the traffic arrival rate, $\lambda(t)$, when applied to sources (messages sent). The information length, $L(t)$, is called the call holding time in telephone systems or the packet length in data networks. We write $\phi_{in}(t) = \lambda(t) L(t)$ when focusing on the incoming (arriving) information flux. The information rate is called the throughput, $\gamma(t)$, when applied to destinations (messages received). An example of a source is a typist ($\lambda(t)$ in characters per second and $L(t)$ in bits per character) and a destination is a printer ($\gamma(t)$ in characters per second).

The beginning and ending states of the information establish the communication problem: How to deliver a volume of information in a form that is recognizable and useful, in a timely manner, and with an acceptable level of accuracy. The performance requirements of a system are simply the detailed expression of the communications problem.

Connections are the information links, trunks, or wires that create a channel between sources (or destinations) and transformation units or storage locations. Connections have length and speed and can be viewed, at their simplest level, as a bit or cycle pipe through which a given number of bits or cycles per second can be transmitted. Connections have a transmission capacity that is not a function of time, C, equal to the transmission rate or bandwidth measured in bits per second (bps), or cycles per second (Hz). Examples are Ethernet (10 Mbps) and television channels (6 MHz). When using a queuing model, connections are servers with capacity, $\mu(t)$, some measures of which are packets per second or calls per second. The terms $\mu(t)$ and C are related through the expression $\mu(t) L(t) = C$.

Several streams of traffic may flow through a single connection by conforming to a discipline that allows the traffic to be distinguished, in a process called multiplexing (e.g., a cable television network is frequency division multiplexed to allow it to carry multiple channels). A connection may be capable of one-way or two-way transmission. The length of a connection creates a propagation delay between the time information leaves one end and arrives at the other end. This delay is proportional to the physical length of a connection and can be substantial if orbital signal paths are used. Similarly, the speed of a connection creates a transmission delay between the times the first and last parts of a piece of information are transmitted.

Transformation units are the information modifiers and can be input devices, processors, or output devices (e.g., keyboard, computer, or monitor, respectively), including any controlling software. They change the state of the information that flows through them. Transformation units have a capacity, *C*, equal to the transformation rate or bandwidth of the unit. When using a queuing model, the transformation units are servers with capacity, $\mu(t)$,[2] which varies depending on function (see Figure 5.4).

If a *transformation* is thought of as requiring an effort (resource expenditure) that results in a change of state, then, as a quantity it is similar to the concept of work, and the *transformation rate* is similar to the concept of power. More specifically, we can define these quantities as:

$$\text{Work} = \text{Effort} \times \text{Change of State}$$

$$\text{Power} = \frac{\text{Work}}{\text{Time}}$$

There are no generally accepted measures of the effort required to change a state and it is often of little interest (e.g., few care how much electrical energy is consumed by a transformation unit to change a state). So the industry typically assumes this to be a constant and uses well-defined changes of state, called "benchmarks" or "workloads," as measures of work. Each type of transformation unit has its own set of benchmarks or workloads. For example, those for a computer are known by names like "SPEC95," "Vortex," "Hanoi," "Prime," "Linpack"; for a fax machine they are known by names like "IEEE Facsimile Test Chart."

	Transformation Unit	Function	Measures of Transformation Rate	
			$\mu(t)$ (server capacity)	C (continuous capacity)
Probabilistic Information Flows	**1. Input:**			
	Keyboard	Translate keystrokes into alphanumeric data.	Characters per second (cps)	Bits per second (bps)
Queuing Model Applies	Automated teller machine	Translate function buttons into bank account deposit, withdrawal, and inquiry requests.	Transactions per second (tps)	Bits per second (bps)
	Telephone (rotary)	Translate rotary number dials into pulses.	Numbers per second	Pulses per second
	2. Processor:			
	General purpose computer	Calculate, compare, and copy data.	Tasks per second	Millions of instructions per second (MIPS)
	Transaction processor	Complete transaction and keep up to date record of account activity.	Transactions per second (tps)	Millions of instructions per second (MIPS)
	Telephone switch	Connect telephone calls.	Calls per second	Bits per second (bps)
	3. Output:			
	Printer	Convert an electronic data file into hardcopy.	Pages per minute (ppm)	Bits per second (bps)
	Display	Translate numeric data into a readable line.	Lines per second	Bits per second (bps)
	Internet TV	Translate HTML code into web pages.	Web pages per minute	Bits per second (bps)
Deterministic Information Flows	**1. Input:**			
	Antenna	Convert electromagnetic waves into electrical signals.		Hertz (Hz)
Fluid-Flow Model Applies	Microphone	Convert remote sound vibrations into electrical signals.		Thousands of Hertz (KHz)
	TV camera	Convert pictures into electrical signals.	There is no need to introduce the concept of a server since the system is deterministic.	Millions of Hertz (MHz)
	2. Processor:			
	Rectifier	Convert an alternating waveform to unidirectional one.		Hertz (Hz)
	Amplifier	Increase signal strength.		Thousands of Hertz (KHz)
	Multiplexor	Combine signals.		Millions of Hertz (MHz)
	3. Output:			
	Transmitter	Broadcast signal.		Thousands of Hertz (KHz)
	Speaker	Reproduce sound vibrations.		Thousands of Hertz (KHz)
	Television set	Receive and reproduce picture.		Millions of Hertz (MHz)

Figure 5.4   Transformation Rate Measures.

When the benchmark or workload is run and timed, the times recorded measure the power of a transformation unit (i.e., its ability to handle the anticipated information flows). A comparison of the times recorded for transformation units from different manufacturers is used to gauge relative power. For example, the IBM Model A computer may run "Vortex" in 203 seconds and the Control Data Model B computer may run it in 362 seconds. When a transformation unit is general purpose, meaning it is intended to handle a variety of information transformations, a series of benchmarks may need to be run to typify the mix of work.

If we rewrite the previous expression for power as the work done per cycle multiplied by the number of cycles per unit time,

$$\text{Power} = \left(\frac{\text{Work}}{\text{Cycle}}\right) \times \left(\frac{\text{Cycle}}{\text{Time}}\right)$$

then, in the case where transformation units share identical designs and differ only in speed, this expression reduces to:

$$\text{Power} = \text{Constant} \times \left(\frac{\text{Cycle}}{\text{Time}}\right)$$

This shows that a simple comparison of the underlying clock rates of the different transformation units can be used to gauge relative power. For example, an Intel 466MHz microprocessor should be twice as fast as one operating at 233MHz.

Storage locations are the information repositories that preserve the state of the information they contain. They share a number of the properties of transformation units, to the point where many people don't distinguish between the two. Storage locations have volume, figured in bytes or time. Storage locations also have a capacity, C, equal to the transfer rate, including latency, measured in bytes per second or cycles per second (Hz). When using a queuing model, storage locations are servers with capacity, $\mu(t)$, equal to the I/O rate measured in transfers per second. They may store information temporarily or permanently, and may allow reading and writing of data or be read-only. Examples are digital video disk drives (8.5 Gbytes of volume on a single-sided double-layered disk, 1.1 Mbytes/sec nominal transfer rate) and cassette tape drives (120 minutes of volume, 20 KHz bandwidth).

■ 5.2 FLOW DIAGRAMS

Sources & destinations, connections, transformations, and storage locations are assembled into a flow diagram, with the basic form shown in Figure 5.5. For deterministic systems, sources generate an information flux, $\phi_{in}(t)$, which arrives at a connection, transformation unit, or storage location with

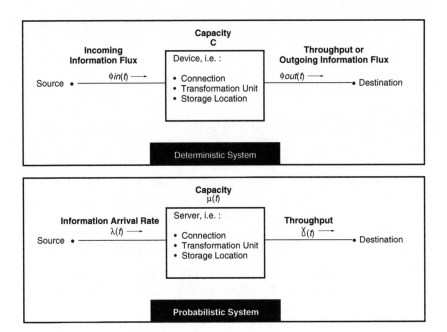

Figure 5.5   Basic Flow Diagram.

capacity, C, that in turn generates a throughput, $\phi_{out}(t)$, which is received at the destination.

For probabilistic systems, sources generate information at a rate, $\lambda(t)$, which arrives at a connection, transformation unit, or storage location any one of which acts as a server with capacity, $\mu(t)$, that in turn generates information at a rate, $\gamma(t)$, the throughput. For probabilistic systems, we do not focus on the information flux, $\phi_{in}(t) = \lambda(t)L(t)$. Instead, we use the information rate, $\lambda(t)$. We can do this by having the server capacity, $\mu(t)$, reflect message length. Letting $\mu(t)$ be the rate at which an incoming message is served, using the same units as that for $\lambda(t)$, accomplishes this. Then $\mu(t)$ changes according to the message length. Long messages result in a reduced rate of service and short messages result in an increased rate of service. Intuitively this makes sense because $1/\mu(t)$ is the service-time for a message. This length of time multiplied by a constant capacity, C, is equal to the length of the message, $C/\mu(t) = L(t)$. With the preceding definition of $\mu(t)$, there is no longer a need to include $L(t)$ in the picture, since it can be described in terms of $\mu(t)$, simplifying analysis.

The lines in the flow diagrams merely show which sources and destinations are assigned to a device or server. They should not be interpreted as wires: a wire is represented by a box since a wire acts as a device or server. Sometimes these lines are called "arcs" in the literature to emphasize this distinction.

The basic flow diagram applies wherever a connection, transformation unit, or storage location is found. *Complex systems can be constructed by chaining this basic form allowing the creation of systems with scales ranging from the micro to the mega* (see Figure 5.6).

For both deterministic and probabilistic information flows, the amount of incoming information does not have to equal the amount of outgoing information. Specifically, the information flux, $\phi_{in}(t)$, does not have to equal $\phi_{out}(t)$, and similarly, the information rate, $\lambda(t)$, does not have to equal the throughput, $\gamma(t)$. This is because information is

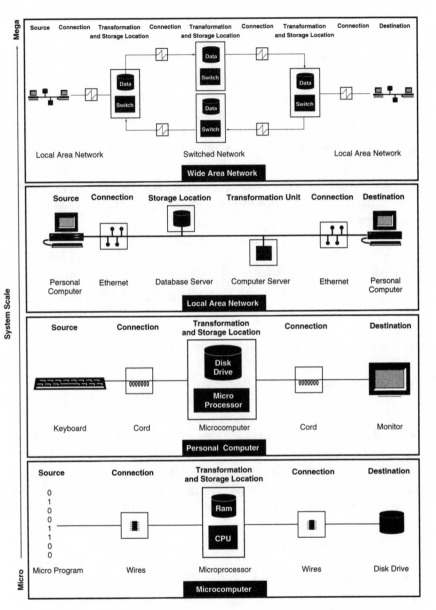

Figure 5.6 High-Level Applications of Basic Flow Diagram.

not conserved. For example, more telephone calls may arrive at a network switch than it can handle, resulting in some calls being blocked.

Consistent units must be used to analyze information flows. The incoming information flux, $\phi_{in}(t)$, the device capacity, C, and the outgoing information flux, $\phi_{out}(t)$, must be expressed in like units. Similarly, the information rate, $\lambda(t)$, the server capacity, $\mu(t)$, and the throughput, $\gamma(t)$, must be expressed in like units. For data systems, we might have $\lambda(t)$ in packets per second and $L(t)$ in bits per packet, so $\mu(t)$ and $\gamma(t)$ must be in packets per second with $\phi_{in}(t)$, C, and $\phi_{out}(t)$ in bits per second.

For telephone systems, we might have $\lambda(t)$ in calls per second and $L(t)$ in seconds per call, so $\mu(t)$ and $\gamma(t)$ must be in calls per second with $\phi_{in}(t)$, C, and $\phi_{out}(t)$ fundamentally dimensionless, though for telephony applications they are expressed in units called Erlangs or hundred call-seconds per hour (CCS). A system with a call rate of 2 calls per second with each call lasting 2 seconds has an information flux of 4 Erlangs. Since 1 CCS represents 100 call-seconds per hour, 1 Erlang corresponds to 36 CCS.

Sometimes conversion from analog to digital units must be performed because the world is mostly analog and the technology often digital. For example, if a source is faxing at a rate $\lambda(t)$, equal to a single page of graphics every 26.67 seconds, we must convert a page of graphics into an equivalent number of bits to calculate $\phi(t)$ in bps. Using one page of graphics as equivalent to 256,000 bits after data compression, we have $\phi = 256,000/26.67$ seconds $= 9,600$ bps. A conversion table for many of the information types encountered is shown in Figure 5.7. Conversion factors for analog objects will change over time as data compression (coding) techniques improve.

One more point should be made before proceeding to the next section. Information flows are the product of the interests of parties having a stake in the system. Customers have preferences for certain types and amounts of information. Regulators impose laws and standards governing content. Suppliers offer on request certain types of data. Employees expect a certain level of detail. Competitors provide substitutes.

Communication Type	Analog Form	Digital Equivalent	Degree of Equivalance*
Symbolic	1 character	8 bits	Exact; assumes extended ASCII coding
	8.5" x 11" typewritten page (80 lines x 66 characters)	42 kbits	Approximate; density of text varies and assumes extended ASCII coding
Aural	Voice: 4 kHz	64 kbps	Approximate; technology advances are reducing this to 32 kbps or less
	Music: 20 kHz	1.5 Mbps	Approximate; compact disc technology assumed here
Visual	8.5" x 11" graphic (1728 x 2376 pels)	256 kbits	Approximate; facsimile with 16-fold compression assumed here
	Black & White image (480 lines x 512 pels x 8 bits/pel)	1 Mbit	Approximate; assumes coded at 0.5 bits per pel
	Color image	1.15 to 1.25 Mbits	Approximate; color increases black/white bit count by 15% to 25%
	Videoconferencing/VCR	384 kbps to 1.5 Mbps	Approximate; depends on coding scheme
	Television	10 to 45 Mbps	Approximate; depends on coding scheme
	HDTV	20 to 100 Mbps	Approximate; depends on coding scheme

*Approximate conversion factors will change over time as coding technology improves. The numbers shown here are current as of 1999.
Definitions: 1 byte = 8 bits; bps = bits per second; G (Giga) = billion; M (Mega) = million; k (Kilo) = thousand.

Figure 5.7 Conversion Table.

Investors have a required rate of return. An information flow will reflect these combined interests.

■ 5.3 REENGINEERING

If an information flow currently exists, it should be diagrammed to reveal any area of inefficiency that can be corrected by a new information technology system. Examples of information flow inefficiencies are redundancy, delay, and error. The information flow should then be reengineered to eliminate as many inefficiencies as possible.[3] This reengineered information flow should become the basis for the system design.

To illustrate this, consider a universally recognizable office telephone system. An existing information flow diagram for this type of system might look like Figure 5.8.

Closer inspection of the information flows would usually reveal a large fraction of the destination telephones are within the offices of the company. This type of traffic is intralocation calling (or intercom calling), in contrast to incoming calls and outgoing calls, and can be dialed using only four digits instead of the seven digits for local outgoing calls. This traffic is inefficiently handled:

➤ Calls must travel offsite and be handled by the local telephone company, which simply reroutes them back to the office. When multiplied by the number of telephones, the amount of redundancy in the connection path is large.

➤ The time required to establish a connection is longer than needed, especially during busy periods.

➤ Some important types of intralocation traffic are discouraged because of lack of call forwarding, call transfer, or conference calling capabilities.

A reengineered information flow to address these inefficiencies would look like Figure 5.9.

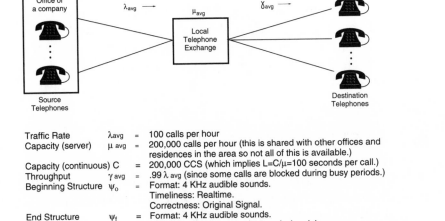

Traffic Rate λ_{avg} =   100 calls per hour

Capacity (server) μ_{avg} =   200,000 calls per hour (this is shared with other offices and residences in the area so not all of this is available.)

Capacity (continuous) C   =   200,000 CCS (which implies $L=C/\mu=100$ seconds per call.)

Throughput γ_{avg} =   .99 λ_{avg} (since some calls are blocked during busy periods.)

Beginning Structure ψ_o =   Format: 4 KHz audible sounds.
                                 Timeliness: Realtime.
                                   Correctness: Original Signal.

End Structure ψ_f =   Format: 4 KHz audible sounds.
                                   Timeliness: <.005 second transmission delay.
                                   Correctness: <.00016 errored–seconds. (An errored–second is a 1–second interval during which one or more bit errors occur. We assume digital telephony. For analog telephony, a signal to noise ratio could be used.)

Figure 5.8   Office Telephone System Information Flow.

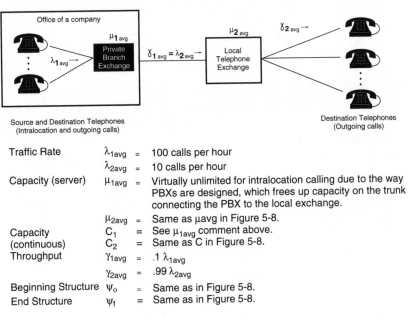

Traffic Rate λ_{1avg} =   100 calls per hour
                      λ_{2avg} =   10 calls per hour

Capacity (server) μ_{1avg} =   Virtually unlimited for intralocation calling due to the way PBXs are designed, which frees up capacity on the trunk connecting the PBX to the local exchange.

                      μ_{2avg} =   Same as μ_{avg} in Figure 5-8.

Capacity C_1 =   See μ_{1avg} comment above.

(continuous) C_2 =   Same as C in Figure 5-8.

Throughput γ_{1avg} =   .1 λ_{1avg}

                      γ_{2avg} =   .99 λ_{2avg}

Beginning Structure ψ_o =   Same as in Figure 5-8.

End Structure ψ_f =   Same as in Figure 5-8.

Figure 5.9   Reengineered Office Telephone System Information Flow.

A transformation unit, called a "private branch exchange," has been added to handle the intralocation traffic more efficiently. It allows four-digit dialing, reduces the length of the connection path significantly, and supports call forwarding, call transfer, and conference calling. These are readily available in the market.

■ 5.4 DETERMINISTIC FLOWS

A deterministic system is analyzed by applying the basic flow diagram (Figure 5.5), treating the information as if it were a fluid. Complex systems can be thought of as chains of this basic flow diagram and analyzed by partitioning them into these components. The quantities of interest for a given $\phi_{in}(t)$ are the device utilization, $\phi_{in}(t)/C$, the throughput, $\phi_{out}(t)$ and the backup time that can occur when the incoming and outgoing information flux differ, which we will call T_{backup}.

A little reflection will lead to the realization

$$\phi_{out}(t) = \begin{cases} \phi_{in}(t) \text{ if } T_{backup}(t) = 0 \\ C \text{ if } T_{backup}(t) > 0 \end{cases}$$

This leaves us with the task of finding the backup time, $T_{backup}(t)$, which depends critically on the ratio of the load to the capacity of the system. There are three ways to calculate this quantity: (1) arithmetic, (2) mathematical integration, and (3) computer programming. The arithmetical solution lays out the thought process for the other two methods. Let's focus on a time interval Δt that starts at $t_o + (k\text{-}1)\,\Delta t$ and ends at $t_o + k\Delta t$. If we define

$n_a(k)$ = number of arrivals during the kth interval

$n_d(k)$ = number of departures during the kth interval

$N_{backup}(k) = \dfrac{\text{cumulative number backed up}}{\text{between the first and the } k^{th} \text{interval}}$

and set $t_o = 0$ for the start time, then approximating the information flux, $\phi_{in}(t)$, by its value at the midpoint for the interval, we have for the number of arrivals during an interval (see Figure 5.10).

$$n_a(k) = \phi_{in}\left(\frac{(k-1)\Delta t + k\Delta t}{2}\right)\Delta t$$

where the parentheses mean the value of $\phi_{in}(t)$ at time t.

The maximum number of departures possible during an interval is $C\Delta t$. However, the amount of information available during the interval may be less than this, in which case the number of departures is equal to the cumulative number backed up at the start of the interval plus the number of arrivals during the interval $N_{backup}(k-1) + n_a(k)$. The number of departures during an interval is therefore the minimum of these two quantities

$$n_d(k) = \min\left\{C\Delta t, N_{backup}(k-1) + n_a(k)\right\}$$

The cumulative number of arrivals, of departures, and backed up at time t, where $t = \kappa\Delta t$ corresponds to the κth time interval, is then

$N_{arrivals}(\kappa) = $ cumulative number of arrivals $= n_a(1) + n_a(2) + \dots + n_a(\kappa)$

$N_{departures}(\kappa) = $ cumulative number of departures $= n_d(1) + n_d(2) + \dots + n_d(\kappa)$

$N_{backup}(\kappa) = $ cumulative number backed up $= N_{arrivals}(\kappa) - N_{departures}(\kappa)$

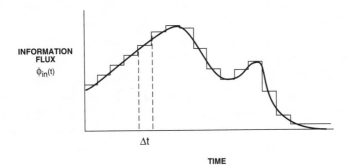

Figure 5.10 Midpoint Approximation.

The expression for $N_{backup}(\kappa)$ is a recursive formula, which means the next term in the sequence is determined from preceding terms. This arises because $n_d(\kappa)$ is determined by the value of $N_{backup}(\kappa - 1)$. This makes evaluating it well-suited for computers.

The task of finding the backup time, $T_{backup}(t)$, can be concluded by dividing the cumulative number backed up, $N_{backup}(\kappa)$, by the device capacity, C, which gives the time it would take to work this backup off.

$$T_{backup}(t) = T_{backup}(\kappa \Delta t) = \frac{N_{backup}(\kappa)}{C}$$

The value of this expression depends critically on the quantity

$$\rho(t) = \frac{\phi_{in}(t)}{C}$$

which can be seen by recognizing that $T_{backup}(t)$, is a function of terms that look like $n_a(\kappa)/C$ and $n_d(\kappa)/C$.

The quantity, $\rho(t) = \frac{\phi_{in}(t)}{C}$ with its probabilistic flow counterpart, $\lambda(t)/\mu(t)$, which we will call the connection, transformation unit, or storage location *utilization,* represents the ratio of information load to capacity. It plays a key role in determining the performance of a system for both deterministic and probabilistic flows. For equilibrium to exist, the information flux must be less than or equal to the capacity, $\rho(t) \leq 1$. If the reverse is true, $\rho(t) > 1$, traffic will build up in time if there is a buffer, or will not be served if the buffer is full or does not exist. These conditions are sometimes acceptable, even though they may not be desirable. For example, several channels of television broadcasts constantly arrive at a television receiver, but only one channel is watched at a time. The other channels' broadcasts are "spilled" into the ambient electromagnetic field, never being tuned in by the television receiver, due to lack of viewer interest.

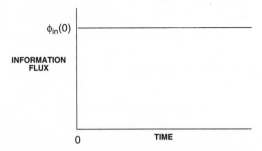

Figure 5.11 Constant Flow Condition.

This illustrates a general point: *The capacity requirements of a system are determined not just by the information load, but by the grade-of-service (performance level) that is acceptable.* Another way of stating this is that the offered load does not need to equal the carried load.

We are now ready to evaluate the expression for backup time, $T_{backup}(t)$, for a given $\phi_{in}(t)$. The simplest case is when we have a constant flow condition, $\phi_{in}(t) = \phi_{in}(0)$ (see Figure 5.11). We start with this because some information flows can be approximated by a constant level, and the effort involved in hand calculations is apparent even in this simplest of cases, which motivates the exploration of software programs for doing the mathematics by computer.

Assuming the system starts with no backup initially, $N_{backup}(0) = 0$, for the first interval, $\kappa = 1$, we have

$$T_{backup} \text{ (at end of first time interval)} = \frac{\phi_{in}(0)}{C}\Delta t$$
$$- \min\left\{\Delta t, \frac{\phi_{in}(0)}{C}\Delta t\right\}$$

As anticipated, the value of this expression depends critically on the term $\rho = \dfrac{\phi_{in}(0)}{C}$:

$$T_{backup}\text{(at end of first time interval)} = \begin{cases} 0 & \text{if } \rho \leq 1 \\ (\rho-1)\Delta t & \text{if } \rho > 1 \end{cases}$$

So for the simple case of constant flow, no backup occurs when the load on the system is less than or equal to the capacity, whereas it rises linearly with time when the load is greater than the capacity. This is exactly what you would expect.

Returning to our earlier illustration of an office telephone system (Figure 5.9), treating it for the moment as a deterministic flow with constant incoming information flux, and setting a grade-of-service of 1% of calls blocked, then the load to capacity requirement of the private branch exchange is

$$\rho_1 = \frac{\phi_{1in}}{C_1} = \frac{\lambda_{1avg}}{\mu_{1avg}} \leq 1.01$$

Similarly, if the PBX is well behaved, the outgoing information flux is constant and the load to capacity requirement of the local telephone exchange is also

$$\rho_2 = \frac{\phi_{2in}}{C_2} = \frac{\lambda_{2avg}}{\mu_{2avg}} \leq 1.01$$

The case just examined assumed a constant flow condition. Information rates or lengths, however, are usually dynamic, fluctuating over time, in which case we have a time-dependent flow condition, $\phi = \phi(t)$. The degree of fluctuation observed depends on the time interval, Δt, that is chosen (see Figure 5.12). The shorter Δt is, the less the observed range of fluctuation. For the largest possible time interval, Δt, equal to the lifetime of a system, the maximum degree of fluctuation is observed.

This raises the question: Which information flux (load) should be used to apply a grade-of-service criterion against? This requires engineering and business judgment. For a critical information service, the peak information flux is often appropriate; for a noncritical one, the average information flux may be appropriate (see Figure 5.13). Sometimes a grade-of-service criterion is established for both the peak

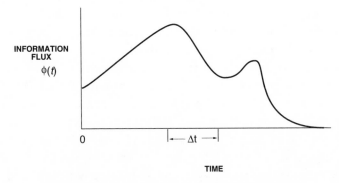

Figure 5.12   Time-Dependent Flow Condition.

and the average. For example, the grade-of-service for telephony is based on the busy hour (peak) and the busy season (average).

Once this choice is made, the variation in information flux within the time interval must be considered. This variation can be estimated based on the anticipated customer usage patterns, peaks, and averages from the market research results of Chapter 3, or measured using network analyzers to collect load characteristics in the case of existing traffic.

If the variation in the information flux within the time interval can be considered negligible or ignored from a

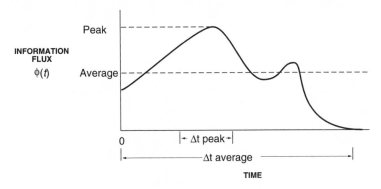

Figure 5.13   Load Intervals of Interest for Applying a Grade-of-Service Criterion.

grade-of-service standpoint, we have the constant flow condition discussed previously and the capacity requirements of the system can be derived accordingly. If it is not negligible, we need to calculate the backup time using the function $\phi(t)$ that describes how information flux behaves within the time interval. If we don't have an explicit description of $\phi(t)$, we can try to approximate it with linear, polynomial, exponential, sinusoidal, or other functions. The method of least-squares for curve fitting can be used for data on existing traffic.

Let's examine the case where we have a ramped flow, which is a simple model of an information system with a rush hour. This can be described by the linear function

$$\phi_{in}(t) = \phi_{in}(t_m) - \left(\frac{\phi_{in}(t_m) - \phi_{in}(0)}{t_m} \right) | t - t_m |$$

for the interval $0 < t < t_f$. A picture of this is shown in Figure 5.14.

Assuming the system starts with no backup initially $N_{backup}(0) = 0$, the backup remains zero until $\phi_{in}(t)$ increases to equal C for the first time at time t_1. At this point, the backup begins to grow reaching its maximum at time t_3 when $\phi_{in}(t)$ again equals C. Thereafter, it declines until it reaches zero again. A plot contrasting the cumulative number of arrivals and departures shows the growth and decline of the level of backup (see Figure 5.15).

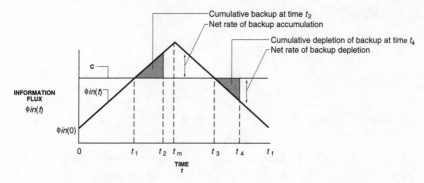

Figure 5.14 Ramped Flow Condition—"Rush Hour."

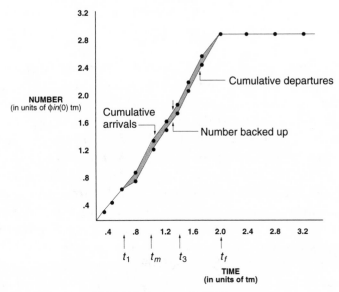

NOTE: $\phi in(tm)$ has been set to $2\phi in(0)$

Figure 5.15 Cumulative Arrivals and Departures.

This is a good place to show how integration can be used to calculate the backup time, $T_{backup}(t)$, partitioning $\phi_{in}(t)$ into periods where it is larger and smaller than C. Replacing the previous sums with integrals, after some effort, results in

$$T_{backup}(t) = \begin{cases} 0 & \text{for } 0 < t < t_1 \\[2ex] \left(\dfrac{\phi_{in}(t_m)}{C} - 1\right)\left[\dfrac{(t-t_1)^2}{2(t_m - t_1)}\right] & \text{for } t_1 < t < t_m \\[3ex] \left(\dfrac{\phi_{in}(t_m)}{C} - 1\right)\left[\dfrac{(t-t_1)^2 - 2(t-t_m)^2}{2(t_m - t_1)}\right] & \text{for } t_m < t < \dfrac{\left(\dfrac{\sqrt{2}}{2}t_f + t_1\right)}{\sqrt{2} + 1} \\[4ex] 0 & \text{for } \dfrac{\left(\dfrac{\sqrt{2}}{2}t_f + t_1\right)}{\sqrt{2} + 1} < t \end{cases}$$

Note. For these formulas to be valid, t_1 must be greater than $.29t_f$, otherwise working off the backlog will take longer than t_f and $\phi_{in}(t)$ could become negative in the process. This is equivalent to requiring $C > 1.58\phi_{in}(0)$.

A plot of $T_{backup}(t)$ shows the rush hour pattern for an information system that should be familiar to most of us (see Figure 5.16).

The information system operates smoothly until the beginning of the rush hour, t_1. Delays are then encountered that reach a peak at t_3, when incoming flows have returned to levels below the capacity of the system. At this point, the rush hour is over. However, even though levels have returned to normal, a substantial backup has to be worked off while newly arriving information is handled. Thus, the backup continues for some time longer, finally dropping to zero. These comments apply to any information flow, where the incoming flux at times exceeds the capacity of the system.

If you worked through the mathematics of calculating the backup time for the preceding constant and ramped flow examples, you will be keenly aware of how tedious this can be. A recommended alternative is to use a software program for doing the mathematics by computer. *Mathematica*® is one such program that will take a nearly direct formulation of a mathematical problem and solve it automatically. If you can write down the mathematics, you can

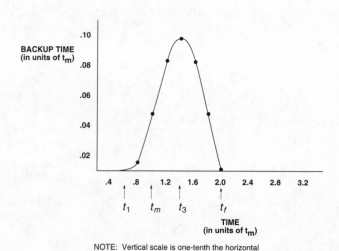

NOTE: Vertical scale is one-tenth the horizontal

Figure 5.16 Backup Time.

operate this software, so long as you stay within the limits of its capability. A program written in *Mathematica* for automatically calculating the backup time is shown in Figure 5.17. It can be seen to be a close copy of the arithmetical formulation developed at the beginning of this section. This program is written in a general form, so that users can specify whatever function they wish to represent the incoming information flux along with the other parameters of the

Definitions

$t = K \Delta t =$ time at which the expression for backup time is to be evaluated, which corresponds to the Kth time interval.

$t_f =$ final time marking the end of the period of interest, assuming a start time of zero.

$K =$ total number of time intervals the period of interest is divided into; a larger number increases resolution of detail, but increases calculation time.

$\Delta t = t_f \div K =$ length of a time interval.

$\emptyset_{in}[k] =$ function representing the incoming information flux, evaluated at the midpoint of the kth time interval.

$C =$ continuous capacity of device

$n_a[k] =$ number of arrivals during the kth time interval

$n_d[k] =$ number of departures during the kth time interval

$N_a[K] =$ cumulative number of arrivals at time $t = K \Delta t$

$N_d[K] =$ cumulative number of departures at time $t = K \Delta t$

$N_b[K] =$ cumulative number backed-up at time $t = K \Delta t$

$N_b[0] =$ initial amount of backup

$T_b[K] =$ the backup time at time $t = K \Delta t$

Calculation of Backup Time

$n_a[k\_] := n_a[k] = \emptyset_{in}[k] \; \Delta t$

$N_a[K\_] := \text{Sum}[n_a[k], \{k, 1, K\}]$

$N_b[0] = 0$

$n_d[k\_] := n_d[k] = \text{Min}\,[C \, \Delta \, t, \, N_b[k\text{-}1] \, + \, n_a[k]]$

$N_d[K\_]:= \text{Sum}[n_d[k], \{k, 1, K\}]$

$N_b[K\_] = N_a[K] - N_d[K]$

$T_b[K\_] := N_b[K] \div C$

Figure 5.17 Mathematica® Program for Automatically
Calculating Backup Time.

flow. The output for a square pulse, ramped flow, sinusoidal flow, and exponential flow is shown in Figure 5.18.

The significant time savings and the improved accuracy in getting results makes use of computer programs for doing mathematics the preferred way to calculate information flow quantities such as backup time.

The last case of deterministic flows we will discuss is a complex system arranged as a network (see Figure 5.19).

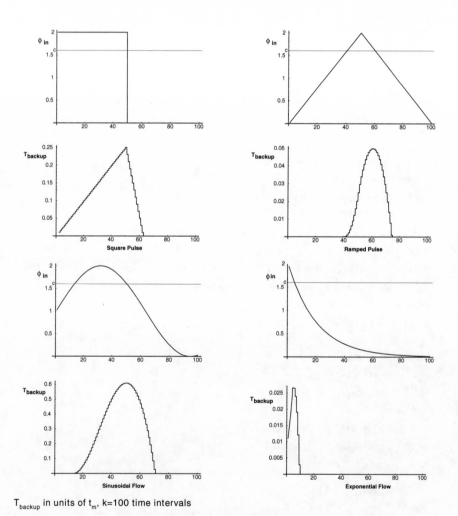

T_{backup} in units of t_m, k=100 time intervals

Figure 5.18 Some Output from Program.

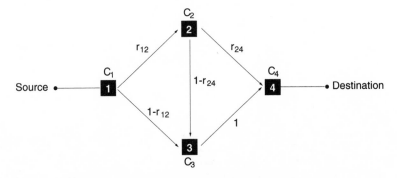

Figure 5.19 Networked Deterministic System.

This can arise if there are many steps involved in processing information, or if a system is geographically dispersed. In network arrangements, flows may be split between multiple devices so we introduce the term r_{ij} representing the flow from device i to j, expressed as a percentage of the capacity of device i.

The problem here is understanding what the capacity of this system is for flows traveling from the source to the destination. The answer is given by the maximum-flow minimum-cut theorem.[4] To state this theorem, we must first define the concept of a cut as a set of flows that, once removed from a network, will separate all flow from the source to the destination. A simple way to identify all possible cuts is to draw lines through the network that divide it in two. The flows across this line that are directed toward the destination are a cut. An example is shown in Figure 5.20.

You can think of a deterministic network as equivalent to a pipe of varying width and a cut as a cross-section of the pipe. Obviously the capacity of a pipe is determined by its smallest cross-section, which is essentially what the maximum-flow minimum-cut theorem states: the maximum flow between a source and a destination is the minimum capacity of all cuts.

In practice, many networks can be approximated by a deterministic model. Analytic and simulation studies of

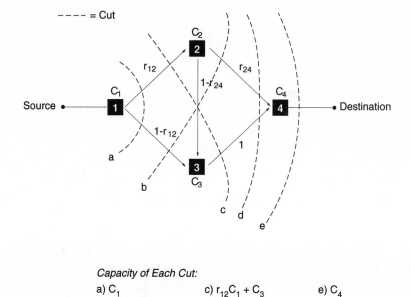

Capacity of Each Cut:
a) C_1
b) $(1-r_{12}) C_1 + C_2$
c) $r_{12}C_1 + C_3$
d) $r_{24} C_2 + C_3$
e) C_4

Figure 5.20 Cuts.

networks, including the Internet, have shown that delays are small and nearly that of an unloaded network until the load approaches the capacity of the minimum cut. Then the delay increases rapidly in an unbounded fashion.[5]

Two comments need to be made about applying the maximum-flow minimum-cut theorem. First, this theorem applies when it is not necessary to distinguish among the units of information flowing in the network. If there are some units of information that have to be directed to a particular device, we have what is called a multi-commodity network flow which is much more difficult to solve. Second, for complex networks with a large number of possible cuts, a procedure known as the labeling algorithm can be used to compute the network capacity and identify the particular cut associated with it. For both of these circumstances the reader is referred to the literature for further discussion.[6]

■ 5.5 PROBABILISTIC FLOWS

A probabilistic system is analyzed by applying the basic flow diagram (Figure 5.5), treating the information as if it were a series of discrete intermittent blocks that can vary in length. The quantities of interest for a given $\lambda(t)$ are the server utilization, $\rho(t) = \lambda(t)/\mu(t)$, the throughput, $\gamma(t)$, and the time spent waiting for service which we will call $T_{wait}(t)$. These quantities are random variables whose values cannot be known in advance since they follow a probability distribution of occurrence.

Complex systems can be thought of as chains of the basic flow diagram. A complex probabilistic system can only be analyzed at the present time: (1) by reducing it to a single basic flow diagram and certain variations of it; (2) by making complicated approximations such as merging information flows restores their original character (Kleinrock approximation); or (3) by constructing a computer simulation. Deriving exact expressions for the information flows of complex probabilistic systems is, unfortunately, beyond the current state-of-the-art in mathematics.

To avoid this problem, often only the most critical part of a probabilistic system is analyzed and the rest is modeled as simply a constant flow under worst case conditions, which conforms to (1). This works well for a large number of systems. For example, with a local area network the information flows in an individual's personal computer can be ignored since it is rarely overloaded and the analysis confined to bottlenecks such as printer, database, or communication servers where contention is found. We confine our discussion to this approach in the remainder of this section and will address computer simulation in the next section.[7]

To analyze a probabilistic system, we must first determine the time intervals for which the load on the system is stationary. By *stationary load,* we mean the information arrival rate and service time probability distributions do not change their form and therefore the parameters that describe the distribution, such as the mean and variance, remain constant.

For example, in the telephone system the stationary interval is usually taken to be an hour, since empirical data supports the assumption that telephone traffic distributions can be considered stationary over an hour's time.

A grade-of-service criterion can then be applied to the stationary load interval of interest such as the one where the peak information rate occurs.

Deciding what probability distribution to use to describe the information arrival and service time within a stationary interval can be difficult. One possible approach is to simply replace a probability distribution with its average value, which effectively treats the flow as a deterministic system (see Figure 5.21). This is sensible if we know the average value but little about the range or frequency of occurrence of different values for $\lambda(t)$, $\mu(t)$. The validity of the approximation, however, is limited to situations where the variation from the average of information and arrival rates is negligible or can be ignored from a grade-of-service standpoint. Where the performance of a system is sensitive to these vari-

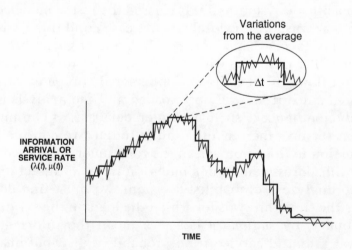

Figure 5.21 Average Value Approximation During Stationary Load Intervals.

ations, such as occurs when systems are running near capacity, $\rho(t) \approx 1$, this assumption cannot be made.

The reason for this is the probabilistic variability of the arrival and service rates can cause the information to arrive in clumps or the service time to elongate, which can lead the system to become congested.

We are therefore still left with the task of deciding what probability distribution to use, through we have narrowed things down slightly. There are four cases to consider:

1. Existing flows can be measured.
2. The underlying information generation process is understood.
3. Estimates of the parameters of a distribution are available.
4. There is an absence of data.

The first case is restricted to existing flows only. The other three cases can arise with both new and existing flows.

For Case 1, with existing flows we can collect data on the quantity of interest and either use these values as is, directly in our analysis; derive an empirical distribution from which random values can be generated; or fit a known theoretical distribution to the data such as the normal distribution. Shortcomings can be found with each of these approaches, though their severity depends on the situation. Using the data as is limits the analysis to a consideration of what has happened historically. The empirical distribution may have a form that differs from its long-term time average, and may not generate extreme values that are infrequently encountered yet substantial in impact. The theoretical distribution may be a poor fit to the observed data. A trade-off that minimizes these shortcomings must be made in deciding which of these approaches is preferable.

For Case 2, an understanding of the underlying process of information generation can be used to select a distribution that conforms to it. In the commonly occurring situation where a large number of potential users are acting independently, and the percentage of users actually generating information arrivals is small compared with the maximum possible, a Poisson distribution has been shown to describe the information arrival rate well. This usually applies to calls, transactions, and packets. When the probability of completion of service in a small interval of time is directly proportional to the length of the interval, no matter how long service has already been in progress, the negative exponential distribution or the geometric distribution describes the service time well. The former is usually applied to calls and is an example of a *continuous* distribution, which means the probability the service time is within a range of values can be given. The latter is often applied to transactions and is the *discrete* form of the negative exponential distribution, which means the probability the service time assumes a specific value can be given. A listing of some of the more important distributions can be found in Appendix B.

For Case 3, sometimes the available data is limited to estimates of the parameters of a distribution such as the mean, variance, minimum, maximum, and particular aspects of its shape. Frankly, the most efficient approach to selecting an appropriate distribution in this case is to scan through listings of probability distributions and pick the one with the closest match. Additional sophistication can be added by performing statistical tests, such as checking to see if the mean is equal to the median, which would suggest a symmetric continuous distribution should be chosen.

For Case 4, when there is an absence of data only the crudest of approximations can be made. One is to pick a range where it is felt that the information rate will fall with almost certainty. A uniform probability distribution can then be assumed where all values within this range have equal probability. This first approximation can be refined by estimating the most frequently occurring value within this range. A triangular distribution that peaks at this point can then be assumed. Other possibilities are to try to find an upper and lower bound for the system. So, for example, the system might be examined under the assumption of a totally random process using the negative exponential distribution, and the results contrasted with those found if a constant value is assumed. Since all other distributions produce probabilities between these two extremes, the results provide a direct indication of the range of possible outcomes.

A pictorial description of what we are doing when we use a particular distribution to represent the arrival or service rate is shown in Figure 5.22.

This may seem to be a lot of trouble to go through to simply build a model that reconstructs actual information rates. The problem is, we rarely know the actual information rate since this requires a continuous history be recorded and that the system lifetime be over. However, we can often estimate the parameters characterizing the information rate such as the average, and derive a reasonable probability distribution of information rates to apply. *This allows us to address the practical problem of forecasting what the actual information rate will be in some future time interval.* The average information rate and other parameters can be estimated from the results of the market research of Chapter 3 on customer usage demand patterns. If one is fortunate enough to be able to observe actual information rates, measuring the information rate over a time interval of interest (e.g., the busiest

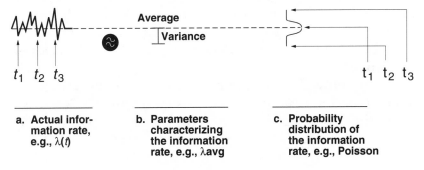

a. Actual information rate, e.g., $\lambda(t)$

b. Parameters characterizing the information rate, e.g., λavg

c. Probability distribution of the information rate, e.g., Poisson

Figure 5.22 Pictorial Description of Probabilistic Information Flow Model.

hour of the day) will give an estimate of these parameters. Building these models of information flows is challenging, but necessary. For, if you don't, you are likely to build a system that is obsolete or wasteful because it has been under- or overengineered for the load it actually experiences.

Now we can turn our attention to calculating the server utilization, $\rho(t)$, the throughput, $\gamma(t)$, and the time spent waiting for service, $T_{wait}(t)$ for a given flow. The last two quantities generally depend on the level of server utilization, $\rho(t) = \lambda(t)/\mu(t)$.

There are a large number of possible system configurations for which these quantities can be calculated. So many, in fact, that *Kendall notation* A/B/C/D/E/F is used to classify these different systems by their characteristics. The symbol A stands for the information arrival rate distribution, B is the service time distribution, C is the number of servers, D is the buffer capacity, E is the size of the source population, and F is the service discipline. We haven't spoken about D, E, F and will not because of the unnecessary complexity they add to the discussion. Normally, D and E are assumed to be infinite and F is first-in, first-out.

Applying a telemarketing call-center analogy to illustrate, A is the number of calls, B is the length of the calls, C is the number of agents, D is the number of calls that can be put on hold, E is the maximum number of customers making calls, and F is the order in which the calls are handled.

Deriving results for each of these configurations is covered by a rich, and remarkably complex, body of technical literature.[8] For our purposes, we only care about the results found for these systems. A listing of selected results is found in Appendix C.

Let's apply some of these results to four illustrations: a home banking system that could support the bank-for-kids opportunity of Chapter 2; an airline messaging system; an office telephone system like that of Chapter 5; and an Internet access system (see Figure 5.23). The system part of interest in all three cases will be the connecting trunk that provides a communications link for remote devices. The

| Application | Flow Diagram Components for the System Part Analyzed | | | Flow Model | Comment |
	Source	Server	Destination		
1. Home Banking	Concentrator/ Multiplexor	Connecting Trunk	Bank Transaction Processing System	M/D/1	Packet Switched System
2. Airline Messaging	Communica- tions Switch	Connecting Trunk	Airline Flight Operations System	M/M/1	Message Switched System
3. Office Telephone	PBX	Central Office Trunk Group	Local Telephone Exchange	M/M/N	Circuit Switched System
4. Internet Access	Network Computer/ Set Top Box	Cable Television Channel	Cable Headend	M/M/N	Packet Switched System

Figure 5.23 Comparison of Probabilistic Flow Illustrations.

level of utilization and an appropriate grade-of-service criterion will be used to calculate the required capacity of the connecting trunk.

The home banking system part can be modeled as an M/D/1 flow, meaning traffic arrivals follow a Poisson distribution, service times are constant, and there is a single server. This is the case of Category B information flows in Figure 5.3. The reason this model is sensible is that the arrival rate should be approximately random, bank transactions are typically fixed in length with a few transaction types (e.g., account withdrawal) making up the bulk of the traffic, and a single communication line can be purchased that will economically provide the capacity needed. The flow diagram is shown in Figure 5.24. Assume the network is *packet-switched,* a technology where messages are broken into strings of bits called packets that are individually transmitted through a network and reassembled into messages at the destination. This technology is well suited for data communications. Depending on the particular implementation, packets can be fixed- or variable in length.[9] Lets say the bank transactions are loaded into fixed length packets of 1,000 bits, which is about as much information as a name, address,

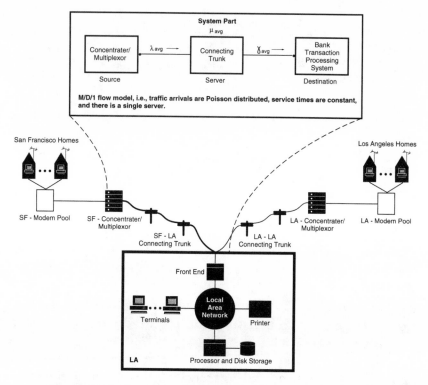

Figure 5.24 Home Banking System Part Information Flow.

and telephone number. This further reinforces the deterministic nature of the traffic. A fairly stringent grade-of-service criterion must be chosen because banking customer satisfaction levels depend on quick system response and there are other sources of delay whose effects are additive such as service times, processing time, and propagation times. Setting the grade-of-service so that the probability is less than 1% that the time spent waiting for service is more than 3 seconds should be adequate to take into account these factors. To ensure the system is operating at an efficient level, the condition of 90% communications trunk utilization will also be imposed. Applying both criteria to the formula for the probability distribution of waiting time for an M/D/1 system (see Appendix C), we find that Probability (T_{wait} > 3 seconds) < .01 when

$$\frac{3 \text{ seconds}}{\dfrac{1}{\mu_{avg}}} > 22$$

Since $\mu_{avg} L_{avg} = C$, we have

$$\frac{3 \text{ seconds}}{1,000 \text{ bits}} C > 22$$

or the capacity of the connecting trunk, C, must be greater than 7.3 kbps. A 9.6 kbps modem connection would therefore be suitable. The low rate of speed found here is due to the short length of banking transactions. However, this capacity requirement is sensitive to high levels of utilization. This can be seen if we let $\rho \approx .95$, which is about a 5% increase. Then the capacity requirement rises to about 15 kbps or a 100% increase! There is a clear need to control loads to avoid this "butterfly effect" where a small increase in utilization at high levels can have a significant impact on the capacity requirements of a system. *Flow control* to regulate the load on a system through blocking, scheduling, and rate restrictions is a major aspect of the design and operation of packet switching networks.

The airline messaging system part can be modeled as an M/M/1 flow, meaning traffic arrivals follow a Poisson distribution, service times follow a negative exponential distribution, and there is a single server. This is the case of "Category C" information flows in Figure 5.3. The reason this model is sensible is that the airline messages resemble e-mail. They concern flight operations, administrative matters, commercial activities, and technical issues. These messages arrive randomly, their lengths are random, and a single communications line can be purchased to provide the capacity needed. The flow diagram is shown in Figure 5.25. Assume the network is *message-switched,* which is a technology where complete messages are transported as a unit, without stringent time requirements since the messages are nonconversational.

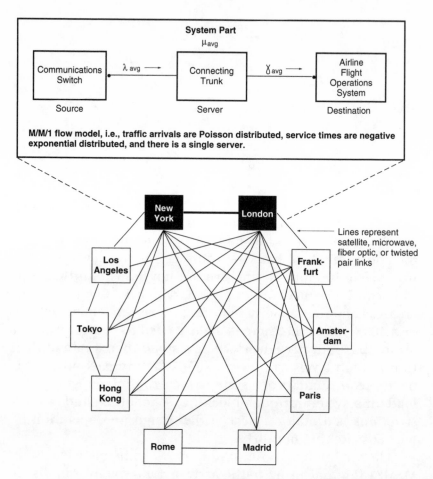

Figure 5.25 Airline Messaging System Part Information Flow.

Let's say the messages have an average length of 5,000 bits, or about a paragraph of information.

The nonconversational aspect of these messages means a much more relaxed grade-of-service criterion can be chosen. Setting the grade-of-service to be that the probability is less than 1% the time spent waiting for service is more than 10 minutes, should ensure the messages are received when they are needed yet without an undue rush. Applying this grade-of-service criterion, under the condition of 90% communications trunk utilization, to the formula for the waiting time distribution for an M/M/1 system (see Appendix C), we find that Probability ($T_{wait} >$ 600 seconds) < .01 when

$$\frac{600 \text{ seconds}}{\frac{1}{\mu_{avg}}} > 45$$

As before, since $\mu_{avg} L_{avg} = C$ we have

$$\frac{600 \text{ seconds}}{5{,}000 \text{ bits}} C > 45$$

or the capacity of the connecting trunk, C, must be greater than .4 kbps. This is an extremely low rate of speed and is due to the relaxed grade-of-service criteria. This result has led airlines to share the communications lines for their messaging systems with their reservation systems, so both message and reservation traffic is carried over the same link. These shared links have historically had a capacity of 9.6 to 14.4 kbps.

The office telephone system part can be modeled as an M/M/N flow, meaning traffic arrivals follow a Poisson distribution, service times follow a negative exponential distribution, and there are N servers. This also is a case of "Category C" information flows. The reason this model is sensible is that analysis of telephone call traffic has shown a remarkable correspondence between the Poisson distribution and arrival rates, as well as between the negative exponential distribution and observed call holding times. In addition, central office trunk groups provide many telephone circuits (servers) to improve service response. The flow diagram is shown in Figure 5.26. Assume the network is *circuit-switched* which is a technology where a dedicated communications path is temporarily set up between a source and a destination, with messages between them traveling over it until it is no longer needed. This is the way most telephone calls have historically been handled. This technology forces us to rethink our approach to the problem of determining what the

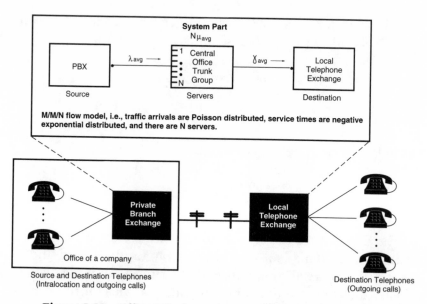

Figure 5.26 Office Telephone System Part Information Flow.

capacity of the connecting trunk must be, because a telephone call cannot be sped up. A telephone call will hold on to a circuit for the duration of a call, which lasts on average about 3.5 minutes, regardless of the capacity of the circuit (so long as it is above the minimum required to transmit a voice signal). Therefore, the problem becomes one of determining how many voice-quality circuits are needed for a particular grade-of-service. A grade-of-service criterion in line with service levels of telephone companies is that the probability be less than 1% that the time spent waiting for a circuit to become available is more than 1 second. Measurements have shown the average telephone is in use about 7.5% of the time during the busy hour, so for 100 phones the total load on the system is about 7.5 Erlangs. For this system, we have N servers so

$$\rho(t) = \frac{\lambda_{avg}}{N\mu_{avg}}$$

where μ_{avg} is the service rate of an individual server.

The term ρ can be thought of as the utilization per trunk. The total load on the system is represented by Nρ.

At this point, we know that at least 8 voice-grade circuits are needed since we have an overloaded system, ρ > 1, if N < 8. To get the exact number of circuits, we need to use the formula for the waiting time distribution for an M/M/N system (see Appendix C), under the conditions Nρ = 7.5 Erlangs and that the wait time is less than 1 second or, in units of the average call holding time, is less than 1 second/3.5 minutes = 1 second/210 seconds = .0048. This occurs when N = 15. A typical voice-quality digital circuit has a capacity of 64 kbps so the total capacity requirement here is nearly 1 Mbps. A 1.5 Mbps T1 line with 24 voice-quality circuits would be more than adequate for this application.

An interesting question arises with multiple server systems: Which is more efficient—systems with a low number of servers or a high number? *The answer, it will turn out, is that a lower number of faster or larger servers is usually preferred over a higher number of slower or smaller servers, from a performance standpoint.* This is a very general result, applicable to any type of server, whether man or machine. Two formulations of this problem are worth exploring. The first applies broadly, and we will continue to use the office telephone system as an illustration. The second applies to systems other than those that are real-time circuit-switched, which rules out telephony-like systems. We will turn to the cable television network to illustrate this second formulation.

First consider the case where several office PBX systems are connected to the local telephone exchange. The formulation of the problem here is: Which is more efficient—a single common trunk group or several separate trunk groups? (See Figure 5.27.) Consider dividing the PBX call volume across k separate trunk groups. The common trunk group corresponds to $k = 1$ and the separate trunk groups correspond to $k = 2, 3 \ldots$ A plot of the number of servers needed for a given load on the system, keeping the grade-of-service constant, is shown in Figure 5.28. We use the term server in

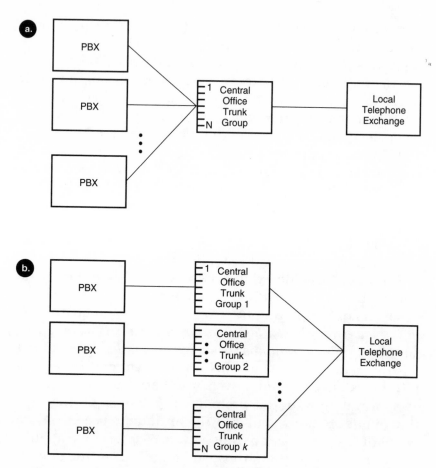

Figure 5.27 Office Telephone Systems: (a) Common Trunk Group;
(b) Separate Trunk Group.

this chart to express the generality of the result and only need to replace it with the word "trunk" to interpret the chart for our example. Fewer trunks are needed with a common trunk group for any offered load on the system. An economy of scale effect is at work here, with consolidated groups of servers more efficient than distributed groups. The reason for this is that all servers are available to incoming traffic with consolidated groups, so that only the very largest variations in flux will use the full capacity of the system.

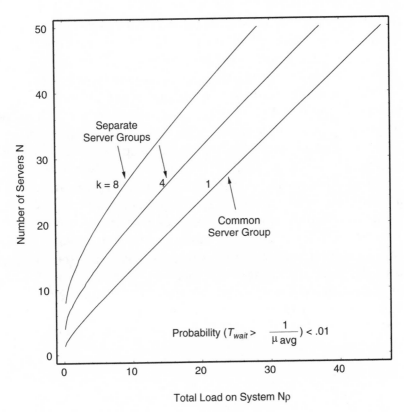

Figure 5.28 Common Server Group Advantage in an M/M/N System.

This effect has profound implications for network design. It is helping to propel the formation of integrated networks that carry video, voice, and data traffic together. Today's separate television, telephone, and data networks could be made more efficient if grouped together. The term "convergence" is often used to describe this integration process. It is also an important force behind shaping networks into a monopolistic and hierarchical structure.

By hierarchical, we mean a radiating pattern formed by the tendency for traffic to be concentrated as a result of this economy of scale. This pattern is so common it has been given the name star network, and at the center of the network the largest switching systems can be found. The cost of these switching systems must be weighed against the savings in trunks as well as reliability and other considerations. These trade-offs often shape larger networks into the form of a constellation of interconnected stars (see Figure 5.29).

The second formulation of the problem is: Which is more efficient—a multiple server system with N servers each of capacity μ_{avg}, or a single server with equivalent capacity $N\mu_{avg}$? To answer this question, we must drop real-time circuit-switched systems from consideration. As earlier, the reason for this is that for these systems the communication, such as a telephone call, cannot be sped up. Let's take the case of a network computer (set top box) attached to the cable television network for Internet access, using packet switching. The cable channel for providing Internet access can be divided into N separate channels of capacity μ_{avg} (see Figure 5.30a), or consolidated into a single channel of capacity $N\mu_{avg}$ (see Figure 5.30b). We have to be careful here because the capacity of the individual servers is not identical. The service

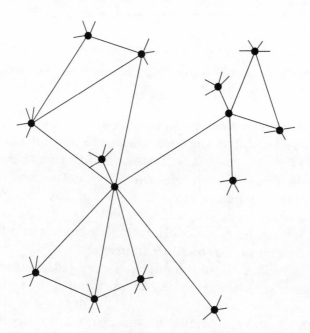

Figure 5.29 Constellation of Interconnected Star Networks.

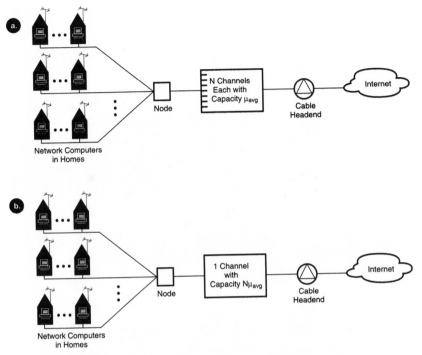

Figure 5.30 Network Computer System over Cable:
(a) Multiple Circuits; (b) Single Circuit.

times are therefore different in the two systems, which means we must take into account both the wait time and the service time in any comparison. In the previous examples, the capacities of the servers were identical so service time did not matter in comparing them. The expression for the probability distribution of the time spent in the system is complicated[10]; the problem can be simplified by using the average value of the time spent in the system as our measure. This quantity provides an aggregate comparison and is equal to the average time spent waiting for service (see Appendix C), plus the average time spent in service, $1/\mu_{avg}$. A plot of the time spent in the system and the portion of this time spent waiting for service is shown in Figure 5.31. This demonstrates that the shortest amount of time is spent in the single server system. The multiple server systems do have shorter

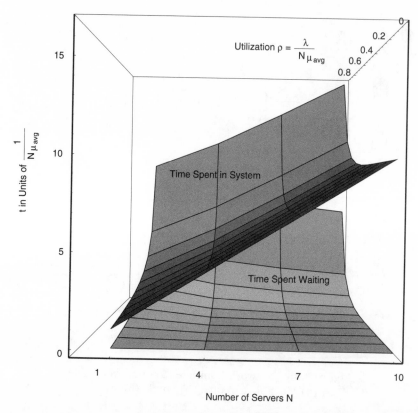

Figure 5.31 Single Server Advantage over Equivalent Capacity Multiple Server Systems.

waiting times, but this is more than offset by longer service times. As in the previous discussion, the implications of this for network design are profound. The comments on propelling the integration of video, voice, and data, as well as the formation of hierarchical networks are reinforced here. We can expect both of these developments to occur in cable television networks. In addition, two other observations can be made. First, a system design that shares high performance server resources, rather than dedicates low performance resources, is advantageous. This approach is widely used in the traditional telephone and television networks. The concept of an inexpensive network computer in the home connected over cable television lines to substantial computer server power therefore has real merit. Second, R&D efforts to build high performance communication, processing, and storage servers are of strong economic, and not just academic, interest. The backbone and headends of cable television networks will become populated by this type of equipment, in step with the provision of advanced services such as switched video, digital telephones, and Internet access.

One final comparison should be made before moving on to the next section. Since we have compared single server with multiple server systems and found the single server systems have a performance advantage, it is reasonable to inquire about how the various single server systems compare among themselves. This is shown in Figure 5.32, which plots the average time spent in each system, M/D/1, M/M/1, and deterministic, keeping the server capacity constant. As can be seen, the more deterministic the system, the shorter the amount of time spent in the system. The difference can be substantial at high levels of utilization.

We now turn to software simulation of information systems, which provides some relief from the mathematical

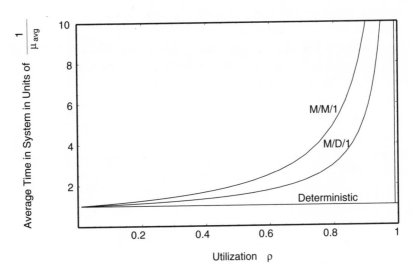

Figure 5.32 Comparison of Single Server Systems.

acrobatics of queuing theory while providing practical results for actual information systems.

■ 5.6 SIMULATION

In the real world, modeling a complex probabilistic system from end-to-end usually cannot be done exactly. Many system parts can be involved and useful expressions for quantities of interest do not exist. Simulation must be used instead where the system is represented in computer software and its operation by the running of a software program. Powerful software packages such as Comnet[11] are available for just this purpose. Those with graphical user interfaces let you point and click on preconstructed components from a palette to assemble the system desired. A dialog box captures the specific parameters for each component. Once the system is assembled on the computer screen, the simulation can be run. Statistics on utilization, throughput, and delay are automatically collected and can be viewed in the form of animation, snapshots, real-time plots, and reports.

To illustrate this, we can construct a simulation of the home banking system of Figure 5.24. *First* we must define an objective for the simulation. Assume we want to know the delay in getting a response from the bank's transaction processing system that a kid banking at home would observe. The key issue is whether the system design will result in a 1-second or less response time during the peak busy hour. *Second,* we need to assemble the data to be used as input and lay out the information flows. Here we will assume that at peak service 100 home computers in each city are active, with each generating an M/D/1 flow with a peak arrival rate of 1 transaction per minute per home, of length 1,000 bits. The modem pool will be conservatively set to be made up of 100 modems, each capable of 33–56 kbps. The connecting trunk will be a simple 9.6 kbps telephone line. The concentrator/multiplexor and front end will be modeled as standard routers. The local area network will be taken as a 4 Mbps token ring. The processor will be assumed to have unlimited capacity, but create a delay of .2 seconds to process each transaction (i.e., the processor is rated at 5 TPS). *Third,* the model must be built using a simulation software package suitable to the task. The result of a package with a graphical user interface is shown in Figure 5.33. The layout of the system is shown as it would look on an actual computer screen, surrounded by the palette of preconstructed components and the main menu bar. *Fourth,* a number of test runs should be conducted to validate the model and shape the scenarios that will be considered. We could select certain input conditions that coincide with a known result such as the previous analysis of the home banking system of Figure 5.24, or compare the test runs against systems that might be similar, such as an automated teller machine network. *Fifth,* and finally, production runs should be made and the results reported so they can be analyzed. Since samples from probability distributions are used to complete each run of the model, the results themselves form a probability distribution. Therefore, a number

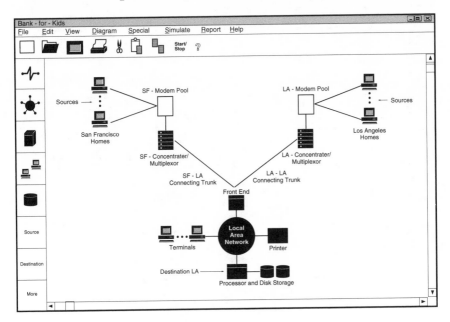

Figure 5.33 Simulation Software Screen Layout.

of replications should be conducted to calculate averages and confidence intervals. A report on the delay in getting a response from the bank's transaction processing system is shown in Figure 5.34. The average response time meets our criterion of being 1 second or less. This is the time it takes for a transaction to be sent from one of the home computers, processed at the bank, and then received back at the home computer from which it came. It does not include modem connect or session setup times, and rounds off the negligible propagation time to zero. A calculation of confidence intervals based on 10 replications shows that there is a 99% probability that the average response time is between .6 seconds and .8 seconds.

The best way to learn how to use packaged simulation software is to determine how to enter input, re-create some known examples, experiment by changing these examples in interesting ways, and then pick a system you understand well and model it. After you have simulated a few such systems you should become familiar enough with the program to attempt to simulate complex systems. At the end of this

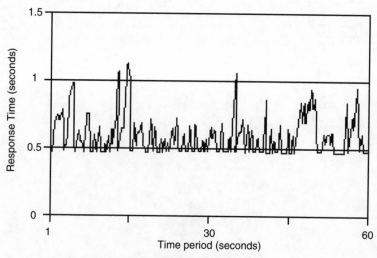

Source. Comnet III, CACI Products Company. Used with Permission.

Figure 5.34   Report on Response Time of Bank's
Transaction Processing System.

process, you will discover just how powerful these simulators are. Learning how a simulator works is essential, for otherwise the user can be fooled into a false sense of security about the quality of the results they are generating. A sample of some of what these simulations can do is described in Figure 5.35.

Simulation is an iterative and interactive process in which building a model is itself a source of learning about a

Building Blocks	Simulation Software Package Features
Sources and Destinations	Sources can be individual or grouped together. The traffic they generate can be packets, messages, sessions, responses, workloads, and calls. Transport protocols, flow control methods, and priorities can be set. Destinations can be chosen based on how busy they are, whether the information is being broadcast, on a random basis, on a preferred basis, or by direct assignments. Information arrival rates and service times can be described by standard probability distributions such as the Poisson, Erlang, exponential, geometric, normal, triangular, and uniform, or by user-defined distributions. Units can be either packets, calls, sessions, or bytes.
Connections	Several types of connections are available. Point-to-point connections can be applied when linking two locations together and multiaccess connections when linking multiple locations. The latter can be random access, such as Ethernet, or polled access, such as token ring. A wide range of established vendor equipment offerings can usually be selected from within these categories. The number of connections, their capacity, propagation delay, error rates, failure rates and repair times can be set. Capabilities exist for modeling combined data and call traffic over a common line.
Transformation Units	Transformation units can be computers, switches, routers, hubs, and other devices. These units can be individual or grouped together. Processing times, buffer sizes, bus rates, routing tables, priority schemes, failure rates, and repair times can be set. Libraries of device parameters can be referenced for a wide range of established vendor equipment offerings. Application software execution can be modeled.
Storage Locations	Storage locations can be modeled as having a disk controller alone or with a processor. Read/write commands and file transfers can be executed. Processing times, buffer sizes, disk sizes, sector sizes, transfer times, seek times, transfer overhead, failure rates and repair times can be set.

Figure 5.35   Implementation of Building Blocks in a
Simulation Software Package.

system's properties. As an example, a check of the number of busy modems in the home banking simulation suggests that only 70 to 80 are actually needed, instead of 100. A worthwhile iteration would therefore be to run the model with, say, 75 modems in the modem pool. For this reason, it is recommended that a system be modeled starting at a high level, followed by successively lower levels of detail. This way, you will retain your focus on what is important and not get lost in a sea of complexity.

So far, we have discussed mathematical models of a system. Physical models can also be built that represent a scaled-down version of an actual system. Studying physical models of systems is not standard practice. Perhaps this is because it can often be nearly as expensive to build a scale model as an actual system, and simulators can be accurate. Equipment vendors routinely build working prototypes, however, to experiment with before committing to volume manufacture. The key to physical model building is to determine the important similarities that must be maintained between the actual system and the scale model. The engineering literature on the topic is called dimensional analysis, with the most common types of similarities being geometric (length-scale), kinematic (length-scale and time-scale), and dynamic (length-scale, time-scale, and workload-scale). Traffic generators used to test these models are the information system equivalent of the wind tunnel. The tools for mathematically modeling systems are becoming increasingly powerful so the need for physical models will continue to decline. This means that putting the first prototype of a system into service as a production system is likely to become a common occurrence.

■ PROBLEMS AND SOLUTIONS

Problem 5.1: Can a transformation unit, storage location, or connection be a source or destination?

Solution: Yes. When a system is made up of a chain of basic information flows, a server in the chain acts as a destination for the previous server and as a source for the following server, assuming it is not located at the end points of the chain.

Problem 5.2: Character legibility requirements lead to a facsimile resolution of typically 7.7 dots per millimeter. For a page of 8½″ × 11″ paper, how many bits of information are there? If the entire page is covered with characters at 7 characters per inch, with 5 lines per inch and each character is encoded in 8-bit extended ASCII, how many bits of information are required? What is the effective compression ratio? What is the effective compression ratio of the page as an image represented by 256,000 bits?

Solution: 3.577 million bits. 26,180 bits. 137:1. 14:1.

Problem 5.3: Draw an information flow diagram for broadcast television.

Solution:

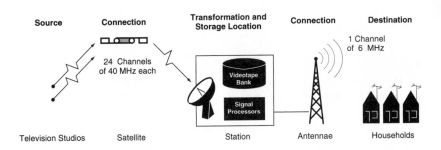

Problem 5.4: Describe some of the information flows that were ignored in our analysis of the office telephone system. Why can they be ignored?

Solution: Digit dialing, signaling (dial tone, busy signal, ringing), billing. These information flows do not drive the economics of the office telephone system, though they are essential to its operation. The office telephone system is designed from the perspective of the company purchasing it. Telephone equipment and service is offered by suppliers to handle calls, which includes the associated digit dialing, signaling, and billing. If these suppliers split out the costs for digit dialing, signaling, and billing, then we would have to consider these information flows.

These information flows we have ignored are important in the right context. From the perspective of the supplier of telephone sets, the digit dialing process is of considerable economic interest. From the perspective of the supplier of switching service, the signaling process is of considerable economic interest. From the perspective of the supplier of the billing system, the billing process is of considerable economic interest.

Given the right context, the engineering of information flows should be governed by Amdahl's law, which states that the performance improvement from a design change is limited by the fraction of the time the design change can be used. Amdahl's law can serve as a guide to how to distribute resources to improve cost/performance.

Problem 5.5: Assume there is a constant information flow, $\phi_o = \lambda_o L_o$, and a propagation delay, t_p, representing the time it takes to transmit the information from the server to the destination. If the maximum time the information can take to flow through the system is t_{max}, find the capacity requirement C.

Solution: The time it takes for information to flow through the system is

$$\frac{L_o}{C} + t_p$$

So we have

$$C = \frac{L_o}{t_{max} - t_p}$$

Problem 5.6: What happens to the system's capacity requirement if we simply increase λ_{avg} by a constant factor, $\lambda_{avg} \rightarrow a\lambda_{avg}$ while holding L_{avg} constant?

Solution: We have

$$\phi_{avg} = \lambda_{avg}L_{avg} = C$$

Substituting, we have

$$C' = a\lambda_{avg}L_{avg}$$

The capacity requirement is simply $C' = a\lambda_{avg}L_{avg}$. In other words, an increase in λ_{avg} requires an identical increase in C. This is a useful result if growth in information flows is expected.

Problem 5.7: Derive the expression for the backup time, $T_{backup}(t)$, for the ramped flow condition (rush hour) described in Figure 5.14.

Solution: See Section "Deterministic Flows" in this chapter.

Problem 5.8: Show that the information flow in the second stage of a chained system can follow an entirely different process than the first stage.

Solution: Assume $n + 1$ arrivals of identical length, L_o, reach the first server almost instantaneously, the $(k-1)^{th}$ arrival separated from the kth ($k \leq n + 1$) by Δt, where $n\Delta t << 1/\mu_1$. In other words, $n\Delta t$ is much smaller than the time it takes for the server, μ_1, to process an arrival.

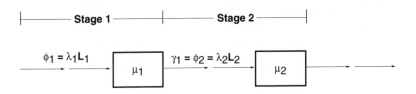

For the information flow in the first stage, we then have

$$\phi_1 = \frac{n+1}{n\Delta t} L_o$$

The arrivals in the first stage simply queue up and are served one right after the other, keeping μ_1 continuously busy. This means the throughput γ_1 is simply a constant information flow μ_1 and therefore,

$$\phi_2 = \mu_1 L_o$$

Comparing ϕ_1 to ϕ_2, we have

$$\frac{\phi_1}{\phi_2} = \left(\frac{n+1}{n\Delta t}\right)\frac{1}{\mu_1}$$

But, $n\Delta t << 1/\mu_1$, which implies $\phi_2 << \phi_1$. In other words, the high intensity burst flow, ϕ_1, results in a low intensity constant flow ϕ_2.

Problem 5.9:   The following statement is from a technical publication in the 1970s about a 2-stage chained system: "If the information rate is Poisson and the information lengths are exponentially distributed for the information flow of the first stage with an infinite buffer for both stages, the output of the first stage reduces to a Poisson stream identical to the input. When this Poisson stream is fed into stage 2, the result is the same as if the original traffic had bypassed stage 1 and fed directly into stage 2." Is this true or false? Why?

Solution: True, but it is far from obvious and should never be assumed ad initium. The information rate at the second stage becomes correlated with the length of the information, violating the Poisson distribution requirement that the information rate does not change as a result of previous or future events. Consider the 2-stage chained system:

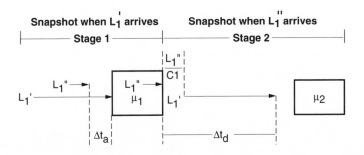

Snapshot when L_1' arrives   Snapshot when L_1'' arrives

Two messages arrive, of length L_1', L_1'', in stage 1, within Δt_a of each other. Since the arrival process is Poisson, they arrive independently of one another in the first stage. Assume L_1' is sufficiently long that L_1'' arrives before L_1' has been completely served. Then the two messages depart stage 1 (which is the same as arriving in stage 2) within Δt_d of each other, which has become lengthened, $\Delta t_d > \Delta t_a$, as a result of the arrival of the previous message. More generally, all messages flowing into the second stage must have arrival times that are separated by at least the time it takes for the trailing message to be served (L_1''/C_1). The correlation between information rate and information length should now be clear.

Despite this difficulty, it has been shown (see, e.g., R.L. Disney and P.C. Kiessler, *Traffic Processes in Queuing Networks*, Baltimore: Johns Hopkins University Press, 1987) that the arrival process in stage 2 is Poisson, with the same arrival rate λ_{avg} as in stage 1. This is a special circumstance, where the Poisson process depends on the length of the information in a specific manner that yields this result. More generally, the fact that the information rate becomes correlated with information length, after traversing the first stage, creates enormous difficulty in analyzing chained systems. The Kleinrock independence approximation, Jackson's theorem, and computer simulations are some ways that have been employed to overcome this difficulty.

Problem 5.10: The probability distributions for the arrival rate and service times can be combined to determine the joint probability of a particular load on the system. Is this very useful?

Solution: No, except in simulations. The rate for joint probabilities is:

$$\text{Probability}\left(\begin{array}{c}\text{an arrival rate and a}\\\text{service time occur together}\end{array}\right) = \text{Probability}\left(\begin{array}{c}\text{an arrival}\\\text{rate occurs}\end{array}\right)$$

$$\times \text{Probability}\left(\begin{array}{c}\text{a service time occurs, given}\\\text{that the arrival rate occurs}\end{array}\right)$$

For independent events, this is simply

$$\text{Probability (an arrival rate occurs)} \times \text{Probability (a service time occurs)}$$

An explicit expression for the probability of a particular load on a system can therefore be developed. This kind of expression, however, doesn't help much in providing immediate insight into the quantities of interest such as wait time, except when used in simulations.

■ NOTES

1. Various discussions of information architecture and technology architecture, in different contexts, can be found in A. Meijers and P. Peeters, *Computer Network Architectures,* London: Pitman, 1982; J. Hagel III and A.G. Armstrong, *Net Gain: Expanding Markets through Virtual Communities,* Boston: Harvard Business School Press, 1997; and R.S. Wurman, *Information Architects,* New York: Graphis Inc., 1997.

2. Capacity is symbolically represented by the letters $\mu(t)$ or C, where C is fixed. Though they share these symbols in common, there are substantial capacity differences between connections, transformation units, and storage locations arising from their different functions.

3. This is generally true. There are exceptions, however, where inefficiencies may be desirable. For example, broadcasters create a 7-second transmission delay during coverage

of some live events so that censors can expunge objectionable material.

4. See L.R. Ford, Jr. and D.R. Fulkerson, *Flows in Networks,* Princeton, NJ: Princeton University Press, 1962.

5. L. Kleinrock discusses this in *Queueing Systems* (Vol. 2, Sec. 5.6), New York: John Wiley & Sons, 1975–1976.

6. See M. Bazaraa, J. Jarvis, and H. Shevali, *Linear Programming and Network Flows,* New York: John Wiley & Sons, 1990.

7. We refer the reader to L. Kleinrock, *Queueing Systems* (Vols. 1 and 2), for a discussion of approximation techniques.

8. See, e.g., L. Kleinrock, *Queueing Systems* (Vol. 1).

9. An example of a modern fixed-length implementation is an ATM (Asynchronous Transfer Mode) network.

10. See M. Tanner, *Practical Queuing Analysis,* New York: McGraw-Hill, 1995, 176.

11. Comnet is available from CACI Products Company of La Jolla, CA.

C h a p t e r

System Designs

Computer engineering can be thought of as a multivariable mathematical problem in which the engineer searches for an optimum within certain constraints. Unfortunately, an optimum in one variable is rarely an optimum in another, and thus a major portion of computer engineering is the search for reasonable compromises.

—C. Gordon Bell, J. Craig Mudge, John McNamara,
Computer Engineering

If there are no alternatives, you have no problem.

—George Schultz

In this chapter, we focus on the *technology architecture* which is the physical implementation of the information architecture. An information architecture can have many physical implementations, each representing a particular set of priorities and compromises. In theory, an optimum implementation exists; in practice, system complexity limits our ability to find just approximations. The more system design alternatives examined, the better the approximation to the optimum. Therefore, a portion of this chapter is devoted to laying out strongly contrasting system design alternatives before showing how to narrow them down to the one closest to the optimum.

The point of a technology architecture is to describe what equipment and staff goes where and how much is needed.

The design philosophy adopted here is for the technology architecture to be driven by the information architecture. The industry term for this is that the system design is *data-driven*. This recognizes that the information handled by the system is more valuable than the system itself. The information (data) is the asset; the system is the means to employ it.

■ 6.1 COMPONENTS

The components of a technology architecture come in such a wide range of forms that to the casual observer they may not be separable. The difference between a twisted pair cable and a coaxial cable, for example, may be lost on them. This situation is referred to as a "zoo" in other settings, where there is a large collection of things that are confusing because of their similarities as well as their differences. The term is appropriate here. This development is a result of the diversity of the marketplace for information technology. The basis for distinguishing among these components has been laid out in the previous chapter's discussion of the properties of sources and destinations, connections, transformation units, and storage locations. The *differences between components can be determined by comparing vendor's equipment specifications,* which list these properties. Equipment specifications can be found in vendor's product catalogues, web sites, technical notes, and brochures.

Equipment can essentially play any role in a technology architecture. The equipment offered by industry is so varied that describing it all is not possible. The components that we discuss here, however, constitute primary features of the equipment landscape in a digital world: wireline transmission media/networks, computer processors, and disk drives/memory boards.

Wireline transmission media act as connections, with three of the most popular types being twisted pair wire, coaxial cable, and fiber optics. The primary property of digital transmission media components is their speed and length, which when multiplied together can be combined into a single figure of merit, measured in bit-meters per second. Unwanted radiation of energy resulting in relative loss of signal power compared with ambient noise is the primary impediment to increasing speed-length. At low transmission rates, the problem is small; but at only slightly higher rates, say a few kilobits, the problem can be serious. Wireline transmission media components reflect increasingly elaborate techniques for reducing this unwanted radiation of energy. For low speed transmission of information over short distances, simple insulated copper wire is twisted together forming what is called a twisted pair. Vast quantities of this are used for telephone transmission for the home. For higher speed transmission over moderate distances, a copper wire is placed within a cylindrical conductor forming what is called coaxial cable. Large quantities of this are used for cable television transmission. For very high speed transmission over long distances, a thin fiber of optical material is used forming what is called fiber-optic cable. Widespread deployment of this is occurring to support the buildout of integrated networks. A comparison of the properties of twisted pair, coaxial, and fiber-optic digital transmission media is shown in Figure 6.1. The specifications shown are for high-performance applications in 1999 and provide a feel for their relative capabilities. Historically, twisted pair and coaxial cable technology advances over the past 10 years have led to only modest improvements in their capabilities, whereas fiber-optic technology advances have resulted in speed-length increases of about 70% to 80% annually in the laboratory. Actual installed fiber capacity has lagged far behind this rate.

In addition to transmission media, software and other equipment is needed to ensure a successful communication. There are several layers to a connection where functions such as error correction, routing, flow control, multiplexing, authorization, and encryption are performed. These layers,

Twisted Pair	Coaxial Cable	Fiber Optic

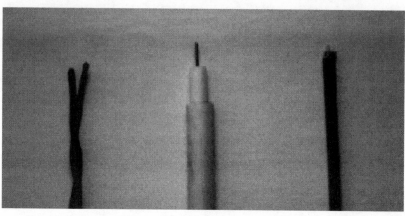

	Approximate			
Transmission Media	Speed	× Length =	Figure of Merit[4]	Relative Performance (twisted pair = 1)
Twisted pair[1]	1.5 Mbps ×	2 km =	3 Mbps-km	1
Coaxial cable[2]	1,500 Mbps ×	.5 km =	750 Mbps-km	250
Fiber optic[3]	2,500 Mbps ×	75 km =	187,500 Mbps-km	250 × 250

[1] T-1 line with repeaters.
[2] @Home service provides about 25 Mbps per 6Mhz channel and cable systems commonly have 60 or more channels.
[3] Sonet OC-48 over a single-mode fiber.
[4] This is commonly referred to as the bandwidth-distance product in the technical literature.

Figure 6.1 Wireline Digital Transmission Media Component Specifications in 1999.

of which transmission media is one, define a communication service or *network* that can be purchased as a complete package from a vendor. Several of the most important examples are shown in Figures 6.2 and 6.3.

Computers act as transformation units with three of the most popular types being personal computers, servers, and multiprocessors, listed in order from lowest to highest performance. In the past, we would have used the categories microcomputer, minicomputer, and mainframe, but

Communication Service	Speed (Mbps)	Typical Transmission Media
Voice-grade circuit	.064	Twisted pair
Fractional T1	.064 x N (where N = 2, ..., 23)	Twisted pair
T1	1.5	Twisted pair
Fractional T3	1.5 x N (where N = 2, ..., 27)	Fiber Optic
T3	45	Fiber Optic
OC-1/STS-1	51	Fiber Optic
OC-3/STS-3	155	Fiber Optic
OC-12/STS-12	622	Fiber Optic
OC-48/STS-48	2488	Fiber Optic
OC-192/STS-192	9792	Fiber Optic

Figure 6.2 Public Networks.

microprocessor advances have been so dramatic that these machines have ceded leadership to computers based on microprocessor designs. The primary property of computer components is their power, which is measured by the rate at which various workloads can be run. Two key factors influence the power of a computer: the technology employed and the machine organization.

Network	Type	Speed (Mbps)	Length (km)	Transmission Media
Token Ring	LAN	4	5	Twisted Pair or Fiber Optic
Ethernet	LAN	10	2.5	Coaxial Cable
FDDI	LAN	100	4	Fiber Optic
ATM	LAN or WAN	155, 622, ...	2	Fiber Optic

Figure 6.3 Private Networks.

Semiconductor technology is the basis of computing, by virtue of its use in creating devices that comprise the logic of a machine. To achieve a given level of performance, computer engineers employ a mix of semiconductor devices, such as bipolar and MOS chips, with different speeds, energy consumption, and density. These devices require time and energy to switch from one logical state to another. For this reason, the rate a computer can process information is related to the energy consumed by a device. Fast computers run hotter than slow computers. Semiconductor devices also have different circuit densities. High density results in higher speeds, since signals travel shorter distances and there is less capacitance in the circuit. So faster computers want to be smaller. Unfortunately, hot things confined in small spaces tend to burn up, so the fastest machines end up being large. Adding energy increases speed more than lowering density reduces it. A semiconductor technology advance that lowers the energy consumption of a device for a given speed or increases device density is noteworthy because of the broad improvement this can have on computer performance.

As a point of comparison, the minimum feature size of an Intel Pentium II™ microprocessor in 1997 was .35 microns, which would allow 7.5 million transistors to be packed on the chip. After two more generations of technology, this should drop to .18 microns and the die size should double. As a result, the total number of transistors should increase by about 8×, the transistor density by 4×, the clock rate by 5×, and the power consumption by 40×. Today's chip already runs hot, so managing a power increase of this magnitude will be a challenge for Intel.[1]

Aside from semiconductors, other technologies influence computer performance to varying degrees, such as those involved in creating software and packaging devices.

Internal organization is the second key factor responsible for performance differences between computers. The most familiar organizational aspect of computers is their proportions. The number of processors, amount of memory, number of I/O channels, and expansion slots can vary. Add-ons like graphics accelerators and floating point arithmetic units provide more special purpose circuitry to the basic processor. At a deeper level, instruction sets, bus structures, pipelining, and other organizational considerations can have a significant effect on computer performance. Advances in machine organization, beyond simply their proportions, continue to be substantial even though the practice of engineering computers is now over 40 years old. A notable recent example is the development of reduced instruction set computers (RISC).

The demands placed on a computer by a workload determine the power of the machine needed to run it. Workloads are now almost universally written in high-level programming languages such as "C," so that in theory they can run on almost any computer. As you would expect, *single-user programs* are the least demanding and so usually run well on personal computers. Examples of single-user workloads are spreadsheets, word processors, and games. *Multiuser programs* are more demanding and so usually run well on servers. Examples of multiuser workloads are database management software, printer-sharing programs, and communication applications. Some single-user and multiuser programs can deviate from these norms and be extremely demanding. If these programs exhibit parallelism, and key software challenges can be overcome, they may run well on multiprocessors. Examples of extremely demanding workloads are complex simulations and transaction processing systems. *Multiprogramming,* where several independent programs are run simultaneously on a machine also works well on multiprocessors. Management information systems comprise many separate programs and so are often run on multiprocessors. Underlying these workloads are operating systems, which follow a similar pattern. Generally speaking, Windows[2] runs best on personal computers. Unix or Windows NT on servers, and MVS on multiprocessors. Software is dynamic, so shifts are occurring in this pattern. Unix and Windows NT in particular are migrating both upward and downward.

	Personal Computer	Server	Multiprocessor
Company	Dell	Sun	IBM
Model	Dimension XPS D233	Enterprise™ 450	S/390 G3 R84®
Operating System	Windows®95	Solaris™2.6 (Unix)	MVS®
CPU	1x Intel Pentium II® 233 MHz	1x Ultra SPARC™ 296 MHz (4x maximum)	8x 9672-R84 CMOS
Memory	32MB (384MB maximum)	1GB (4GB)	8GB (maximum)
Disk	2GB (4 drives maximum)	4GB (over 5TB maximum)	TBs
Electrical Power	200 watts	1,660 watts (maximum)	5,000 watts

Heat Output	.8KBTU/hr. (maximum)	5.7KBTU/hr. (maximum)	17.1KBTU/hr. (maximum)
Footprint	1 sq. ft.	3.4 sq. ft.	19.7 sq. ft.
Weight	30 lbs. (maximum)	205 lbs.	2,068 lbs. (maximum)
Performance Benchmarks	SYSmark = 228	SPECint_base95 = 10.4 SPECfp_base95 = 17.2 SPECint_rate_base95 = 91.8 SPECfp_rate_base95 = 151	Large System Performance Reference (LSPR) Mixed Benchmark Internal Throughput Rate = 4.75
Comment	SYSmark is a benchmark based on the most popular word processing, spreadsheet, database, graphics, presentation, and publishing applications. This benchmark is maintained by Business Applications Performance Corp.	SPECint_base95 is a benchmark based on compute-intensive integer programs, such as simulation, file compression, database, and software development applications using conservative compiler optimization rules. Descriptions of the other benchmarks can be found on the SPEC web sites. The benchmarks are maintained by the Standard Performance Evaluation Corporation (SPEC).	LSPR Mixed is a benchmark based on representative transaction processing, database, timesharing, batch, and scientific applications. It is expressed relative to the IBM 9672-R15 processor (=1). This benchmark is maintained by IBM Corporation.

Source. Photos courtesy of Sun Microsystems and International Business Machines Corporation. Unauthorized use is not permitted.

Figure 6.4 Personal Computer, Server, and Multiprocessor Specifications in 1998.

The combined effect on a computer's power of the technology employed and machine organization, as well as its suitability for a workload, is highlighted in a computer's specification. A comparison of some personal computer, server, and multiprocessor machine specifications in 1998 is shown in Figure 6.4. Historically, advances in computer engineering have led to a 55% to 60% annual increase in the rate at which standard CPU workloads are run. Approximately 35% of this can be attributed to advances in semiconductor technology and 20% to 25% to machine organization.

Disk drives and memory boards act as storage locations, with three of the most popular types being magnetic disks, optical disks, and semiconductor memory boards. The primary properties of disk drive components are their volume, access time, and transfer rate. These are generally determined by two factors: the speed of rotation and the density of the data on the disk. A higher speed of rotation requires a larger motor to turn the disk. As a result, faster disks tend to be larger and consume more energy. To provide a point of comparison, a 3.5-inch hard disk in the 1990s rotates at around 7,200 RPM.

Data density, measured in bits per square inch, is driven by the ability to read small signals over fine geometries. This is a function of the gap size in the heads for magnetic disks and the wavelength of the laser in optical disks. The dimensions here are small, on the order of microns and hundreds of nanometers, respectively.

The combined effect of magnetic disk technology advances has been about a 60% annual increase in data density, a 50% annual increase in transfer rate, and a 5% annual decrease in access times. Optical disk advances over the past 10 to 15 years have been more modest, with the difference between a DVD-ROM and a CD-ROM translating into about a 20% to 30% annual increase in data density, a 15% to 20% annual increase in transfer rate, and a 5% annual decrease in access times.

The primary properties of memory boards are their volume, access time, and cycle time. Since they are based on semiconductor technology, these properties are driven by the same trade-offs between energy consumption, speed, and density as was found in computer logic devices. Memory boards only provide temporary storage in contrast to disk drives, so there is a need to rewrite the memory after it has been read. The cycle time is the time it takes for a memory location to become available again after being read. This only applies to dynamic memories, referred to as DRAMs. Some memories are engineered to eliminate the need to rewrite, so there is no cycle time. These are called static memories or SRAMs. SRAMs require several times the number of transistors as DRAMs.

Semiconductor technology advances have led to about a 60% annual increase in DRAM board density, a 5% to 10% annual decrease in access time, and a 5% to 10% annual decrease in cycle time.

Comparison of semiconductor memory boards, magnetic disks, and optical disks reveals a storage hierarchy. The different types of storage devices can be arranged so that each has greater volume than its predecessor, while simultaneously having a slower access time and transfer rate. The lowest volume but fastest are semiconductor memory boards. This is followed by the medium volume and medium performance magnetic disks. The highest volume but slowest are optical disks. By moving information as needed from the slowest storage devices to the fastest, the overall performance of a system can be made to appear as if it were mostly made up of the fastest storage components. Specifications for magnetic, optical, and semiconductor storage devices in 1998 are shown in Figure 6.5.

Human beings are a component of a technology architecture, most often acting as sources and destinations for information and sometimes as MIS staff. Of course, human beings do not come with specifications, but profiles of their characteristics, such as a resume, perform a similar function. There are mental characteristics of a person that relate to the structure of information, such as the language spoken, the degree of intelligence, and the attention to detail.

	Semiconductor Memory Board	Magnetic Disk	Optical Disk
Company	Chrislin	Seagate	Toshiba
Model	CI-VME80 DRAM	ST39173xx hard drive	SD-M1102 DVD-ROM
Volume (bytes)	32, 64, 128, 256, 512, 1024 MB	9.2 GB	4.7, 8.5, 9.4 17.1 GB
Modes of Operation	Read/Write	Read/Write	Read only
Volatility	Temporary	Permanent	Permanent
Access Time (Seek Time + Rotational Latency)	30 nsec, block read	11.6 msec (average)	190 msec (average)
Seek Time	N/A	7.5 msec	150 msec (average)
Rotational Latency	N/A	4.1 msec (average)	40 msec (average)
Cycle Time	95 nsec, block read	N/A	N/A
Transfer Rate	80 MB/sec (maximum)	20 MB/sec Ultra SCSI 8	1,350 KB/sec, sustained
Power	10 watts, average for 256 MB board	10 watts, idle	6 watts (average)
Dimensions	6.2" H x 9.1" W	1" H x 4" W x 5" D	1.6" H x 5.7" W x 8" D
Weight	1–2 lbs. (approximate)	1.5 lbs.	3.2 lbs.

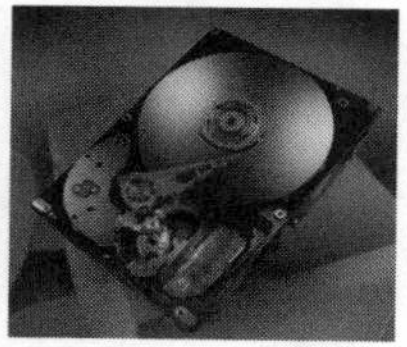

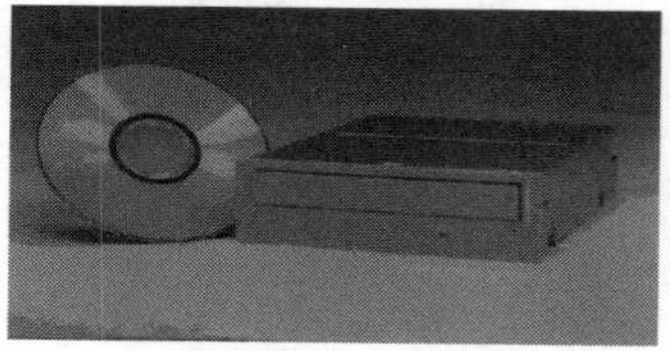

Source. Photos courtesy of Chrislin Industries, Seagate Technology, and Toshiba Corporation. Unauthorized use is not permitted.

Figure 6.5 Magnetic, Optical, and Semiconductor Storage Device Specifications in 1998.

Physiological characteristics relate to the information flux such as eyesight, hearing, balance, touch, taste, and smell. These physiological characteristics can be translated into actual bit rates. One team of researchers has shown that the ultimate display, one in which the viewer would be unable to tell that they were not viewing a real scene, would require a bit rate of 810 gigabits/sec.[3] This figure seems many generations away from being even remotely achievable in other than a laboratory. From a practical standpoint, people can do with far less visual information for normal tastes and are willing to accept such things as a finite size and a 2-dimensional image for television, photography, and so on. As a result, high-quality video can be accomplished with only about 4 Mbps on average by a DVD. This illustrates a general issue that arises with the human components of a technology architecture: What is the maximum information a person can process, and what is the minimum information they are willing to accept? This issue has been extensively studied for eyesight and hearing, but little has been done for the other senses of balance, touch, taste, and smell, or for mental faculties. The answers developed so far have been based on subjective testing and found to be application dependent. A person reading would attach great importance to image resolution, while a television viewer might be more concerned with image color. Our knowledge of ourselves is imperfect, which injects a subjective aspect to the human component of a technology architecture (see Figure 6.6).

So far, the component comparisons we have discussed have been between similar types of equipment, such as twisted pair versus fiber-optic cable. It is instructive to look at whether comparisons between different components can be meaningful. For example, people who want to rent a movie today to watch at home can simply get in their car and rent a DVD at the local video store. Alternately, sometime in the electronic future they may be able to download the movie over a twisted pair, coaxial cable, or fiber-optic network connected to their home. A comparison of the time

Figure 6.6. Child Banking at Home.

to perform this task for each of these approaches is shown in Figure 6.7. Making a trip to the video store ranks second in convenience, surpassed only by fiber-optic transmission. Low-tech components can be remarkably competitive when compared with high-tech.

Rank	Method	Time Required
1.	Fiber optic cable:	(5 GB x 1000 MB/GB x 8 bits/byte)/2500 Mbps = 15 sec.
2.	Person with a car:	(4 miles roundtrip/30mph) + 5 min. for parking + 2 min. for checkout = 15 min.
3.	Coaxial cable:	(5 GB x 1000 MB/GB x 8 bits/byte)/25 Mbps (one channel) = 25 min.
4.	Twisted pair:	(5 GB x 1000 MB/GB x 8 bits/byte)/1.5 Mbps = 7 hours, 25 min.

Note Transmission speeds are from Figure 6.1. Number of bits for a full length, 2-hour movie is assumed to be about 5 GB.

Figure 6.7 Renting a Movie: High-Tech versus Low-Tech Component Comparison.

■ 6.2 SYSTEM PARTS

Creating a technology architecture *is a process of matching component specifications to information flows.* This is done by system part, using the information architecture as a guide. The structure of the information flowing through a system part determines the *function* (F) of a component. The flux determines the *performance* (P).

The interests of parties having a stake in the process, however, limit the component choices available for making a match. Customers have preferences for certain brands of equipment. Suppliers offer a limited product line. Regulators impose laws and equipment standards dealing with safety, compatibility, and commerce. Employees possess given skill levels. Competitors form exclusive alliances. Investors have a required rate of return. A match must reflect these combined interests.

Though our primary focus in developing a technology architecture is the function and performance of each component, their contribution to the *cost* (C) and *schedule* (S) for system construction and operation is worth anticipating now, ahead of a more rigorous examination to follow later. This will improve the prospects for meeting the economic hurdles described in Chapter 8, which represent the interests of shareholders, the most important constituency of all to satisfy. In the process, it will reduce unproductive effort when developing a system.

The home-banking system part illustration in Chapter 5 can be used to show how this matching process works. The system part there was the connecting trunk between the local concentrator/multiplexer and the remote bank transaction processing system.

The structure of the information flows for home banking requires that the connecting trunk function as a reliable and secure communication path. Corruption of deposit, withdrawal, or payment instructions is unacceptable.

The reliability of a connection is measured by the bit-error-rate (BER), which is the number of bits that are perceived to be incorrect after transmission. The BER improves the more shielded the transmission medium is from noise. Twisted pair T1 lines provide better than a 10^{-6} BER, coaxial cable can achieve a 10^{-8} BER, and fiber-optic SONET lines provide better than a 10^{-10} BER. While errors are improbable for all these media, a 100-fold difference separates each, with fiber optics more reliable than coaxial cable which, in turn, is more reliable than twisted pair.

The security of a connection is measured by its ability to thwart eavesdroppers, vandals, and impostors. Security also improves the more shielded the transmission medium, because less radiation or interference of signal can occur. This reinforces the previous transmission media preferences, so on the basis of function a connection made of fiber optics is preferred to coaxial cable is preferred to twisted pair, for home banking.

The flux of the information flow for the home banking illustration in Chapter 5 was found to require the performance of the connecting trunk to be greater than 7.3 kbps. A search of vendor specifications shows that nearly all communications services are capable of supporting this low speed. A single voice-grade circuit can provide up to 64 kbps so this is more than adequate. There is no need to build a private network to create this circuit, since public networks have the capacity in place already. The public networks available for use are those of the telephone and cable television companies. The remaining task is to translate the concentrator/multiplexer's output into signals that can be carried over a voice-grade circuit. This requires the use of a modem that operates at speeds greater than 7.3 kbps, which nearly all can. A cable network and cable modem combination has much more capacity than needed, so a telephone network and telephone modem combination is least wasteful.

At this point, our problem is pretty much solved, with the final choice of voice-grade circuit and modem provider mostly a matter of who offers the closest to a fiber-optic connection at the lowest cost. Given the small amount of fiber deployed in the local telephone network, we are likely to have to settle for the least attractive twisted pair connection.

A little more thought, however, should raise the question: Why have dedicated communication lines, modems, and concentrators/multiplexers in the first place? An alternative is to share this equipment with other services. The system part illustrations of Chapter 5 suggest what some of these other services might be. To home banking, we could add telephony, Internet access, electronic mail, television, and so on. There are several advantages to this over and above the possibility of being able to have a more secure connection:

➤ It should be more convenient for consumers to access an integrated service rather than many fragmented ones.

➤ The performance of the system should be enhanced.

➤ Standardization should enable greater system flexibility.

➤ Services can be linked so, for example, home banking could provide a payment mechanism for home shopping.

➤ Cost efficiencies would be gained by sharing a common infrastructure.

To carry all these services, we will need far more capacity than required for home banking alone. By far and away the most demanding service is providing video. We could drop video-based services for this reason, but it is quite likely that some of the most attractive new services would link home banking with video. So let's assume video services are included. Though it is possible to transmit video over the twisted pair connections used by the local telephone network, they are not designed for the kind of continuous use to be expected with video services. Telephone calls generally last only 3 or 4 minutes while television sets are left on for hours at a time. Coaxial cable connections used by the local cable network, on the other hand, are well suited for video services. Provision for 2-way capability has also been made in cable systems. A promising alternative solution then would be to integrate the home banking service with a cable network. The next section will explore what this kind of system would look like.

■ 6.3 ASSEMBLED SYSTEMS

Putting a system together is a process of assembling system parts. This involves repeated application of the previous matching process, with emphasis on component interactions. The output of this process is a description of what equipment and staff goes where and how much is needed for a working system. Using a real example best shows how a system is assembled. Cable networks cover the main ideas and, as already shown, can provide a platform for a variety of services. Their high speed, wide deployment, and upgradability make them worthy of our attention.

The information flow in a cable system providing television, home banking, electronic mail, telephony, and Internet access is both deterministic and probabilistic. Television broadcasting represents a deterministic flow. A television channel forms a constant 6 MHz load on a cable system. So for 100 channels, we need equipment capable of handling at least 600 MHz. If we add to this some reverse channels, guard bands, and do some rounding off, we wind up at about 750 MHz, which is a standard bandwidth for cable networks. Home banking, telephony, Internet access, and electronic mail, on the other hand, represent probabilistic flows. We need to make some assumptions about how much of this traffic is generated by, say, 5,000 cable subscribers during the peak hour. For home banking, the traffic is negligible, because a load as low as 90% of the 7.3 kbps calculated earlier (see Chapter 5) still amounts to 6.6 banking transactions per second, which should be enough for this size population. For electronic mail, the traffic is also negligible, because a load as low as 90% of the .4 kbps calculated earlier still amounts to 1 message mailed every 14 seconds. For telephony, the average phone is in use about 7.5% of the time during the busy hour; however, we must recognize that this traffic will tend to go over the existing telephone network with perhaps 10% captured by cable. So for 5,000 phones, the total load on the system is 37.5 erlangs, which, following our earlier calculation, translates into 53 voice-quality circuits, or 3.4 Mbps. If we compress these voice conversations, we could reduce this by as much as 8×. Lastly, for Internet access, simulation studies[4] have shown that between 1,000 and 1,800 active Internet users can be supported by each 6 MHz channel. The lower figure assumes the lowest grade of service acceptable is set by cable's next best competitor, a 128 kbps ISDN connection. The higher figure assumes an average delay of about 1 second for viewing a Web page and 4 seconds for video clips. Using measurements from cable modem deployments that about 20% of subscribers are active during the peak hour, an area of about 5,000 to 9,000 Internet access subscribers can be served per channel. Recognizing that the cable channel bit-rate is 25–30 Mbps and that it is unlikely for the peak loads for these multiple services to occur at the same time, a single cable channel should be able to support all four services simultaneously for an area of 5,000 cable subscribers, to within about 10% in the worst case. With these information flows as a backdrop, we can now turn our attention to assembling the cable system part.

A cable system is made up of a headend, trunk, feeder plant, drop line, and subscriber premises equipment. These parts are arranged as a tree-and-branch network to minimize the amount of cable that must be laid. Signals leave the headend over a trunk running down a main street. The signals are then branched out over the feeder plant into the neighborhood streets. The drop line connects the feeder plant to the home. The subscriber premises equipment allows tuning into the services offered. A diagram of a cable network is shown in Figure 6.8.

The *headend* is the central source of programming services for the network. It is where signals are received and combined for transmission. Equipment capable of doing this for 100 television channels is found in the headend of a 750 MHz cable system. This equipment is made up of satellite dishes and over-the-air antennas to receive the television programming, racks of signal processors to clean up the pictures, racks of modulators to transmit the television signals,

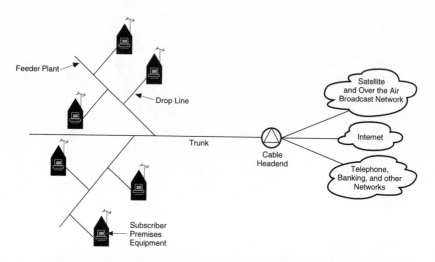

Figure 6.8   Cable System Technology Architecture Diagram.

and a combiner that integrates the signals so they can be sent down the trunk.

Equipment to provide home banking, electronic mail, telephony, and Internet access services is also located in the headend. This equipment comprises headend routers, local content servers, and a cable network manager. Headend routers are special purpose computer servers used to move information between the headend and bank networks, telephone networks, or the Internet. Local content servers are magnetic disk drives that store frequently referenced information at the headend (which is simply an application of the storage hierarchy concept to speed up performance). A cable network manager is a computer workstation running software that services and operates the cable data network.

The equipment in a headend is very reliable and can operate without human intervention. Many cable headends are therefore unattended. A picture of a headend is shown in Figure 6.9a.

The *trunk* carries the signals from the headend through a community, forming a main artery. It is attached to the combiner in the headend and terminated at the far end of a service area. To improve the distance a trunk can cover, special

From Top to Bottom: Main
Lobby, Television Equipment
Racks, Satellite Dish Antennae,
and Internet Access and Other
Service Equipment.

Source. Photos courtesy of Cable Co-op of Palo Alto, CA.

Figure 6.9a Cable Headend.

low-loss large diameter coaxial cable or fiber optics is used. Fiber-optic lines contain many strands of fiber, which has the advantage of enabling partitioning of service areas so that a small number of subscribers can share channel capacity. To maintain signal strength, amplifiers are spaced along a trunk at regular intervals. A picture of a coaxial cable trunk and trunk amplifier is shown in Figure 6.9b.

The *feeder plant* carries signals away from the trunk and down the streets of a neighborhood. It is attached to the trunk by a splitter. Bridger (also called line extender) amplifiers maintain signal strength in the feeder plant. A picture of a feeder line and splitter is shown in Figure 6.9b.

The *drop line* connects the feeder plant to the subscriber premises equipment. It is attached to the feeder plant by a tap. A picture of a drop line and tap is shown in Figure 6.9c.

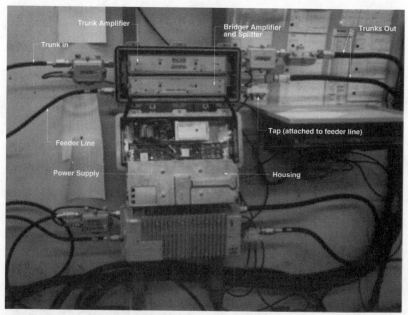

Source. Photo courtesy of Cable Co-op of Palo Alto, CA.

Figure 6.9b Trunk, Trunk Amplifier, Feeder Line, Bridger Amplifier, and Splitter.

Source. Photo courtesy of Cable Co-op of Palo Alto, CA.

Figure 6.9c Drop Line and Tap.

The subscriber premises equipment allows tuning into the signals carried by the cable network. For television, a set-top box is used to receive and descramble the picture. For home banking, electronic mail, telephony, and Internet access, a cable modem is used to convert the downstream and upstream signals for processing by a personal computer or network computer. A picture of subscriber premises equipment is shown in Figure 6.9d.

Maintenance and installation of the trunk, feeder plant, drop line, and subscriber premises equipment requires a staff of technicians. A picture of a cable service technician and truck is shown in Figure 6.9e.

A full description of the system design for a cable network is shown in Figure 6.10. It is similar to a bill of materials listing the type and number of components needed. *The description is detailed enough to allow us to analyze the economics of the system.* This is the test of whether a technology architecture is complete for our purposes. We are now finished laying out the technology architecture for a multi-service cable system.

Source. Photo courtesy of Cable Co-op of Palo Alto, CA.

Figure 6.9d Personal Computer and Cable Modem.

Source. Photo courtesy of Cable Co-op of Palo Alto, CA.

Figure 6.9e Service Technician and Truck.

General: Size of service area is 25,600 households, density 88 homes per mile.
Cable subscriber penetration is 60% of households.
Hybrid fiber-coaxial cable design.
Fiber-optic trunk covers a neighborhood of 1,024 households, resulting in 25 nodes.
750 MHz bandwidth (100 video channels, 1 data channel).
Two-way capability.
Services offered: television, home banking, electronic mail, telephony, and Internet access.

Location	Component	Quantity	Description
Headend (serves 25,600 households)	Tower and building	1	Real estate and structures
	Earth station and over-the-air antenna	1	Satellite dishes and terrestrial antenna including electronics
	Microwave antenna	1	Microwave relay antenna
	FM receivers	1	FM radio reception equipment
	Standby power	1	Backup power system
	Microwave receiver	64	64 channels received by satellite dish and microwave delay antenna. Remaining 36 channels are received over the air or local origination
	Codec	100	Converts analog video to digital video
	Optical transmitter	25	Laser transmitters for 100 channels and 25 nodes
	Power	2,500 watts	Power unit
	Headend router package	1 per 5,000 cable modem subscribers	Computer router to move information between headend and Internet, bank, and telephone networks
	Local content server	5 per 5,000 cable modem subscribers	Magnetic disk drives for local storage
	Cable network manager	1 per 5,000 cable modem subscribers	Computer workstation and network management software
	Router for T3 line	1 per 8,333 cable modem subscribers*	Links cable network to Internet, bank, and telephone networks
	General manager, administrators	1,4 FTE	Management, community relations, administration
	Accounting and finance staff	4 FTE	Payroll, accounts receivable/payable, MIS
	Sales and marketing staff	6 FTE	Direct sales, telemarketing, promotion, guides
	Customer service representatives	3 FTE	Billing, installation, dispatch
	Engineering staff	2 FTE	Headend maintenance, system design
	Programming staff	2 FTE	Local origination, commercial production
	Human resources staff	2 FTE	Benefits, recruiting

*Assumes a bit rate of 27 Mbps per cable channel and each channel serves 5,000 cable modem subscribers. The capacity of a T3 line is 45 Mbps.

Figure 6.10 Cable System Technology Architecture Description.

(continued)

Location	Component	Quantity	Description
Trunk (serves 1,024 households)	Single mode fiber	4 fibers of 3,072 m.	Fiber backbone
	Cable sheath	3,072 m.	Protective wrapper
	Underground installation	3,072 m.	Buried cable
	Inner duct	3,072 m.	Protective duct
	Splice, connector	Each fiber spliced 3x, 2 connectors	Splice labor, connector hardware
	Optical receiver	1	Broadband detector
	Amplifier, accessories, housing	1	Signal strength booster
	Power	340 watts	Power unit
	Technical operations	.32 FTE	Maintenance, construction (8 FTE total)
Feeder Plant (serves 1,024 households)	Coaxial cable	22,820 m.	1/2-inch diameter coaxial cable
	Bridge amplifier	64	Signal strength booster
	Passive components	256 splitters, 128 connectors	Attachments to trunk
	Underground installation	17,550 m. of trench	Buried cable
	Underground conduit	17,550 m.	Protective conduit
	Power	16 stations	Power unit
	Technical operations staff	(included in trunk above)	Maintenance, construction
Drop Line (serves 1 subscriber)	Coaxial cable	27 m.	1/4-inch diameter coaxial cable
	Tap, connector	1, 1	Portion of tap, coaxial cable
	Cable installation	11 m. trench	Buried cable
	Installation staff	.00026 FTE	Home installation (4 FTE total)
Subscriber Premises Equipment (serves 1 subscriber)	Addressable converter	1	Set-top box
	Hookup and installation	1	Labor
	Second converter	.2	20% request second converter
	Cable modem	1x	High speed cable network connection, where x = penetration
	Ethernet connector	1x	10 Base-T Ethernet port, where x = penetration
	Installation staff	(Included in drop line)	Home installation

Adapted from Leland L. Johnson and David P. Reed, *Residential Broadband Services by Telephone Companies? Technology, Economics, and Public Policy.* Santa Monica, CA: Rand Corporation, June 1990, Tables A1, C1, G2. Used with permission.

Figure 6.10 *(Continued)*

The economic analysis of a system is the subject of Chapters 7 and 8. Before we can take this subject up, however, we need to look at system design alternatives. This has already come up naturally in our comparison of a telephone versus cable network design for home banking. A more formal treatment will be the focus of the remainder of this chapter.

■ 6.4 SYSTEM DESIGN ALTERNATIVES

The two highest level design decisions are to choose the underlying technology and the basic organization of a system. These decisions determine, respectively, the range of components and the arrangement of components that will be used in a system. The decision possibilities result in strongly contrasting system design alternatives.

Lower-level design decisions rapidly become system-specific and therefore are best treated on a case-by-case basis. The view adopted here is that system design is a series of successive refinements. By focusing on the highest level, we expose the structure of a system to which the subsequent layers of detail conform.

➤ Underlying Technology

The most fundamental design decision is the choice of underlying technology. A system can be based on high technology, hybrid technology, or low technology components. These terms are distinguished by time, with high technology representing the newest generation of components, hybrid technology a mixture of new and old, and low technology the oldest still in use. An example of technology generations is shown in Figure 6.11.

It is often possible to build attractive systems out of each underlying technology (high, hybrid, and low) which is why they all need to be considered initially. A high-tech online service distributed over a network might find competition from a hybrid-tech CD-ROM product sent through the mail

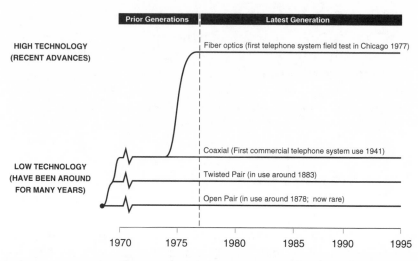

Figure 6.11 Technology Generations—Wireline Transmission Media for Telephony and Computing Over the Past 25 Years.

which, in turn, might find competition from a low-tech print catalog distributed through the mail.

The choice of underlying technology is a limiting one that determines the range of components that can be used in the system. The underlying technology obviously constrains component choice in the case of a high-tech or low-tech design. For hybrid-tech, the mixed case, the component choice is limited by the requirement that high-tech and low-tech components work together.

Six classes of components can be aligned against the building blocks of the information architecture. These classes are distinguished by their function: Is the component a connection, transformation unit, or storage location? Is software providing control or is hardware equipment performing the action? A choice of underlying technology must be made for each component class. This is shown in Figure 6.12.

➤ Basic Organization

Once the underlying technology is chosen, the basic organization of the system needs to be addressed. The basic

		Connections	Transformation Units	Storage Locations
Software (control)	High Tech ↑ ↓ Low Tech	Stored Program	Network control programs (NCP)	Application software and operating systems	Database software
		Feedback loop	Samplers and comparators	Samplers and comparators	Samplers and comparators
		Direct control	Policies and procedures	Policies and procedures	Cataloguing and circulation procedures
Hardware (equipment)	High Tech ↑ ↓ Low Tech	Optical	Fiber-optic cable	Optical computer (under development)	Optical disk
		Electronic	Satellite transponder Terrestrial antenna Coaxial cable Twisted pair wire	Multiprocessor Server Personal computer	Magnetic disk Magnetic tape Semiconductor memory
		Mechanical	Postal network	Slide rule	Paper Film

Figure 6.12   Underlying Technology Choice Framework—Computing.

organization can affect the choice of underlying technology, demonstrating an iterative aspect to the design process. By basic organization, we mean how the components of the system are distributed. For software, this is the distribution of control; for hardware, this is the distribution of equipment. Many other aspects of system organization, such as the number, mix, and interconnection of components, need to be addressed in a complete description of system organization. We will not cover them here.

If sources & destinations do not need to share components, then the organization is trivial with components clustered locally at each site. If sources & destinations need to share components, then the shared components must be located remotely (from one or the other or both) and, in the ideal case, the apparatus in-between made transparent. In other words, components should appear to a source or destination as if they are local, even though they may actually be remote.

The main question, when components are shared, is whether they should be distributed in a centralized or decentralized manner. The reasons are manifold. First, many information technology components exhibit economies of scale and, therefore, centralization can have a substantial positive impact on *costs* (C). Second, sources & destinations can exhibit shifts in the desired *functions* (F) to be done, which decentralized systems can often respond to more quickly. Third, *performance* (P) is often improved if components are as decentralized (i.e., local) as possible. Fourth, the technical challenge of constructing decentralized systems can slow down *schedules* (S); for example, a distributed database is hard to build. The preceding is illustrative; it is by no means comprehensive. The choice matrix for basic organization is shown in Figure 6.13.

The choice of basic organization further limits and defines the components that make up a system, influencing their type, size, number, mix, interconnection, and so on.

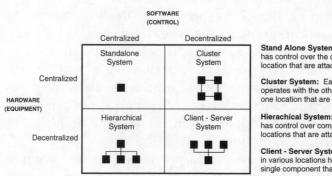

Figure 6.13   Basic Organization Choice Framework—Computing.

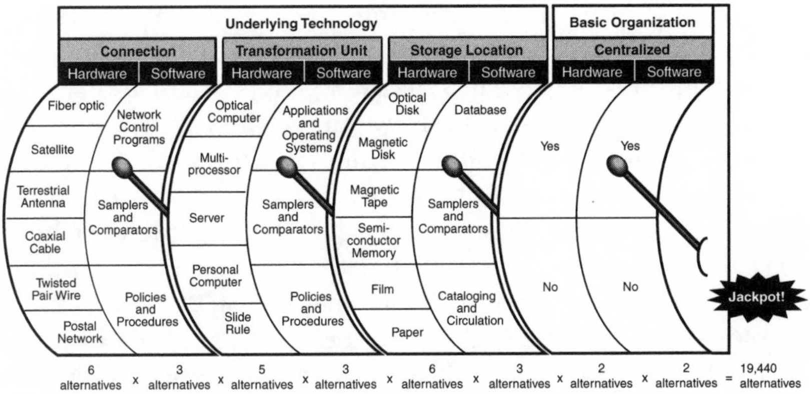

Figure 6.14 System Design Alternatives Based on Underlying Technology and Basic Organization.

➤ Combinations of Choices

Combining the underlying technology and business organization choices results in a large number of distinct system design alternatives. In Figure 6.14, we have taken the examples from Figures 6.12 and 6.13 and shown all the combinations of choices that are possible, which amount to about twenty thousand. Nearly all these alternatives are suboptimal system designs, and some hybrid-tech combinations would not normally even work (e.g., high-tech optical-type connections with low-tech mechanical-type transformation units). These should be removed from consideration.

■ 6.5 SYSTEM DESIGN ASSESSMENT

An index of the attractiveness of a system design is the ratio of function (F) and performance (P) to the cost (C) and schedule (S). There are a number of difficulties in applying this index, however, on more than a qualitative basis. First, FPC&S are expressed in different units and may be weighted differently in importance (e.g., performance may be more important than cost), so it is not possible to evaluate trade-offs between FPC&S on more than a subjective basis. Second, each element of FPC&S has many aspects (performance can include setup time and thereby encompass ease-of-use; or recovery time and thereby include maintenance . . . aside from the obvious aspect of the time it takes to perform main functions) and conversely, may not be complete (where does size get consideration?). Third, it is difficult to find an objective and summary unit of measure of FPC&S. For example, with F and P issues of number, type, and mix of functions arise that are difficult to resolve. All these difficulties come with the quantitative assessment of complex information systems. They are compounded because a design decision must occur before the system is even built, so one is relying on projections, not actual data.

The assessment of system design alternatives is then, an inherently qualitative and imperfect process that is guided by an awareness of system priorities and constraints. To sort through the alternatives, we need a set of heuristics to apply that will allow us to approximate the optimal system design. These are statements expressing the relationship between a particular choice and the system design priorities and constraints (FPC&S). These take the form of "rules of thumb," such as "Moore's Law," which states that the number of bits per chip for MOS memory doubles every 18 to 24 months, and is used to predict levels of F, as well as P and C, over time. They may also be very specific to a system, such as paper being preferred over electronic or optical media by a target customer segment. By applying these heuristics, the number of system design alternatives worth examining can often be reduced to a handful. Some commonly used heuristics are shown in Figure 6.15.[5] Heuristics must be used carefully. A heuristic like "processing power and storage will be so cheap, they will become virtually free" is used to stimulate thinking about what may be possible in the future, but it would be a big mistake to take this literally in a system design that must conform to real economic constraints.

	Underlying Technology
Connections	"The major cost of installing wireline transmission media (e.g., fiber-optic cable, coaxial cable, twisted pair wire) is labor, not materials."
	"Fiber-optic cable can support transmission speeds in the Gbps range, coaxial cable in the 10s to 1000s of Mbps, and twisted pair in the 10s to 1000s of Kbps."
Transformation units	"The performance of computers improves about 55%–60% per year."
	"Electronic devices are significantly more reliable than mechanical."
Storage locations	"Most programs use only a small, relatively invariant, subset of stored information and therefore designs with small amounts of fast storage and large amounts of slow storage often perform well."
	"Moore's Law: The number of bits per chip for MOS memory doubles every 18 to 24 months."
	"Memory is cheap and software isn't, so larger program sizes are likely."
	Basic Organization
Hardware	"Centralized hardware results in a lower cost system."
	"Decentralized hardware can increase performance by putting the processing power where it is needed."
Software	"Centralized software results in a system that is less responsive to changing user needs (application development backlog)."
	"Decentralized software can create significant data compatibility problems."

Figure 6.15   Commonly Used Heuristics in Computing.

Finally, a system design needs to be examined from the perspective of its entire life cycle. The system life cycle comprises five phases:

1. *Concept*   The recognition of an opportunity and determination of technical and economic feasibility.

2. *Development/Procurement*   The development or procurement of equipment and staff.

3. *Operation*   The operation and management of the system.

4. *Maintenance and Upgrade*   The periodic adjustment, repair, replacement, and enhancement of the system.

5. *Retirement*   The decommissioning and storage or scrapping of the system.

Consideration of the entire life cycle in a system design will help ensure it is close to optimum. Most systems have designs centered around their operation; less are designed for maintainability or upgrade; almost none are designed with retirement in mind. Yet substantial resources are often consumed in system maintenance, upgrade, and retirement. For example, the portion of effort spent on software maintenance is greater than that spent on software development, as a general trend.[6] Similarly, it is often more costly to retire a system than it is to develop it, because its use gets ingrained into an enterprise.

■ PROBLEMS AND SOLUTIONS

Problem 6.1:   What is a source of information on the capacity of system components?

Solution: Technical specification sheets from the manufacturer.

Problem 6.2:   What are some major design choices that have to be made, aside from underlying technology and basic organization?

Solution: Type, size, number, mix, and interconnection of the components. Compatibility, scalability, and modularity of the system.

Problem 6.3:   Develop a technology architecture for the PBX system of Chapter 5, Figure 5.26.

Solution:

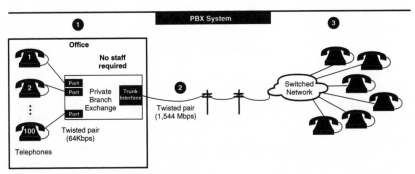

Overview of Operation

Step 1: Calls are sent to the PBX where they are multiplexed onto a 1.544MBPS trunk
Step 2: Calls are transported to the switched network
Step 3: Calls reach their destination

Private Branch Exchange (PBX) Bill of Materials

Item	Quantity	Description	Capability
1.	100	Digital phones	Comply with ISDN S/T interface
2.	100	Port	Comply with ISDN S/T interface
3.	1	PBX	Call handling capacity of 7.5 erlangs
4.	1	Trunk interface	Comply with ISDN U interface
5.	1	Manuals, software, etc.	Provide various features

There is no need for additional staff.

■ NOTES

1. See Gordon Moore, "An Update on Moore's Law," *Intel Developer Forum Speech,* delivered September 30, 1997, and Carver Mead and Lynn Conway, *An Introduction to VLSI Systems,* Reading, MA: Addison-Wesley, 1980.

2. Windows® and WindowsNT™ are registered trademarks of Microsoft Corporation. Unix™ is a trademark of Bell Laboratories, Inc., MVS™ is a trademark of IBM Corporation.

3. Barry Haskell and Arun Netravali, *Digital Pictures,* New York: Plenum, 1988, 567.

4. S. Beauchamp, "Throughput Analysis of Com21 Service Levels and ISDN," *Com21 Application Note,* August 4, 1997, and "Series 2000 Cable Down-Telephone Return System Capacity," S. Varma, *Hybrid Networks, White Paper* February 10, 1998.

The user activity traffic model in these simulations is based on observations of Web clients and servers, which for one study can be summarized as follows:

Item	HTML	Images	Sound	Video	Dynamic	Formatted	Other
% Requests	51.1	48.1	0.2	0.1	0.01	0.006	0.484
% Bytes	51.1	36.0	3.5	6.2	0.06	0.2	2.94
Mean Size (bytes)	12,950	9,679	197,605	594,796	6,535	369,590	103.783

Each active user requests Web pages at a rate of 3 per minute. This model of Web-browsing traffic is likely to become obsolete, however, as communication speed increases enable more video and sound traffic to occur. Changes in Web traffic patterns will have to be monitored to gauge the effect on network capacity plans.

5. See also D. Patterson and J. Hennessy, *Computer Architecture: A Quantitative Approach,* San Mateo, CA: Morgan Kaufmann, 1996.

6. B. Boehm, *Software Engineering Economics,* New York: Prentice Hall, 1981, 18.

Part IV

Economic Value

Chapter 7

Cost Estimation

Which of you, intending to build a tower, sitteth not down first, and counteth the cost, whether he have sufficient to finish it?

—*The Holy Bible*
Luke 14:28

Diligence is the mother of good fortune.

—Miguel de Cervantes, *Don Quixote*

There is no royal road to geometry.

—Euclid, c. 300 B.C.

We are now prepared to begin the analysis of the economics of the most promising information technology system designs. In this chapter, we will focus on how to estimate their costs. A comparison of costs is needed to narrow down the alternatives to just one, if we assume each has the same probability of generating the same revenue. An understanding of costs is also needed to perform a system design valuation.

There are three main cost components: investment costs, operating costs, and allocated costs. They will be discussed in turn. These costs should be measured on an incremental basis. This will ensure that we are considering the amount of wealth created or destroyed by a system in our assessment. Also, costs are a function of capacity, so capacity targets must be set if we are to make a good estimate. This requires fixing on the results derived in Chapters 2, 3, 4, and 5 before beginning.

179

■ 7.1 INVESTMENT COSTS

Investment costs are capital outlays to create assets that support business activities for a prolonged time period, comparable to the system life cycle. This includes capital expenditures, capitalized intangibles, and working capital to fund operations.

Capital expenditures are property, plant, and equipment, and can be derived directly from the system design and a knowledge of what may be in place already. The bill of materials describes the necessary equipment. Property and plant is merely an extension of the bill of the materials to include real estate. An estimate of these costs can be made by identifying sources for each piece of property, plant, or equipment and obtaining a quote. Tax and installation costs should also be included, where appropriate.

Capitalized intangibles are the expenditures on software development, research and development, planning, patents, and so on. These must be estimated, if not fully known. For complex software development efforts, it is sometimes worthwhile to obtain a quote from a vendor to estimate this cost, since it can be large and errors are easily made. The capitalization of intangible costs must be done carefully to comply with accounting rules.

Working capital to fund operations is the cash tied up in receivables, inventory, and elsewhere and represents a genuine investment requirement. It can be estimated by examining working capital requirements of similar businesses, usually as a percentage of sales. The change in working capital represents the investment requirement for a period.

Investment costs can be incurred throughout the system life cycle; for example, as capacity requirements change or system upgrades occur. The timing of the incurring of investment costs is important information that must be determined to truly understand the cost requirements of a system.

Once the data on investment costs has been obtained, it should be organized and totaled. The organization should reflect the system design to help understand how the design and its associated costs are related. Arraying the costs of property, plant, and equipment and capitalized intangibles by underlying technology function (hardware/software, connection, transformation unit, storage) and location does this well. Working capital does not directly reflect the system design and therefore should be shown separately. Costs can be ordered from highest to lowest within this overall framework if desired (see Figure 7.1).

If there is some uncertainty about the investment costs, a contingency should be included to provide a safety factor against underestimates. The dominant costs should also be noted to improve the understanding of the primary cost drivers and aid in project management.

Returning to our earlier illustration of a cable television system, the investment costs look like those shown in Figure 7.2.

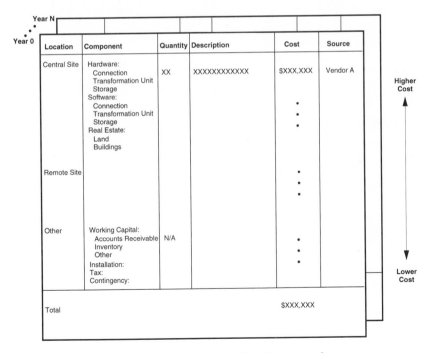

Figure 7.1 Investment Cost Framework.

General: Same as Figure 6.10, except we assume cable modem penetration is 30% of cable subscribers.

Location	Component	Quantity	Description	Unit Cost ($)	Calculation	Cost ($) per Subscriber		Source
						Cable	Cable Modem	
Headend (serves 25,600 households)	Tower and building	1	See Figure 6-10	55,000	55,000/25,600(.6)	3.5	—	Vendor quotes, engineering contractors
	Earth station and over-the air antenna	1		50,000	50,000/25,600(.6)	3.5	—	
	Microwave antenna	1		25,000	25,000/25,600(.6)	1.5	—	
	Microwave receiver	64		7,000/channel	7,000(64)/25,600(.6)	29.0	—	
	FM receiver bank	1		8,000	8,000/25,600(.6)	.5	—	
	Codec	100		125/channel	125(100)/25,600(.6)	1.0	—	
	Optical transmitter	25		3,500	3,500(25)/25,600(.6)	5.5	—	
	Power	2,500 watts		10 per watt	2,500(10)/25,600(.6)	1.5	—	
	Standby Power	1		15,000	15,000/25,600(.6)	1.0	—	
	Headend router package	1		75,000	75,000/25,600(.6)(.3)	—	16.5	
	Local content server	5		10,000	50,000/25,600(.6)(.3)	—	11.0	
	Cable network manager	1		5,000	5,000/25,600(6)(.3)	—	1.0	
	Router for T3 line	1		30,000	30,000/25,600(.6)(.3)	—	6.5	
	Installation fee for T3 line	1		50,000	50,000/25,600(.6)(.3)	—	11.0	
					Subtotal	47	46	
Trunk (serves 1,024 households)	Single mode fiber	4 fibers of 3,072 m.	See Figure 6-10	.10 per m.	4(3,072)(.1)/1,024(.6)	2	—	Construction contractors
	Cable sheath	3,072 m.		2 per m.	3,072(2)/1,024(.6)	10	—	
	Underground installation	3,072 m.		6 per m.	3,072(6)/1,024(.6)	30	—	
	Inner duct	3,072 m.		1.15 per m.	3,072(1.15)/1,024(.6)	6	—	
	Splice, connector	Each fiber spliced 3x, 2 connectors		15,25 each	4[3(15)+2(25)]/1,024(.6)	.5	—	
	Optical receiver	1		700	700/1,024(.6)	1	—	
	Amplifier, accessories housing	1		2,550	2,550/1,024(.6)	4	—	
	Power	340 watts		15 per watt	340(15)/1,024(.6)	8.5	—	
					Subtotal:	62	—	

Feeder Plant (serves 1,024 households)						
Coaxial cable	22,820 m.	See Figure 6-10	1.6 per m.	22,820(1.6)/1,024(.6)	59.5	—
Bridger amplifiers	64		350	350(64)/1,024(.6)	36.5	—
Passive components	256 splitters, 128 connectors		70, 14	256(70)+128(14)/1,024(.6)	32	—
Underground installation	17,550 m. of trench		4 per m.	17,550(4)/1,024(.6)	114.5	—
Underground conduit	17,550 m.		.75 per m.	17,550(.75)/1,024(.6)	21.5	—
Power	16 stations		1000	16(1,000)/1,024(.6)	26	—
				Subtotal:	290	—
						Construction contractors

Drop Line (serves 1 subscriber)						
Coaxial cable	27 m.	See Figure 6-10	.2 per m.	27(.2)	5.5	—
Cable installation (buried)	11 m. trench		1 per m.	11(1)	11	—
Tap, connector	1,1		10,10	10-10	20	—
				Subtotal:	36.5	—

Subscriber Premises Equipment (serves 1 subscriber)						
Addressable converter	1	See Figure 6-10	100	100	100	—
Hookup and installation	1		50	50	50	—
Second converter (incl. installation)	.2		150	150(.2)	30	—
Cable Modem	1		150 per cable modem subs.	150	—	150
Ethernet connector	1		75 per cable modem subs.	75	—	75
Cable modem hookup and installation	1		50 per cable modem subs.	50	—	50
				Subtotal:	180	275

Other						
Working Capital	10% of annual revenue		35 per cable modem subs. 47 per cable modem subs.		35	47	Value Line

Contingency						
None					0	0
				Subtotal:	35	47
				Total:	$650	$368

Figure 7.2 Cable System Investment Costs.

Note. Includes field engineering, installation, and testing costs as well as taxes. Adapted from Leland L. Johnson and David P. Reed, *Residential Broadband Services by Telephone Companies? Technology, Economics and Public Policy.* Santa Monica, CA: Rand Corporation, June 1990. Tables A1, C1, G2. Used with permission.

■ 7.2 OPERATING COSTS

Operating costs are ongoing expenses incurred in the course of ordinary business activities throughout the system life cycle. This includes labor, material, service, and occupancy charges.

Labor costs are salaries, wages, and fringes and can be derived from the staffing requirements of the system design, as well as marketing, service, and administrative personnel requirements. Analysis of work flow will pin these requirements down. A cost estimate can be obtained by multiplying labor rates by headcount levels. Fringes are usually estimated as a percentage of the total.

Material costs are raw materials and consumables including media, supplies, and replacement parts. Service costs are maintenance, transportation, mail, and utilities. An estimate of these costs is often made by examining the projected load on the system and examining the requirements of similar businesses.

Occupancy charges are such things as leases and can be determined by consulting local real estate management companies.

The preceding discussion is illustrative, not comprehensive, since operating costs obviously differ in composition among systems. In addition, operating costs will often change as system capacity requirements change. An important exception here is that the cost to physically reproduce and distribute information can be close to zero. This is because the cost of media such as CD-ROM and the cost of downloads over networks are very low. This creates significant scale economies, with a high cost to manufacture the first copy, and a low cost for subsequent copies.

The suggested organization of operating costs is similar to that used earlier for investment costs (see Figure 7.3). As before, a safety factor should be included to guard against underestimates in case of uncertainty, and the dominant operating costs noted.

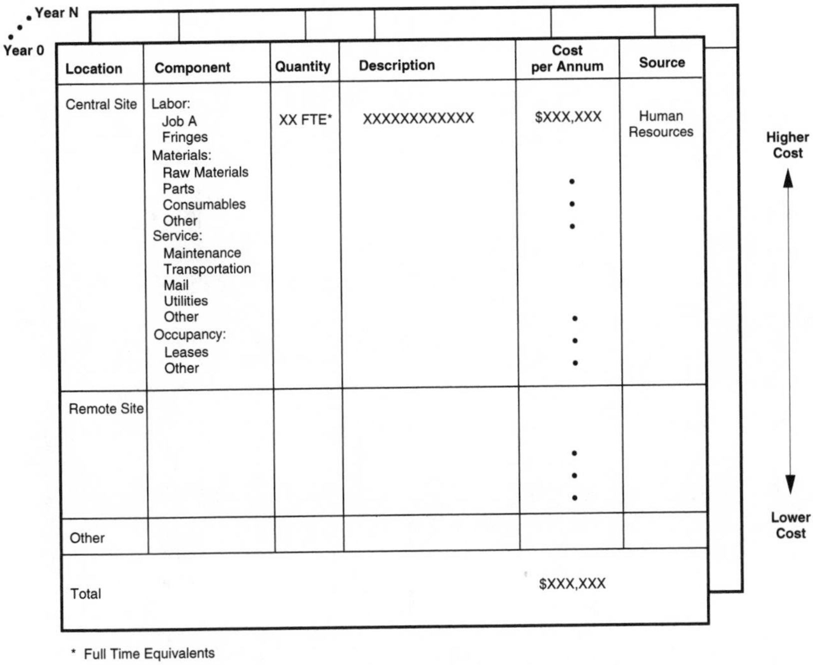

Figure 7.3   Operating Cost Framework.

To illustrate, for our cable television system, the operating costs look like those shown in Figure 7.4.

■ 7.3 COST ALLOCATION

Allocated costs are costs that are shared. Some costs may be shared if the system is part of a larger enterprise. This raises the problem of how to allocate these costs in a way that best reflects the actual consumption of resources by the system. The key here is to find a basis for allocating costs that exhibits a genuine cause-and-effect relationship. For example, if a connection is shared, its cost might be allocated on the basis of the total number of bits transmitted. Allocation basis can involve subtle reasoning. Fortunately, much has been written on the subject, to which the reader is referred.[1]

General: Same as Figure 7.2.

Location	Component	Quantity	Description	Cost per Annum $	Cost ($) per Subscriber			Source
					Calculation	Cable	Cable Modem	
Headend	General and administration	1.4 FTE	Administrative costs	285,000	285,000/25,600(.6)	18.5	—	Annual budget
	Accounting and finance	4 FTE	Payroll, accounts receivable/payable, MIS	185,000	185,000/25,600(.6)	12.0	—	
	Sales and marketing	6 FTE	Subscription and advertising sales, incl. materials	310,000	310,000/25,600(.6)	20.0	—	
	Customer service	3 FTE	Billing and service support	120,000	120,000/25,600(.6)	8.0	—	
	Engineering	2 FTE	Headend maintenance, system design	130,000	130,000/25,600(.6)	8.5	—	
	Programming expenses	100 channels	Programming fees	1,820,000	1,820,000/25,600(.6)	118.5	—	
	Programming (local origination)	2 FTE	Local origination, commercial production	80,000	80,000/25,600(.6)	5.0	—	
	Human resources	2 FTE	Benefits, recruiting	90,000	90,000/25,600(.6)	6.0	—	
	Advertising	N/A	Cable service advertising	40,000	40,000/25,600(.6)	2.5	—	
	Franchise fees	—	Licensing payment	140,000	140,000/25,600(.6)	9.0	—	
	Bad debts	—	Unpaid bills due	80,000	80,000/25,600(.6)	5.0	—	
	Internet, bank, and telephone network connection	1	Fractional T3 lines providing 30 Mbps*	540,000	540,000/25,600(.3)	—	117	Telephone co. rates
	Cable modem service calls	2,300 service calls per year	Service calls @ 50% of cable modem subscribers per year and $50 each	115,000	115,000/25,600(.6)(.3)	—	25	
	Cable modem marketing and sales	2 FTE	Cable modem marketing and sales, incl. materials	125,000	125,000/25,600(.6)(.3)	—	27	Vendor estimates
	Cable modem billing	4,600 bills per month	Billing services @ $1 per subscriber per month	55,000	55,000/25,600(.6)(.3)	—	12	
	Cable modem telephone support	1 FTE	Cable modem customer service	40,000	18,000/25,600(.6)(.3)	—	8.5	
	Cable modem equipment maintenance charges and software licensing fees	N/A	Maintenance and s/w licensing fees @ 10% of cable modem headend equipt. costs	18,000	18,000/25,600(.6)(.3)	—	4	
Trunk, Feeder plant	Technical operations	8 FTE	Construction and maintenance	215,000		14.0	—	Annual budget
Drop Line, subscriber premises equipment	Installation and hookup (churn related)	2 FTE	Installation, incl. maintenance	115,000		7.5	—	Annual budget
	Cable modem installation and hookup (churn related)	1 FTE	Cable modem installation, incl. maintenance	30,000		—	6.5	
					Total:	**$235**	**$200**	

Figure 7.4 Cable System Operating Costs.

* Many cable networks take advantage of fiber-optic infrastructure used to transport cable television signals from a consolidated headend facility to other headends within a region, which allows avoiding this high cost of leasing high-speed communications services from telephone companies. Adapted from T. Baldwin and D. McVoy, *Cable Communications* (2nd ed.). Prentice Hall 1988, p. 417. Used with permission.

Moreover, if we keep in mind that our interest is in the incremental costs of a system, we can often avoid the allocation basis issue entirely. In the case of a shared connection, the capacity consumed by a system may be on a preexisting and underutilized connection, and so the incremental cost is zero and there is no allocated cost to consider.

As before, if there is some uncertainty about allocated costs, a contingency should be included to provide a safety factor against underestimates. The refrain that the dominant costs should be noted to improve the understanding of the primary cost drivers and aid in project management holds here as well.

■ 7.4 COST VARIATIONS

Each component of a system will exhibit some degree of variation over time in cost. Sometimes this variation is substantial and efforts should be made to account for it. Major sources of cost variation are technology progress, which tends to decrease costs over time; inflation, which tends to increase costs; and the level of supply and demand, which can increase or decrease costs. Technology progress can be measured by plotting the cost/performance ratio for a component over time. Sometimes an exponential relationship will be observed which translates into a constant percentage improvement per year. These historical rates of improvement can be applied to estimate costs for future time periods.

Inflation is tracked through the producer price index. Though future levels are unknown, a reasonable approximation is to extrapolate from recent levels. Supply and demand is much more difficult to adjust for. In most cases, this becomes one of many sources of risk in the economic analysis (see Figure 7.5).

It is suggested that cost projections be kept in nominal (not constant dollar) form since most people think in these terms, cost data is usually provided this way, and it simplifies the valuation effort of Chapter 8.

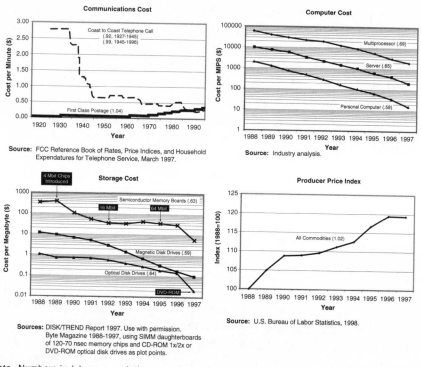

Note. Numbers in ( ) are cumulative annual growth rates over period shown.

Figure 7.5 Cost Variation—Examples.

■ 7.5 COST EQUIVALENCY

Investment costs and operating costs are fundamentally equivalent (Figure 7.6), with investment costs expressible as operating costs and vice versa. That this is true can be shown by determining the value today of amounts to be paid later. This is done by simply calculating the present value, C_{pv}, of an arbitrary series of operating costs:

$$C_{pv} = \sum_{n=1}^{N} \frac{C_n}{(1+r)^n}$$

where C_n = operating cost in year n
r = rate of return that could be earned on investments of similar risk per year
N = last year of the economic lifetime

This means the stream of operating costs C_n, for years $n = 1, 2, \ldots, N$ is equivalent to a capital outlay at the present time ($n = 0$) of magnitude C_{pv}. But, by our earlier definition, this capital outlay can be viewed as an investment cost, creating an asset that supports ordinary business activities throughout the system life cycle.

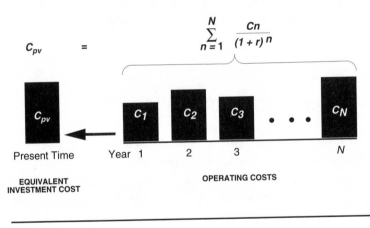

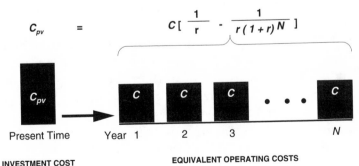

Figure 7.6   Equivalence of Investment and Operating Costs.

Conversely, we can determine the amounts to be paid later for the value of an investment today, where the investment has an economic lifetime of N years. This can be done by simply calculating the annual payment C, for each year $n = 1, 2, \ldots, N$ that is equivalent to an arbitrary investment cost, C_{pv}. Setting $C_n = C$ in the preceding equation and doing some rearranging gives[2]

$$C = \frac{C_{pv}}{\dfrac{1}{r} - \dfrac{1}{r(1+r)^N}}$$

The present value formula converts investment costs into an equivalent series of operating costs and a series of operating costs into an equivalent investment cost. This proves to be very useful in comparing costs of system design alternatives.

■ 7.6 COST COMPARISON

A cost comparison of the system design alternatives can now be made to identify the one with the most attractive economics. Using relative cost as a discriminant assumes that the revenue potential of each system is identical. This is often a reasonable assumption since the system design is driven by the requirement to address a specific customer opportunity.

To compare the cost of the system design alternatives, we must adjust for differences in the mix of investment and operating costs. Transformation of operating costs into investment costs results in a single figure by which systems can be compared (see Figure 7.7a).

Sometimes, however, one of the system alternatives is an existing one in which the investment is a sunk cost and the primary issue is whether a new design has lower equivalent operating costs. In this case, it is more convenient to

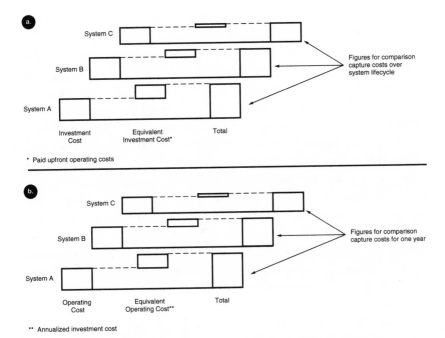

Figure 7.7 Cost Comparison of System Design Alternatives.

transform investment costs into equivalent operating costs as the basis of comparison (see Figure 7.7b). Operating costs can vary from year to year, however, so a single figure for comparison may not be possible here.

Two illustrations show how a cost analysis can be used to narrow down the number of system design alternatives to just one. The first is a comparison of a modern hybrid fiber-coaxial cable system design with a traditional cable system design, from the standpoint of the cable system owner. The second is a comparison of telephone modem service and cable modem service, from the standpoint of the consumer.

A hybrid fiber-coaxial cable system uses a fiber-optic backbone in the trunk that requires few amplifiers between the headend and the subscriber. This improves network reliability and reception, increases system capacity, and provides greater flexibility for offering new services, especially 2-way interactive. This design results in an investment cost of $650 per cable subscriber (Figure 7.2) and an operating cost of $235 per cable subscriber (Figure 7.4).

A traditional cable system uses coaxial cable in the trunk with a large cascade of amplifiers to maintain signal strength. This design results in an investment cost of $695 per cable subscriber (Figure 7.8). The operating costs are identical to the hybrid fiber-coaxial cable design (Figure 7.4), except in the trunk and feeder plant where they are approximately double, rising to $430,000 per annum. This gives an operating cost of $249 per cable subscriber.

A comparison of the hybrid fiber-coaxial with the traditional cable system shows that the former has lower investment and operating costs. The magnitude of this cost advantage can be measured by converting the investment costs into an equivalent series of operating costs, or converting the operating costs into an equivalent investment cost. We will do both to show how this is done.

The additional information needed to apply our conversion formulas is the rate of return that could be earned on investments of similar risk per year by a cable owner and the economic lifetimes of the cable network components. A typical rate of return for a cable operator is 9.5% to 12.5% per year. Ibbotson Associates and Stern Stewart & Company publish rates of return that could be earned on capital (also called the cost of capital) for companies. We will use 12.5% for our calculations. With regard to economic lifetimes, engineering experience has shown the physical portions of cable networks should have a useful life of 20 years and the electronic portions 10 years.

Laying out the costs over a 20-year period, which is the point in time when the cable system would be mostly rebuilt, we get Figure 7.9. We assume cost increases due to inflation are offset by cost declines due to technology advances. The calculation of equivalent investment cost can now be made. The hybrid fiber-coaxial cable system has an equivalent investment cost of $2,443, which is about 5% less than the traditional cable system. The equivalent operating cost is $337, which is also about 5% less. The cable owner will therefore

Cable System Description:

- Size of service area is 25,600 households, density 88 homes per mile.
- Cable subscriber penetration is 60% of households.
- Traditional coaxial cable design.

- 750 MHz bandwidth (100 video channels, 1 data channel).
- Two-way capability.
- Services offered: Television, home banking, electronic mail, telephone, and Internet access.

Location	Component	Quantity	Description	Unit Cost ($)	Cost ($) per Subscriber Calculation	Cable	Source
Headend (serves 25,600 households)	Tower and building	1	See Figure 6-10	55,000	55,000/25,600(.6)	3.5	Vendor quotes, engineering contractors
	Earth station and over-the-air antenna	1		50,000	50,000/25,600(.6)	3.5	
	Microwave antenna	1		25,000	25,000/25,600(.6)	1.5	
	Microwave receiver	64		7,000/channel	7,000(64)/25,600(.6)	29	
	FM Receiver bank	1		8,000	8,000/25,600(.6)	.5	
	Codec	100		125/channel	125(100)/25,600(.6)	1	
	Power	2,500 watts		10 per watt	2,500(10)/25,600(.6)	1.5	
	Standby power	1		15,000	15,000/25,600(.6)	1	
					Subtotal:	41.5	
Trunk (serves 25,600 households)	Coaxial cable	58.5 km	See Figure 6-10	3 per m	(58,500)(3)/25,600(.6)	11.5	Construction contractors
	Trunk amplifiers	100 sites		1,550+620 to install	100(2,170)/25,600(.6)	14	
	Passive components	100 sites		230	100(230)/25,600(.6)	1.5	
	Underground installation	58.5 km		6 per m	(58,000)(6)/25,600(.6)	23	
	Underground conduit	58.5 km		1.1 per m	58,500(1.1)/25,600(.6)	4	
	Power systems	414 units		1,000	414 (1,000)/25,600(.6)	27	
					Subtotal:	81	
Feeder Plant (serves 25,600 households)	Coaxial cable	570.5 km	See Figure 6-10	1.6 per m	570,000(1.6)/25,600(.6)	59.5	Construction contractors
	Bridger amplifiers	1,600		250 +100 to install	1,600(350)/25,600(.6)	36	
	Passive components	6,400 splitters, 3,200 connectors		70,14	6,400(70)+3,200(14)/25,600(.6)	32	
	Underground installation	439.5 km		6 per m	439,000(6)/25,600(.6)	171.5	
	Underground conduit	439.5 km		.75 per m	439,000(.75)/25,600(.6)	21.5	
					Subtotal:	320.5	
Drop Line (serves 1 subscriber)	Coaxial cable	27 m	See Figure 6-10	.2 per m	27(.2)	5.5	Construction contractors
	Cable installation (buried)	11 m trench		1 per m	11(1)	11	
	Tap, connector	1,1		10, 10	10+10	20	
					Subtotal:	36.5	
Subscriber Premises Equipment (serves 1 subscriber)	Addressable converter	1	See Figure 6-10	100	100	100	Vender quotes
	Hookup and installation	1		50	50	50	
	Second converter (incl. installation)	.2		150	150(.2)	30	
					Subtotal:	180	
Other	Working capital	10% of annual revenue per subsciber	–	35 per cable		35	Value line
	Contingency	None	–	–		0	
					Subtotal:	35	
					Total:	$695	

Note. Includes field engineering, installation, and testing costs as well as taxes.

Source. Adapted from Leland L. Johnson and David P. Reed, *Residential Broadband Services by Telephone Companies Technology, Economics, and Public Policy.* Santa Monica, CA: Rand Corporation, June 1990, Tables A1, C1, G1. Used with permission.

Figure 7.8 Traditional Cable System Investment Costs.

Rate of return = 12.5%

HYBRID FIBER-COAXIAL CABLE SYSTEM

	Present Time	1 to 9	10	11 to 20
INVESTMENT COSTS: ($ per cable subscriber)				
20-Year				
Tower and building	4			
Earth station and over-the-air antenna	3			
Microwave antennae	2			
Single mode fiber	2			
Cable sheath	10			
Underground installation	30			
Inner duct	6			
Splice, connector	1	0	0	0
Coaxial cable (feeder plant)	59			
Passive components	32			
Underground installation	114			
Underground conduit	21			
Coaxial cable (drop)	5			
Cable installation (buried)	11			
Tap, connector	20			
Subtotal	320	0	0	0
10-Year				
Optical transmitter	6		6	
Microwave receiver	29		29	
FM receiver bank	1		1	
Codec	1		1	
Power	2		2	
Standby power	1		1	
Optical receiver	1	0	1	0
Amplifier, accessories, housing	4		4	
Power	8		8	
Bridger amplifiers	36		36	
Power	26		26	
Addressble converter	100		100	
Hookup and installation	50		50	
Second converter	30		30	
Subtotal	295	0	295	0
One-Time				
Working Capital	35	0	0	0
Subtotal	35	0	0	0
Total	650	0	295	0
OPERATING COSTS ($ per cable subscriber per year)				
Total	235	235	235	235
Equivalent Investment Cost [1] ($ per cable subscriber)	2443			
Equivalent Operating Cost [2] ($ per cable subscriber per year)	337			

TRADITIONAL CABLE SYSTEM

	Present Time	1 to 9	10	11 to 20
INVESTMENT COSTS: ($ per cable subscriber)				
20-Year				
Tower and building	4			
Earth station and over-the-air antenna	3			
Microwave antennae	2			
Coaxial cable (trunk)	11			
Passive components	1			
Underground installation	23			
Underground conduit	4			
Power system	27	0	0	0
Coaxial cable (feeder plant)	59			
Passive components	32			
Underground installation	172			
Underground conduit	21			
Coaxial cable (drop)	5			
Cable installation (buried)	11			
Tap, connector	20			
Subtotal	396	0	0	0
10-Year				
Microwave receiver	29		29	
FM receiver bank	1		1	
Codec	1		1	
Power	2		2	
Standby power	1		1	
Trunk amplifiers	14	0	14	0
Bridger amplifiers	36		36	
Addressble converter	100		100	
Hookup and installation	50		50	
Second converter	30		30	
Subtotal	264	0	264	0
One-Time				
Working capital	35	0	0	0
Subtotal	35	0	0	0
Total	695	0	264	0
OPERATING COSTS ($ per cable subscriber per year)				
Total	249	249	249	249
Equivalent Investment Cost ($ per cable subscriber)	2579			
Equivalent Operating Cost ($ per cable subscriber per year)	356			

1. $650 + \dfrac{295}{(1+.125)^{10}} + \displaystyle\sum_{n=1}^{20} \dfrac{235}{(1+.125)^n}$

2. $235 + \left[650 + \dfrac{295}{(1+.125)^{10}}\right] \times \left[\dfrac{1}{.125} - \dfrac{1}{.125(1+.125)^{20}}\right]$

Figure 7.9 Comparison of Hybrid Fiber-Coaxial and Traditional Cable System Designs from the Standpoint of the Owner.

only enjoy a small cost saving with the modern hybrid fiber-coaxial cable system design compared with a traditional cable system design. The primary advantage of the hybrid fiber-coaxial cable system lies in improved network reliability and reception, increased system capacity, and greater flexibility to offer new services.[3]

For our second illustration, we compare telephone modem service with cable modem service, from the standpoint of the consumer. This is essentially an analysis of two price offers. We will assume the consumer would use either service regularly, staying logged on in sessions that can last an hour or more. This leads to the requirement for an additional telephone line to the home. The economic lifetime of the telephone and cable modem investments is estimated to be 5 years. We use a rate of return that could be earned on investments of similar risk of 5.5%, which is what a consumer would receive (when this was written) if they put their money in a 5-year Treasury note. An itemization of costs is shown in Figure 7.10. As before, we assume cost increases due to inflation are offset by cost declines due to technology advances.

Rate of return = 5.5%

CABLE MODEM SERVICE			TELEPHONE MODEM SERVICE		
	Present Time	Year 1 to 5		Present Time	Year 1 to 5
INVESTMENT COSTS: ($ per modem subscriber) 5-Year			INVESTMENT COSTS: ($ per modem subscriber) 5-Year		
Cable modem*	200		Telephone modem	100	
Ethernet connection*	100		Second telephone line installation charge	75	
Installation charge	50				
Total	350		Total	175	
OPERATING COSTS ($ per modem subscriber per year)			OPERATING COSTS ($ per modem subscriber per year)		
Cable modem service monthly charge x12		360	Telephone service dial tone charge		84
			FCC line charge		60
Total		360	Local calling charges		39
			Internet service provider monthly charge x12		240
			Total		423
Equivalent Investment Cost [1] ($ per modem subscriber)	$1,887		Equivalent Investment Cost ($ per modem subscriber)	$1,980	
Equivalent Operating Cost [2] ($ per modem subscriber per year)	$442		Equivalent Operating Cost ($ per modem subscriber per year)	$464	

*Assumes the cable operator marks up the cost of the cable modem and ethernet connection by 33%. Installation costs are passed on unchanged.

$$1.\ 350 + \sum_{n=1}^{5} \frac{360}{(1+.055)^n}$$

$$2.\ 360 + 350 \left[\frac{1}{\frac{1}{.055} - \frac{1}{.055(1+.055)^5}} \right]$$

Figure 7.10 Comparison of Cable Modem and Telephone Modem Service from the Standpoint of the Consumer.

The cost picture here is mixed, with the operating cost for cable modem service lower than for telephone modem service, while the investment cost is higher. So it is not obvious at first glance which has a cost advantage. Converting the investment costs into an equivalent series of operating costs (or vice versa), however, reveals the cable modem service has a slight advantage. The cable modem service has an equivalent investment cost of $1,887 compared with $1,980 for telephone modem service and an equivalent operating cost of $442 compared with $464. This is rather remarkable when one considers that the cable modem is capable of delivering speeds of 10 Mbps or more to the home, while the telephone modem is limited to speeds of about 56 kbps, more than a 100x difference! The telephone companies are trying to meet this challenge with ISDN and ADSL technologies. ISDN, however, is appreciably slower than a cable modem and ADSL suffers from significant distance limitations as well as a design that prevents costs from being shared to the degree found in cable systems. These technologies are likely to be most successful in areas not served by cable.

The previous two illustrations show how cost estimates can be used to narrow down the system design alternatives to one that looks most promising. Several key considerations, however, have not been taken into account, such as revenues, taxes, and depreciation, which is necessary to measure the economic value of a system. Performing a system design valuation will be covered in the next, and final chapter.

■ PROBLEMS AND SOLUTIONS

Problem 7.1: What are some ways to estimate the cost of a component?

Solution: Obtaining quotes from external suppliers or an internal purchasing department.

Problem 7.2: How can the annual improvement in the cost-performance ratio of a component be determined if it is approximately constant?

Solution: A constant annual improvement means we have a relation of the form

$$\frac{\text{Cost}}{\text{Performance}} = R_0 \alpha^n$$

where α = constant annual improvement
n = number of years
R_0 = cost/performance ratio in year 0

Taking the logarithm of both sides gives:

$$\log\left(\frac{\text{Cost}}{\text{Performance}}\right) = \log R_0 + (\log \alpha)n$$

But this is the equation of a straight line $y = b + ax$. So all we need to do is obtain the data on the cost and performance of a component over a number of years and then plot the cost/performance ratio on a logarithmic scale and the years on a linear scale. The line that results will have a slope equal to the logarithm of the constant annual improvement, $a = \log \alpha$, and a y-intercept, $b = \log R_0$.

Problem 7.3: A component can be supplied by two different vendors, A and B. Vendor A will provide the component for \$100,000, and it costs \$10,000 per year to operate and lasts four years. Vendor B will provide the component for \$75,000 and it costs \$1,000 per year to operate, but it only lasts two years. Which vendor should be chosen? Assume $r = 10\%$ per year, and the system life cycle is four years.

Solution: The annualized investment costs are,

$$C = \frac{C_{pv}}{\dfrac{1}{r} - \dfrac{1}{r(1+r)^N}}$$

For vendor A, we have

$$C = \frac{100,000}{\dfrac{1}{.1} - \dfrac{1}{.1(1.1)^4}} = \$31,547 \text{ per year}$$

So the total annual operating cost for vendor A for each year of the system life cycle is \$41,547 per year.

For vendor B, we must first recognize the component must be purchased in year 0 and again in year 2, so:

$$C_{pv} = 75,000 + \frac{75,000}{(1.1)^2} = \$136,983$$

Therefore,

$$C = \frac{136,983}{\dfrac{1}{.1} - \dfrac{1}{.1(1.1)^4}} = \$43,214 \text{ per year}$$

So the total annual operating cost for vendor B for each year of the system life cycle is \$44,214 per year. Vendor A should be chosen.

Problem 7.4: Consider replacing the point estimates of investment and operating costs (see Figures 7.1 and 7.3) with curves that are valid for a range of information loads. In other words, replace the cost values with cost functions.

$$C \rightarrow C(\rho)$$

Is this useful? When is it most practical? When does it get impractical?

Solution: If time allows, replacing C with $C(\rho)$ can be very useful when a range of loads must be considered, which is frequently the case. Investment and operating costs can then be automatically calculated for any load of interest. This can be done if the design is fixed in its essentials, with changes in load only affecting things like the number and capacity requirements of the components. It gets to be impractical when the design must change with changes in load. In this case, the relationships between components can shift in complex ways. For example, finding a set of cost functions that can be applied to both a low-tech design that uses mechanical equipment and a high-tech design that uses optical equipment would be extremely time consuming. Instead, each of these designs must be fixed and a separate set of cost functions developed for each.

Problem 7.5: Develop a cost estimate for our earlier illustration of a PBX office telephone system, using the bill of materials from Problem 6.3, the call volumes from Figures 5.8 and 5.9, and vendor quotes.

Solution: The investment costs (circa 1996) look like those shown in Figure 7.11.

Year 0

Location	Component	Quantity	Description	Cost	Source
Central site		(provided by the Telephone Company)			
Remote site	5562	100	Digital phones	$8,000	
	RSTU	13	Port (13 cards each supporting 8 phones)	6,500	
	DK 280	1	Private Branch Exchange	4,500	Telecom Systems Inc.
	RDTU/NDTU/CSU	1	Trunk interface	1,800	
	Software/Manuals	1	Various	Included	
	Miscellaneous	1	Wire, connectors, screws, etc.	Included	
Other	Installation	_	_		
	Tax	8.25%		1,716	
			Total	$22,516	

Figure 7.11 Investment Cost of Office Telephone System.

Years 1–5

Location	Component	Quantity	Description	Cost per Annum	Source
Central site	Calls, Type 1	10 CCS	Interlocation Calls	$18,000	L-D, Inc.
	Calls, Type 2	90 CCS	Intralocation Calls	($32,000)	RBOC, Inc.
Remote site	Maintenance	1	Maintenance Agreement	$3,000	Telecom Systems Inc.
			Total	($11,000)	

Figure 7.12   Operating Costs of Office Telephone System.

The operating costs (circa 1996) look like those shown in Figure 7.12. There are substantial operating cost *savings* due to the elimination of intralocation call handling. We have assumed there are no savings in year 0, which is highly conservative, since it should not take 12 months to install the system (3 months is more likely).

■ NOTES

1. For example, see C.T. Horngren, *Cost Accounting,* New York: Prentice Hall, 1977.

2. This discussion assumes the operating costs are incurred at the end of each year. If they are incurred at the beginning of each year, we must include an operating cost for the present time, Co. The formulas then become:

$$C_{pv} = \sum_{n=0}^{N} \frac{C_n}{(1+r)^n} \qquad C = \frac{C_{pv}}{1 + \dfrac{1}{r} - \dfrac{1}{(1+r)^N}}$$

The value of C_{pv} is always less and C always greater if the end-of-year assumption is made.

3. We did not compare the cable modem subscriber costs of the two cable systems designs. It is difficult to get a traditional

cable system to provide cable modem service due to signal ingress noise on the upstream channels. To get around this, some vendors offer a return path over the telephone network. The extra costs with this approach make the hybrid fiber-coaxial design even more attractive.

Chapter 8

Valuation

val-u-a-tion (val´ you a´ shen), n. 1. the act of estimating the value of something; appraisal. 2. an estimated value or worth. 3. the awareness or acknowledgment of the quality, nature, excellence, or the like of something: the public valuation of the importance of education.

floc-ci-nau-ci-ni-hil-i-pil-i-fi-ca-tion (flok´ se wo´ se ni´ hil e pil´ e fi ka´ shen), n. Rare. the estimation of something as valueless (encountered mainly as an example of one of the longest words in the English language).

—*Random House Dictionary of the English Language*
Second Edition, Unabridged

It is time to look back at how far we have come. The first and second steps of the analytical framework have now been completed: a revenue estimate has been developed by assessing the customer opportunity, and a cost estimate has been developed by aligning the information technology system with it. We now turn our attention to the third and final step, which is to determine the shareholder value of the information technology system.

■ 8.1 DESCRIPTION OF VALUATION MODEL

As stated early on, the objective of an information technology system is to create value for shareholders. The concept

203

underlying shareholder value is that the cash flow generated from the assets of a business belong to the shareholders and debtholders. Shareholder value is measured as follows.[1] The present value of the cash flow from corporate assets, V, is calculated. From this is subtracted the present value of the cash flow to debtholders, D. What remains is the present value of the cash flow to shareholders, E, because, by definition, equity represents the residual claim of owners after debtholders have been satisfied. We can write this as simply

$$E = V - D$$

The shareholder value created by an information technology system is represented by the *change* in the present value of the cash flow to shareholders caused by the system.

$$\Delta E_{System} = \Delta V_{System} - \Delta D_{System}$$

If we think of the present value of the cash flow from corporate assets, V, as the sum of the net present value, NPV, of the cash flow from projects the company has or will commit to (where any investment to date is viewed as a sunk cost), plus the present value of the uncommitted capital available to fund these projects, I, then we can write (see Figure 8.1):

$$E = (NPV + I) - D$$

$$\Delta E_{System} = (\Delta NPV_{System} + \Delta I_{System}) - \Delta D_{System}$$

What do these terms mean? Well, ΔNPV_{System} is the difference in the NPV of all the projects of a company before and after the information system project in question. In other words, it is the NPV of the information system itself. As for ΔI_{System}, this represents the additional investment capital needed to fund the system. Lastly, ΔD_{System} is the portion of ΔI_{System} that is new debt.

The primary driver of the shareholder value created by an information technology system is the term ΔNPV_{System}

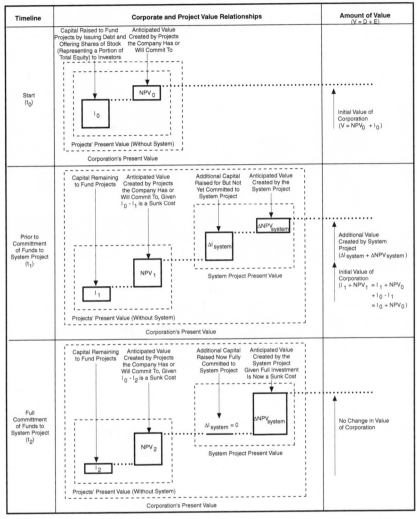

Figure 8.1 Valuation Dynamics.

which is the same as the *NPV* of the system itself. That this is so can be seen by assuming $\Delta NPV_{System} = 0$. Then $\Delta E_{System} = \Delta I_{System} - \Delta D_{System}$, but this is just equal to the present value of the portion of ΔI_{System} that is new equity. In other words, ΔE_{System} equals the amount of equity capital raised to fund the system in the first place. To create value beyond the capital raised to fund the system, we must have $\Delta NPV_{System} > 0$.

It is a common occurrence for a company to have enough capital on hand so that no additional investment capital is needed to fund the system. This makes determining the effect of a system on the share price especially easy. In this case, $\Delta I_{System} = 0$ and so the change in shareholder value $\Delta E_{System} = \Delta NPV_{System}$. If we divide this result by the number of shares outstanding, we get the effect of the system on the share price.

The *net present value* is calculated by discounting expected cash flows from operations to the present at a rate equal to the opportunity cost of capital, making sure that investment costs have been subtracted from gross cash flow (hence the term *net*).[2] *NPV* essentially represents the excess of an investment's value over its cost. The inputs to *NPV* are: cash flow from operations; the required rate of return; and the period. They are combined into a net present value according to the following expression (see Figure 8.2):

$$NPV = \sum_{n=0}^{N} \frac{CF_n}{(1+r)^n}$$

where CF_n = incremental expected cash flow from operations in year n

r = rate of return that could be earned on investments of similar risk per year

N = last year of the system life cycle

All inputs should be expressed in nominal (inflation included) terms. A nominal approach simplifies the valuation effort because the data is most often provided this way and people tend to think in nominal terms. Whether a nominal or a real approach is chosen, it must be consistently applied everywhere once adopted.

Getting a sense of how *NPV* behaves with changes in the inputs can be accomplished by applying the technique used

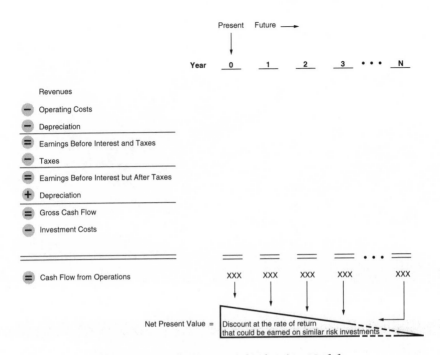

Figure 8.2   Description of Valuation Model.

to show the equivalency of investment and operating costs in Chapter 7. Cash flows from operations that vary from year to year can be transformed into a series of constant cash flows having the same *NPV*. We can therefore express an *NPV* of arbitrary cash flows as an *NPV* of constant cash flows. Measuring *NPV* in units of this constant cash flow results in *NPV* being a function of the required rate of return and the system life cycle, for a given cash flow. This general plot of *NPV* is given in Figure 8.3.

As the plot shows, a rate of return close to 1 causes the *NPV* to be close to 1. This means that the initial years of cash flow make meaningful contributions to the *NPV* while the later years do not. On the other hand, a rate of return close to 0 causes *NPV* to increase in direct proportion to the length of the system life cycle. This means the later years of cash flow make nearly as much of a contribution to the *NPV* as the initial years.

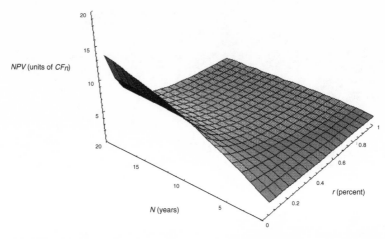

Plot of $NPV = \sum_{n=0}^{N} \dfrac{CF_n}{(1+r)^n}$ with $CF_n = 1$

Figure 8.3 Net Present Value for a Wide Range of Rates of
Return and System Lifetimes.

This has a profound effect on the management of information technology systems. If the rate of return that could be earned on capital is high, (1) schedule delays in constructing an information technology system can destroy enormous value so a strong emphasis on time-to-market is called for and (2) a short product life generates about as much value as a long product life so there should not be much compunction against replacing earlier generations of systems. The high-growth vendors of technology components such as Intel, Microsoft, and Hewlett-Packard have high rates of return and exemplify this management style.

If the rate of return is low, (1) delays have little effect on value so a more deliberate approach to system development can be tolerated and (2) the longer the product life the better, so an effort should be made to "get it right the first time." The companies in mature businesses such as Bell Atlantic and Kroger have low rates of return and exemplify this management style.

When these two different types of companies have to work together, a clash of cultures can occur. Managers of fast-moving companies with high rates of return in the computer industry have characterized their slow-moving customers and suppliers with low rates of return as following not Moore's Law but "Moron's Law." It seems more the case that they are both following the laws of economics.

The plot also shows that whether a company enjoys a high or low rate of return, *NPV* is directly proportional to cash flow. The effect is the same no matter what the rate of return or system lifetime might be. Efforts to increase revenues and decrease costs are therefore universally valuable. This creates a counterforce to moderate time-to-market, obsolence, delay, and perfection tendencies that, if taken to an extreme, could decrease cash flow. For example, an excessive focus on time-to-market could result in higher cost information systems.

■ 8.2 INPUTS

➤ Cash Flow from Operations (CF_n)

Cash flow is simply the amount of cash received minus cash spent, for a given period. Cash flow from operations is the cash flow generated by a system, independent of financial structure. It must be measured on an incremental basis so we can isolate the effect of a decision to move forward with a system on the value of an enterprise. The accounting definition of cash flow from operations is earnings before interest but after taxes plus depreciation minus investment costs (see Figure 8.2). It does not include any financing related cash flow such as interest expense. Earnings before interest but after taxes are simply revenues minus operating costs minus depreciation minus taxes. We therefore have five components to the cash flow from operations: revenues, operating costs, depreciation, taxes, and investment costs.

1. *Revenues.* The quantity of the information service purchased multiplied by the price paid for a given period. This is simply the demand for the information service that was examined in depth in Chapter 3. If the demand estimate is based on market research, the result is usually in nominal terms, so an inflation adjustment does not need to be made.

2. *Operating Costs.* The ongoing expenses incurred in the course of ordinary business activities. This includes labor, material, service, and occupancy charges. Operating costs were examined in depth in Chapter 7. They should be adjusted for cost variations, such as inflation and technology progress.

3. *Depreciation.* The allocation of investment costs to the periods of benefit. It is included in taxable earnings because it creates a tax benefit by increasing the accounting expenses in a given period. However, depreciation expense does not involve an actual cash outlay[3] and therefore is added back in the cash flow calculation.

4. *Taxes.* The income taxes on earnings before interest and taxes. This is the total tax that would be paid if there were no debt to be serviced. This is generally, for a system project, the tax rate of the enterprise times the earnings before interest and taxes. An adjustment for tax loss carry forwards, however, should be made where applicable. For example, many system projects involve losses in early years which create tax loss carry forwards that can be applied to profits in later years.

5. *Investment Costs.* Capital outlays that create enduring assets. This includes capital expenditures, capitalized intangibles, and working capital. If capitalized intangibles cannot be depreciated, they should be treated as an expense under operating costs (i.e., they should not be capitalized in the first place). Investment costs were examined in depth in Chapter 7.

➤ Required Rate of Return (r)

The required rate of return is what must be earned just to compensate investors for the use of their capital. The capital they provide may be used to fund either a system project or the entire company.

For a system project, the required rate of return represents what could be earned on capital per year from investments of similar risk to that of the project in question. It is the system project's cost of capital.

For a company, the required rate of return is the weighted average cost of capital (WACC). This represents the opportunity cost of the capital provided by all investors, weighted by their relative contribution to the total capital of the company. The opportunity cost is what could be earned on capital per year from investments of similar risk to that of the company. The use of the WACC is equivalent to requiring that the company pay the after-tax interest rate on the debt used to finance it, and to also generate the expected rate of return on the equity invested in it.

The required rate of return is expressed as a ratio of income to capital. This ratio must be consistent with our cash flow, and therefore, should be measured on a nominal (inflation included), after-tax, basis. A recent study has shown the average WACC used internally by companies in the early 1990s is about 15% (assuming a 3% inflation rate[4]). This is somewhat higher than a standard analysis of WACC would suggest. Ibbotson Associates and Stern Stewart and Co. publish their calculations of the WACC for a large number of companies that are probably more accurate than those you might obtain internally.

➤ Period (N)

A system is an asset with a lifetime that lasts a period of N years. If the period is short, the cash flows are analyzed year-by-year using the net present value formula described previously. If the period is long, the cash flows can be analyzed year-by-year until the discounted value of the remaining cash flows is small enough to ignore.

Alternatively, the period can be split into a transient era (with period, $n < N$), where cash flows are varying year-to-year, and a steady-state era (with period, $N - n$), where cash flows are stable. The transient era is analyzed year-by-year. The steady-state era can be analyzed by calculating the continuing value.

$$\text{Continuing Value in Year } n = \frac{\text{Cash Flow from Operations in Year } n+1}{WACC - g}$$

where g = expected annual growth rate in cash flow from operations during the steady state period. (*Note:* $g < WACC$ is required for this formula to hold.[5])

The continuing value in year n is the value of the operating cash flows in the steady-state era, as of the last year in the transient era. It therefore must be discounted back to the present before it can be added to the net present value of the transient era operating cash flows. It also assumes that N is so large, it can be considered infinite. The formula itself is simply that of a growing perpetuity. It therefore tends to overestimate value somewhat. It should be noted that for high-tech systems, it is common for continuing value to be a large percentage of the total net present value.

■ 8.3 INTERPRETATION OF RESULTS

The result of an *NPV* calculation is a quantity with direction and magnitude. The *direction* is indicated by whether the quantity is positive or negative. The *magnitude* is the quantity's size. A great deal of information is embodied in these two characteristics.

➤ Direction

What direction to take with a system is literally determined by whether its *NPV* is positive or negative. The net present value of cash flows from operations represents the amount of wealth created by a system. If the net present value of a system is positive, it is creating wealth and should be pursued; if negative, it is destroying wealth and should not be pursued.

To decide whether to proceed with a system project, we are specifically concerned with two sources of incremental cash flow from a system: cost savings over an existing system and revenues from new (or enhanced) services. The circumstances under which a system has a positive *NPV*, and therefore can be justified, vary accordingly.

Sometimes a system can be justified on the basis of cost savings. If the system is expected to provide new services in addition to these savings, the case for moving forward can be compelling.

If cost savings alone are not enough to justify a system, then the economics hinge on the demand for new services, which places a premium on developing as accurate understanding of the customer opportunity as possible.

If cost savings alone can justify the system, but no new services will be provided, then a premium is placed on developing as accurate an understanding of the cost estimates as possible.

Finally, if cost savings and the demand for new services cannot justify the project, the project should be abandoned.

Only systems that have a positive *NPV* are of interest, for otherwise they have no importance except as investment mistakes to be avoided.

➤ Magnitude

Once the direction has been established, the question naturally arises of how important is a system with a positive *NPV* to a company. The best way to answer this is to gauge the impact of the system on the share price. To do this, we need to understand how companies are valued.

Corporate Valuation

The fundamentals of corporate valuation have already been laid down in the description of the valuation model at the beginning of the chapter. The key points to remember here are the following. The concept behind corporate valuation is simply that the cash flow generated from the assets of a business belongs to the shareholders and debtholders. If we take the present value of the cash flow, then the following are all equal to the *intrinsic value* of a company: (1) the present value of cash flow from corporate assets, V, (2) the net present value of cash flow from the projects the company has or will commit to, NPV, plus the uncommitted capital available to fund these projects, I, and (3) the present value of the cash flow to shareholders, E, plus the present value of the cash flow to debtholders, D.

The *market value* of a company, also known as the market capitalization, is determined directly from the price the company's shares of stock and debt obligations trade at in the public or private market. It is equal to the market value of equity plus the market value of debt. The market value of equity is the price of a share of stock times the number of shares outstanding. The market value of debt is the price of the debt obligations times the number of debt obligations outstanding.

The market value of a company should ideally equal, but in reality only approximates, its intrinsic value. This is due to nonuniformity of information, resources, skills, access, and psychology among the individuals calculating the intrinsic value and those participating in the marketplace. Comparison of the market and intrinsic value of a company is the basis for describing a company as being undervalued, fairly valued, or overvalued. The relationship between market and intrinsic valuations is pictured in Figure 8.4.

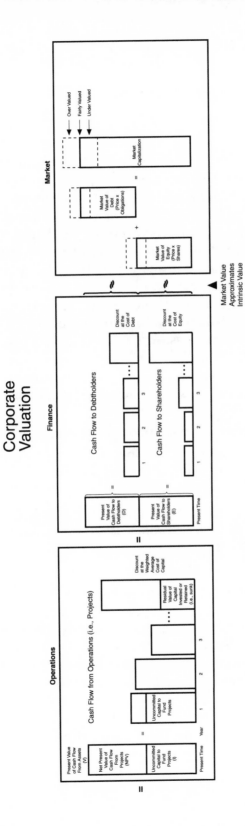

Figure 8.4 Corporate Valuation Perspectives.

From (1) and (3), we have, as before:

$$E = V - D$$

Thus, to find the intrinsic value of shareholder equity, we must first value the total company and then subtract the value of the debt. In both cases, cash flow estimates can usually be made. Alternatively, we could try to determine the value of shareholder equity directly by calculating the present value of the cash flow to shareholders. This, however, is difficult because it requires estimating the dividends that will be paid over a given period, as well as the expected value of the equity at the end of the period. The former can often be done with confidence but not the latter.

Applying the expression $E = V - D$ gives a process of five steps for calculating the intrinsic value of shareholder equity, E, on a per share basis. This represents the intrinsic price at which shares of stock would be expected to trade:

1. Determine the cash flow from operations.
2. Discount the cash flow from operations at the weighted average cost of capital.
3. Add the continuing value, making sure it is discounted to the present. Add the present value of the uncommitted capital. Also, add/subtract miscellaneous items.
4. Subtract the value of debt.
5. Divide the result by the number of shares outstanding.

Step 1 requires estimating the cash flow from operations for the entire company. The method for estimating this cash flow is identical to that described earlier in this chapter.

There is a component of corporate cash flow of special note, namely the capital invested or retained to build the business. This represents the money that investors have sunk into the company throughout the life of a business, with the greatest infusion often in the early years. Example uses of these funds are equipment purchases and working capital.

It is possible that the actual value of the items for which this capital is used will become much lower than the value of the original capital itself. For example, a personal computer rapidly declines in value after purchase. This decline in value does not occur for every item, with working capital, for example, maintaining its value from year-to-year. The sum total of these changes is represented by the *residual value* of the capital invested or retained to build the business, which is a component of the *final* cash flow from operations (see Figure 8.4).

Step 2 involves discounting the estimated cash flow from operations at the weighted average cost of capital. The simplest thing to do to find the weighted average cost of capital is, frankly, to look it up. Sometimes, however, a figure is not readily available for the company and an estimate must be made of the cost of debt, the cost of equity, and the mix of debt to equity from which the weighted average cost of capital can be derived. The expression for the weighted average cost of capital is

$$WACC = r_D(1-t)\left(\frac{D}{V}\right) + r_E\left(\frac{E}{V}\right)$$

where r_D = the cost of debt
r_E = the cost of equity
t = the corporate tax rate
D = the value of debt
E = the value of equity
V = the value of the company

The *cost of debt, r_D,* is the return that lenders require on funds borrowed by the company. A figure for this rate can be obtained by observing how the company's debt, or similar debt, trades in the financial market. The current yield to maturity on these bonds is the interest rate the company must currently pay for debt financing, and, therefore, equals the cost of debt. The interest rate at which any out-standing debt was originally issued, which is called the coupon rate, is irrelevant. This only tells us what the cost of debt was in the past.

The *cost of equity*, r_E, is the return that shareholders require on their equity investment. A figure for this rate can be obtained by applying the capital asset pricing model (CAPM). The CAPM states that the return shareholders require on their equity investments is equal to the risk-free rate of return plus a risk premium for the stock. It is expressed as

$$r_E = r_f + \beta(r_m - r_f)$$

where r_f = risk-free rate of return
r_m = rate of return on a market portfolio of stocks (e.g., Standard & Poor's 500)
β = the systematic risk of the company's stock

The risk-free rate of return, r_f, is given by the interest rate on debt obligations of the U.S. government, which it is assumed will never default. These are 1-year Treasury bills, 10-year Treasury notes, or 30-year Treasury bonds. The one used should have a duration that most closely matches the duration of the cash flows of the company being valued. Rates for these debt obligations are published in the *Wall Street Journal*.

The rate of return on a market portfolio of stocks, r_m, is usually based on the S&P 500 as a proxy for the entire stock market. An average return going back to 1926 for the S&P 500 is often used because of the number of different economic events covered over this period. A current figure for this rate can be found in the *Stocks, Bonds, Bills, and Inflation Yearbook*, published by Ibbotson Associates.

The systematic risk of the company's stock, β, is estimated from historical data on the variability of the return. Figures for the β of a company are published by *Value Line* and *BARRA*.

The corporate tax rate, t, is part of the expression for *WACC* because cash flow is after-tax. The discount rate applied to this cash flow must therefore be expressed on an after-tax basis. Tax rates are published in *Value Line* and annual reports.

The weights to apply to the cost of equity, E/V, and the cost of debt, D/V, so that a weighted average can be computed, are somewhat problematic. The problem is, these weights require knowing the value of the company, but this is why we needed to calculate the *WACC* in the first place! There are two solutions to this dilemma. The first is pick a number for V and iterate until the corporate value (left-hand side) equals the discounted value of cash flow using a *WACC* derived from this number (right-hand side). This is hard, and time consuming. The second is to use a target mix of debt and equity. This is somewhat arbitrary.

As a compromise, we recommend assuming the target mix of debt and equity is to maintain the current mix, and to use the market value of debt and equity to calculate the weights. This is equivalent to picking the market value (market capitalization) of a company as the initial number for V and stopping after a single iteration. Improvements to this approximation can be made by additional iteration, if you are ambitious.

Step 3 is to add the continuing value, making sure it is discounted to the present; to add the present value of the uncommitted capital; and to add/subtract miscellaneous items. The method for calculating the continuing value is identical to that described earlier in this chapter. Uncommitted capital comprises items like excess marketable securities which are short-term cash investments. The miscellaneous cash items that must be taken into account tend to be small, and judgment must be used to decide whether including them is worth the effort. An example that subtracts from the value of a company is unfunded pension liabilities.

Step 4 is to subtract the value of debt. This is determined by discounting the cash flow to debtholders at the cost of debt. Alternatively, we can examine the price at which the company's debt trades in the market and use this to value the debt. The assumption here is that the price at which the debt trades represents fair market value; that is, the market value equals the intrinsic value, which is not unreasonable since the interest payments and default risks for bonds are generally known from the original issuing terms and subsequent debt ratings. The validity of this assumption increases the closer the credit rating of the debt is to investment grade, and decreases with junk bonds.

Step 5 is to divide the result, *E*, by the number of shares outstanding, *S*. This gives the intrinsic value of equity per share, *E/S*, which represents the price at which the shares of stock in the company would be expected to trade.

It is strongly recommended that the resulting valuation be checked against the market, industry rules of thumb, and other alternative methodologies. This will help to surface mistakes and provide insights. It is straightforward to compare the value of equity on a per share basis with the price a share of stock is trading at in the market. Industry rules of thumb can be found by reading trade journals and analyst reports. For example, cable systems have been reported to historically sell for about 11× cash flow, and Internet service providers were selling in 1997 for $100 to $300 per dial-up account, not including assets. Several other alternative methodologies routinely used to value companies are listed in Figure 8.5.

Valuing the shareholder equity of companies is a complicated exercise and can involve taking some shortcuts. For our purposes, we are only trying to establish an approximate value for the shares of a company, so that we can determine the magnitude of the impact an information system has on it. The reader is referred to the excellent references on corporate valuation listed in the Bibliography for a full treatment of this topic, including discussion of preferred stock, junk bonds, CAPM assumptions, and so on.

System Valuation

The process of determining the impact of a system project on the share price is similar to the corporate valuation process. The main difference is that we must consider the need to raise additional capital to support the development and operation of a system. Capital is normally raised in blocks

Valuation Methodology	Description	Advantages	Disadvantages
NPV or Discounted Cash Flow	Determines the present value of future cash flows of a company and owners. (Method adopted in this book.)	Large body of evidence supports the reliability of this approach.	Only as accurate as forecast. Magnitude of terminal value is disporoportionate. Discount rate usually assumed fixed. Option value often ignored.
Real Option Value	Improves upon the NPV method by including the value of the right to take an action in the future.	Captures the value of flexibility.	Relatively new method that is still difficult to implement, except qualitatively.
Market Value	The price at which shares of stock are trading in the market times the number of shares outstanding.	Reflects current market value of equity.	Assumes market value is a good approximation of intrinsic value.
Industry "Rules of Thumb"	This is essentially the same as the comparable company and comparable transaction methodologies below.	See below.	See below.
Comparable Companies	Value established using trading multiples of comparable public companies. e.g., – Price/Earnings – Market Capitalization/ Revenues – Share Price/Book Value	Easy to calculate. More than one data point possible.	Can be misleading to the point of being wrong, e.g., when accounting earnings are used instead of cash flow.
Comparable Transactions	Value established using acquisition multiples of comparable corporate acquisition transactions. e.g., – Multiple of cash flow – Price per subscriber	Reflects what has been paid for companies in the marketplace.	Assumes past prices are a good measure of future prices.
Liquidation Analysis	Estimates liquidation value of corporate assets.	Can establish a worst case estimate.	Often difficult to obtain prices.
LBO Analysis	Estimates the maximum debt capacity of the firm.	Applies to situations where the tax advantages of debt can be fully capitalized on.	Irrelevant if an LBO is not contemplated.

Source. Bankers Trust, 1998.

Figure 8.5 Alternative Corporate Valuation Methodologies.

in response to market conditions, such as a period of low interest rates or a strong stock market. Depending on the circumstances, raising additional capital may or may not therefore be necessary.

As shown in the beginning of the chapter, if no additional capital needs to be raised, determining the effect of a system on shareholder value is especially easy. It is simply equal to the *NPV* of the system. Dividing this by the number of shares of stock outstanding gives the effect of the system on the share price.

The general process for calculating the intrinsic value to shareholders of a system involves the following steps:

1. Determine the cash flow from operations of the system.
2. Estimate the amount of additional long-term and short-term capital needed to fund the system.
3. Subtract the cash flow to the holders of the additional debt from the cash flow from operations of the system.
4. Discount the remaining cash flow to shareholders by the risk-adjusted cost of equity.
5. Add the continuing value, making sure it is discounted by the cost of equity to the present. Add the present value of the additional capital raised but not yet committed to the system project.
6. Divide the result by the number of originally issued plus newly issued shares.

Step 1 is to determine the cash flow from operations of the system. This was covered earlier in Chapter 8.

Step 2 is to estimate the amount of additional long-term and short-term capital needed to fund the system. This is done by taking the cash available at the start of a period and adding the cash flow from system operations during that period. A deficit result represents the amount of additional funds needed for the period. A surplus represents the cash available at the start of the next period.

	Period 1	Period 2	...	Period N
Cash at Start of Period	1	– 1		1
+ Cash Flow from System Operations	– 2	2		2
= Cash at End of Period	–1	1		3

Deficit repre- Surplus
sents addi- represents
tional funds cash available
needed for at the start
the period of the next
 period

The amount of short-term capital needed to close a deficit in the funding of a system is determined by the amount of long-term capital that is raised. At one extreme, companies that have issued a large amount of long-term debt or equity, or retained a large amount of earnings, may never run a deficit and have permanent excess cash. This excess cash would be better placed in the hands of shareholders.

At the other extreme, companies that have issued or retained a small amount of long-term capital may always run a deficit and have a permanent need for short-term debt. This short-term debt comes at a high cost and shareholders would be better off if it were replaced with lower cost long-term capital.

The typical approach taken by most companies lies somewhere between these extremes. *Most companies finance all investment costs with long-term debt and equity. If this is not enough to close the cash flow deficit completely, the remainder is financed with short-term debt.* This is the approach we recommend taking. It follows the general principle of matching the durations of assets and liabilities.

The mechanics of this approach involve calculating the present value of the investment in the system, using the weighted average cost of the *additional* capital. A continuing value of the investment costs should be added if investment costs are expected to be incurred for the foreseeable future.

This represents the amount of long-term debt and equity to be raised for the system. If this amount is enough to cover the deficit, then no short-term capital is needed. If this amount is *not* enough to cover the deficit, then short-term capital will also be needed to close the remaining gap in funding the system.

The mix of long-term debt and equity to be raised can be anything we choose, but the best mix is consistent with the current debt-to-equity ratio of the company. Making this choice will aid our assessment of the effect of the system on the share price by partially eliminating the debt-to-equity ratio as a variable from the comparison. If we make this assumption, then the weighted average cost of the *additional* capital can be taken to be the current weighted average cost of capital, adjusted for the higher or lower risk the system project may pose.

The interest rate and repayment requirements of the long-term debt to be raised are given by the price at which the company's long-term debt, or similar debt, trades in the market and the original repayment terms of this debt. This also applies to any short-term debt that needs to be raised.

The number of new shares of stock to be issued, ΔS is given by the amount of equity that needs to be raised, divided by the price at which shares of the company's stock trade in the market. Actually, the price of a new issue that is realized by a company is usually a few percent below the market price due to underwriting fees, legal expenses, and the need to ensure successful placement. We will ignore this adjustment since it is relatively minor.

We have now finished estimating the amount of additional long-term debt and equity, as well as short-term debt, needed to fund the system.

As an aside, it should be pointed out that very different approaches to financing the system could have been taken. For example, not only could more of the deficit have been funded with long-term debt, but also more of the cash flows from operations of the system could have been used to service issuing a large long-term-debt offering. This would provide much more cash than needed for our system, but would make perfect sense if the company could reinvest the excess proceeds in opportunities that return more than the cost of capital. It is precisely these reinvestment opportunities that allow the potential shareholder value of a company to be almost limitless.[6]

Step 3 is to subtract the cash flow to the holders of the additional long-term and short-term debt from the cash flow from operations of the system. The cash flow to the holders of the additional debt is calculated from the interest and repayment requirements of the debt.

The long-term debtload represents a nearly permanent use of cash. The short-term debtload represents a temporary use of cash, limited to those periods when closing a cash flow deficit requires it.

Step 4 is to discount the remaining cash flow to shareholders by the risk-adjusted cost of equity. The average cost of equity, r_E, is the same as that used in the corporate valuation process. It represents investors' average expectation of return. A risk adjustment, usually amounting to a few percent, is made to the average cost of equity to reflect the relative risk of the system project compared with an average project for the company. This is a shortcut to avoid having to determine the system project β.

Step 5 is to add the continuing value, making sure it is discounted by the risk-adjusted cost of equity to the present. The method for doing this is the same as for calculating the continuing value in the corporate valuation, substituting the risk-adjusted r_E, for *WACC*. We must also add the present value of the additional capital raised but not yet committed to the system project. These funds are usually held as short-term cash investments whose market value equals their present value.

Step 6 is to divide the result, ΔE_{System}, by the number of originally issued and newly issued shares, $S + \Delta S$. This gives the increase or decrease in the price at which shares of stock in the company would be expected to trade as a result of investing in the system. The number of originally issued shares is published in the annual report or Form 10K and by *Value Line*. The number of newly issued shares was calculated in Step 2.

Comparison

To complete our measurement of the impact of the system project on the share price, we need to account for the dilution of shareholder ownership in the corporation that occurred with the issuance of new shares of stock to fund the system project. This will ensure our comparison of the corporate valuation to the system valuation uses the same number of shares of stock as the basis. Accounting for the dilution simply involves repeating Step 5 of the corporate valuation process using the number of originally issued plus newly issued shares of stock as our divisor, $S + \Delta S$.

Adding this result to that obtained from the system valuation gives the intrinsic price at which shares of stock would be expected to trade after a decision is made to invest in the system.

$$\text{Intrinsic Share Price } with \text{ System} = \frac{E}{(S+\Delta S)} + \frac{\Delta E_{System}}{(S+\Delta S)}$$

↑	↑
Repeat of Corporate Valuation Step 5	System Valuation Step 6

This can be compared with our initial result for the intrinsic price at which shares of stock would be expected to trade without the system. This comparison is best used to measure the *relative* impact of the system on the share price.

$$\frac{\text{Percentage Change}}{\text{in Share Price}} = \frac{\text{Intrinsic Share Price } with \text{ System}}{\text{Intrinsic Share Price } without \text{ System}}$$

$$= \frac{\dfrac{E}{(S+\Delta S)} + \dfrac{\Delta E_{System}}{(S+\Delta S)}}{\dfrac{E}{S}} \quad \leftarrow \begin{array}{l}\text{Corporate}\\ \text{Valuation}\\ \text{Step 5}\end{array}$$

We can also compare these results with the current market price of the stock. The difference between the intrinsic price at which shares of stock would be expected to trade, assuming a decision is made to go ahead with the system, and the market price of the stock provides a more *absolute* measure of the impact of the system on the share price.

$$\text{Change in Share Price} = \frac{\text{Intrinsic Share Price}}{\text{with System}} - \frac{\text{Current Market Price}}{\text{at which Shares Trade}}$$

$$= \left(\frac{E}{(S + \Delta S)} + \frac{\Delta E_{System}}{(S + \Delta S)} \right) - \frac{\text{Current Market Price}}{\text{at which Shares Trade}}$$

By absolute we mean an actual number, not an exact number. The analysis of the impact of a system on the share price has involved many assumptions, shortcuts, and estimates. The result is therefore an approximation, which is enough to answer our original question: How important is a system to a company?

Sometimes the absolute measure will show the system will have a small impact on the share price while the relative measure shows the system will have a large impact. This situation suggests the system is already reflected in the share price.

The reverse can also occur, where the absolute measure shows a large impact on the share price while the relative measure shows the system will have a small impact. This situation suggests the corporation is substantially undervalued and the system is inconsequential.

Last, both the absolute and relative measures can be aligned. When this situation occurs, the impact a system will have is clear.

■ 8.4 EXAMPLE

The following illustration shows how to put it all together. We will conduct a valuation of cable modem service from the standpoint of the cable system owner. The company whose shares we will focus on is Tele-Communications, Inc. (NASDAQ symbol TCOMA) because it is a fairly pure play in the cable network industry at the time of analysis. A downloadable file of the three spreadsheets illustrated in this section is available at www.christophergardner.com.

The corporate valuation to determine the intrinsic price of TCI shares *without* the cable modem system is shown in Figure 8.6. Since TCI comprises many separate cable systems, the valuation is first carried out for a single system of average size and expressed on a per subscriber basis. The result is then scaled up to TCI's full size as a multiple system operator. A check of the valuation is performed by comparing the calculated value to a buyer with the price of 11× cash flow that cable systems historically trade for.

The revenue and penetration inputs to the model are from various industry sources. The cost inputs are from Figures 7.2 and 7.4. The financial inputs such as the total number of subscribers, tax rate, debt/equity ratio, β, cost of debt, value of debt,[7] and number of shares of stock are from *Value Line.*

The analysis shows that the intrinsic value of TCI was $25.02 per share as of 9/30/97, compared with a market value of $20.50 on 9/30/97 and $19.50–$33.06 for the 6-month period between 9/30/97 and 3/31/98.

The system valuation to determine the intrinsic change in price of TCI shares *with* the offering of cable modem service is shown in Figure 8.7. As before, the system valuation is first carried out for a single system of average size. The financing of this single system is done as if TCI were broken up into these single system pieces. This allows cash flows to TCI shareholders to be explicitly determined and discounted to get the change in value per share. The result is then scaled to TCI's full size as a multiple system operator, by way of a factor representing the percentage of TCI's systems that are upgraded to provide cable modem service.

The revenue and penetration inputs to the model come from a variety of sources. Revenues to TCI are the costs borne by the consumer, which are summarized in Figure 7.10. The peak penetration and the number of years to reach it are based on consumer surveys, focus groups, trials, and experience. An

CABLE SYSTEM VALUATION- TCI (AS OF 9/30/97)

(excludes cable modem)

SINGLE SYSTEM OPERATION

Number of Households	25,600
Current Cable Subscriber Penetration	60%
Peak Penetration in Cable Subscribers by Year 20	70%
Number of Years to Peak Penetration	20
Cable Service Average Monthly Charge per Subscriber	$35
Inflation Rate	2%
Effective Tax Rate	32%
Average Annual Operating Cost per Cable Subscriber @60% Penetration	$235
Incremental Annual Operating Cost per Cable Subscriber	$139 Programming, billing, bad debt, churn
Average Investment Cost per Cable Subscriber @60% Penetration	$650 This will substitute for capital expenditures to rebuild and upgrade aging cable plant
Incremental Investment Cost per Cable Subscriber @60% Penetration	$252 Subscriber premises equipment, drop line, working capital
Depreciation	Straight line, no salvage value

Year

($ in thousands)	0	1	2	3	4	5	6	7	8	9	10	11	12	13	14	15	16	17	18	19	20
Begin # of Cable Subscribers	15360	15360	15488	15616	15744	15872	16000	16128	16256	16384	16512	16640	16768	16896	17024	17152	17280	17408	17536	17664	17792
Growth in Cable Subscribers	0	128	128	128	128	128	128	128	128	128	128	128	128	128	128	128	128	128	128	128	128
End # of Cable Subscribers	15360	15488	15616	15744	15872	16000	16128	16256	16384	16512	16640	16768	16896	17024	17152	17280	17408	17536	17664	17792	17920
Avg # of Cable Subscribers	15360	15424	15552	15680	15808	15936	16064	16192	16320	16448	16576	16704	16832	16960	17088	17216	17344	17472	17600	17728	17856
REVENUE																					
Current Subscription Fees		$6,580	$6,768	$6,960	$7,158	$7,360	$7,568	$7,781	$8,000	$8,224	$8,454	$8,690	$8,932	$9,180	$9,434	$9,695	$9,963	$10,238	$10,519	$10,808	$11,104
Growth in Subscription Fees		$27	$28	$29	$29	$30	$30	$31	$31	$32	$33	$33	$34	$35	$35	$36	$37	$38	$38	$39	$40
Other Revenue (pay-per-view, etc.)		$661	$680	$699	$719	$739	$760	$781	$803	$826	$849	$872	$897	$921	$947	$973	$1,000	$1,028	$1,056	$1,085	$1,114
Total Revenue		$7,268	$7,475	$7,688	$7,905	$8,129	$8,358	$8,593	$8,834	$9,081	$9,335	$9,595	$9,862	$10,136	$10,417	$10,705	$11,000	$11,303	$11,613	$11,932	$12,258
COSTS																					
-Operating Costs		$3,618	$3,649	$3,679	$3,709	$3,739	$3,769	$3,799	$3,829	$3,859	$3,889	$3,919	$3,949	$3,979	$4,010	$4,040	$4,070	$4,100	$4,130	$4,160	$4,190
-Depreciation		$501	$507	$514	$520	$527	$533	$533	$533	$533	$533	$533	$533	$533	$533	$533	$533	$533	$533	$533	$533
=Earnings Before Interest and Taxes		$3,149	$3,319	$3,495	$3,676	$3,863	$4,056	$4,261	$4,472	$4,689	$4,913	$5,143	$5,380	$5,624	$5,874	$6,132	$6,397	$6,670	$6,950	$7,239	$7,535
-Taxes		$1,008	$1,062	$1,118	$1,176	$1,236	$1,298	$1,364	$1,431	$1,501	$1,572	$1,646	$1,722	$1,800	$1,880	$1,962	$2,047	$2,134	$2,224	$2,316	$2,411
=Earnings Before Interest but After Taxes		$2,141	$2,257	$2,377	$2,500	$2,627	$2,758	$2,897	$3,041	$3,189	$3,341	$3,497	$3,658	$3,824	$3,995	$4,170	$4,350	$4,536	$4,726	$4,922	$5,124
+Depreciation		$501	$507	$514	$520	$527	$533	$533	$533	$533	$533	$533	$533	$533	$533	$533	$533	$533	$533	$533	$533
=Gross Cash Flow		$2,642	$2,764	$2,890	$3,020	$3,154	$3,291	$3,430	$3,574	$3,722	$3,874	$4,030	$4,191	$4,357	$4,528	$4,703	$4,883	$5,069	$5,259	$5,455	$5,657
-Investment Costs	$9,984	$32	$32	$32	$32	$32	$32	$32	$32	$32	$32	$32	$32	$32	$32	$32	$32	$32	$32	$32	$32
=CASH FLOW FROM OPERATIONS	-$9,984	$2,610	$2,732	$2,858	$2,988	$3,121	$3,259	$3,398	$3,542	$3,690	$3,842	$3,998	$4,159	$4,325	$4,495	$4,671	$4,851	$5,036	$5,227	$5,423	$5,625
Buyer Cash Flow	$0	$2,610	$2,732	$2,858	$2,988	$3,121	$3,259	$3,398	$3,542	$3,690	$3,842	$3,998	$4,159	$4,325	$4,495	$4,671	$4,851	$5,036	$5,227	$5,423	$5,625

Figure 8.6 Corporate Valuation—Tele-Communications, Inc.

(continued)

SHAREHOLDER VALUE

Inputs:

Total Number of Subscribers Served by the Company	14,300,000
Debt/Equity Ratio*	1.37
Risk Free Rate of Return (US Treasury 20 Year Bond Yield 1926-1996)**	6.7%
Beta*	1.0
Average Return on Large Company Stocks (1926-1996)**	14.2%
Cost of Debt (pre-Tax)*	8.8%
Number of Shares of Stock*	507,000,000

Derived Numbers:

Cost of Equity	14.2%
Weighted Average Cost of Capital (after-Tax)***	9.5%

SINGLE SYSTEM OPERATION

Valuation Up to Continuing Value	$21,403,184
+Continuing Value	$9,778,575
=Total Valuation	$31,181,759
Value per Cable Subscriber	**$2,030**

MULTIPLE SYSTEM OPERATION

	Value of TCI
Value per Cable Subscriber	$2,030
xTotal Number of Subscribers Served by the Company	14,300,000
=Value for Cable Business	$29,029,892,812

MULTIPLE SYSTEM FINANCING

-Value of Debt (including Preferred Stock)*	$16,343,000,000
=Value of Equity	$12,686,892,812

Value to Stockholders per Share $25.02

Share Price at End of Day 9/30/97 $20.50

Share Price Range from 9/30/97 to 3/31/98 High $33 1/16 - Low $19 1/2

CHECK

*Buyer Weighted Average Cost of Capital*****	*12.3%*
Buyer Value Given Investment in Year 0 is Sunk Cost	*$25,279,327*
+Buyer Continuing Value	*$4,517,101*
=Total Buyer Valuation	*$29,796,428*
Buyer Value per Cable Subscriber	*$1,940*
Cash Flow Multiple (Alternative Valuation Method Used Here as a Check)	*11.0*
Buyer Value at 11x Cash Flow	*$28,710,063*
Buyer Value per Cable Subscriber at 11x Cash Flow	*$1,869*
Percent Difference in Valuations	*4%*

*   *Value Line* (figures as of 9/30/97)
**   *Stocks, Bonds, Bills, and Inflation 1997 Yearbook,* Ibbotson Associates
*** This sets the *WACC* for the entire model, except for buyer valuation
**** This is the median *WACC* for the Transportation, Communications, and Utility Industry Sector
according to Ibbotson Associates 1997
Note: A downloadable file of this spreadsheet is available at www.christophergardner.com

Figure 8.6 *(Continued)*

CABLE MODEM SYSTEM VALUATION- TCI (AS OF 9/30/97)

(excludes cable service)

SINGLE SYSTEM OPERATION

Model is restricted to a maximum 25 years of detailed cash flows

Number of Households	25,600
Cable Subscriber Penetration	60%
Peak Penetration of Cable Modem Service (%Cable Subs)	30%
Number of Years to Peak Penetration	10
Demand Curve: Parameter a	1.2 you want a t+b, where t=0 to 10 years, to fall in the range [-10,10]
Demand Curve: Parameter b	-4 same as above

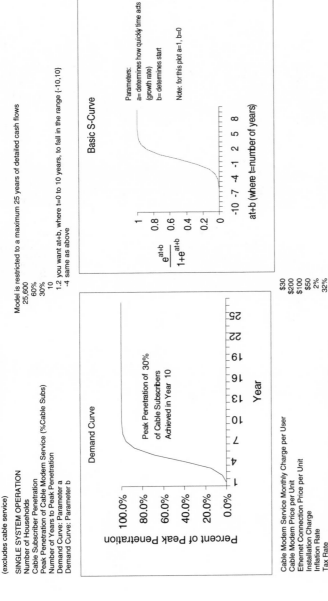

Cable Modem Service Monthly Charge per User	$30
Cable Modem Price per Unit	$200
Ethernet Connection Price per Unit	$100
Installation Charge	$50
Inflation Rate	2%
Tax Rate	32%
Economic Life in Years (model is restricted to one economic life and < 6 generations of replacements)	5
Number of Cable Modem Subscribers per 6MHz Channel	5,000
Annual Equipment Price or Cost Variation (% of Previous Year)	65%
Working Capital (% of Annual Revenue)	10%
Markup	33%

Figure 8.7 Cable Modem System Valuation—Tele-Communications, Inc.

(continued)

Year	1	2	3	4	5	6	7	8	9	10
Demand Curve (Cumulative %)	4.0%	15.3%	39.0%	68.5%	87.9%	96.0%	98.8%	99.7%	99.9%	100.0%
Cable Modem Penetration of Households	0.7%	2.8%	7.0%	12.3%	15.8%	17.3%	17.8%	17.9%	18.0%	18.0%
Cable Modem Penetration of Cable Subscribers	1.2%	4%	11.7%	20.5%	26.4%	28.8%	29.6%	29.9%	30.0%	30.0%
Begin # of Cable Modem Subscribers	0	185	704	1799	3154	4050	4526	4553	4592	4604
End # of Cable Modem Subscribers	185	704	1799	3154	4050	4526	4553	4592	4604	4606
Avg # of Cable Modem Subscribers	92	444	1252	2477	3602	4238	4489	4572	4598	4606
# of Incremental Channels Needed	1	0	0	0	0	0	0	0	0	0
REVENUES										
Subscription Fees	$33,237	$163,171	$468,819	$946,233	$1,403,679	$1,684,427	$1,819,999	$1,890,836	$1,939,558	$1,981,730
Cable Modems	$36,930	$68,876	$96,288	$78,978	$34,614	$9,626	$2,156	$446	$90	$18
Ethernet Connections	$18,465	$34,438	$48,144	$39,489	$17,307	$4,813	$1,078	$223	$45	$9
Installation Charges	$9,233	$26,491	$56,975	$71,896	$48,478	$20,740	$7,146	$2,277	$707	$218
Replacement Cable Modems	$0	$0	$0	$0	$0	$4,731	$5,850	$5,422	$2,949	$857
Replacement Ethernet Connections	$0	$0	$0	$0	$0	$2,365	$2,925	$2,711	$1,474	$428
Replacement Installation Charges	$0	$0	$0	$0	$0	$10,194	$29,833	$65,447	$84,237	$57,936
Total Revenues	$97,866	$292,976	$670,226	$1,136,595	$1,504,079	$1,736,896	$1,868,987	$1,967,361	$2,029,060	$2,041,196
COSTS										
Operating Costs:										
Internet, Bank, PC Telephone Network Connection	$108,000	$108,000	$216,000	$216,000	$324,000	$324,000	$324,000	$324,000	$324,000	$324,000
Cable Modem Service Calls	$2,308	$11,109	$31,293	$61,921	$90,054	$105,947	$112,230	$114,312	$114,958	$115,154
Cable Modem Marketing and Sales	$18,465	$51,943	$109,525	$135,498	$89,572	$37,569	$12,691	$3,964	$1,207	$365
Cable Modem Billing	$1,108	$5,332	$15,020	$29,722	$43,226	$50,855	$53,870	$54,870	$55,180	$55,274
Cable Modem Telephone Support	$923	$4,444	$12,517	$24,768	$36,022	$42,379	$44,892	$45,725	$45,983	$46,062
Cable Modem Equipment Maintenance and Software Licensing Fees	$18,000	$18,000	$18,000	$18,000	$18,000	$18,000	$18,000	$18,000	$18,000	$18,000
Cable Modem Hookup and Installation (i.e., churn-related)	$692	$3,333	$9,388	$18,576	$27,016	$31,784	$33,669	$34,293	$34,487	$34,546
Cable Modems	$27,767	$51,706	$72,397	$59,382	$26,026	$7,237	$1,621	$336	$68	$14
Ethernet Connections	$13,884	$25,853	$36,198	$29,691	$13,013	$3,619	$810	$168	$34	$7
Cable Modem Hookup and Installation	$9,233	$26,491	$56,975	$71,896	$48,478	$30,933	$36,979	$67,723	$84,945	$58,154
Replacement Cable Modems	$0	$0	$0	$0	$0	$3,557	$4,398	$4,077	$2,217	$644
Replacement Ethernet Connections	$0	$0	$0	$0	$0	$1,779	$2,199	$2,038	$1,108	$322
Replacement Installation Charges	$0	$0	$0	$0	$0	$10,194	$29,833	$65,447	$84,237	$57,936
-Total Operating Costs	$200,381	$306,331	$577,314	$665,453	$715,407	$667,853	$675,193	$734,951	$766,424	$710,477
-Depreciation (straight line, no salvage value)	$36,000	$36,000	$36,000	$36,000	$36,000	$4,612	$4,612	$4,612	$4,612	$4,612
=Earnings Before Interest and Taxes	$-138,515	$-49,355	$56,912	$435,142	$752,672	$1,064,431	$1,189,182	$1,227,799	$1,258,024	$1,326,107
Taxes:	$-44,325	$-15,794	$18,212	$139,245	$240,855	$340,618	$380,538	$392,896	$402,568	$424,354
Cumulative Tax Loss Carry Forward (Beginning of Year)	$0	$-44,325	$-60,118	$-41,907	$0	$0	$0	$0	$0	$0
Amount of Tax Loss Carry Forward Applied Against Current Taxes	$-44,325	$-15,794	$18,212	$41,907	$0	$0	$0	$0	$0	$0
Cumulative Tax Loss Carry Forward (End of Year)	$-44,325	$-60,118	$-41,907	$0	$0	$0	$0	$0	$0	$0
-Net Taxes	$0	$0	$0	$97,339	$240,855	$340,618	$380,538	$392,896	$402,568	$424,354
=Earnings Before Interest but After Taxes	$-138,515	$-49,355	$56,912	$337,803	$511,817	$723,813	$808,644	$834,903	$855,456	$901,753
+Depreciation	$36,000	$36,000	$36,000	$36,000	$36,000	$4,612	$4,612	$4,612	$4,612	$4,612
=Gross Cash Flow	$-102,515	$-13,355	$92,912	$373,803	$547,817	$728,425	$813,256	$839,515	$860,068	$906,365
Investment Costs:										
Items Subject to Replacement (5Years)										
Headend Router Package	$75,000	$0	$0	$0	$0	$0	$0	$0	$0	$0
Local Content Server	$50,000	$0	$0	$0	$0	$0	$0	$0	$0	$0
Cable Network Manager	$5,000	$0	$0	$0	$0	$0	$0	$0	$0	$0
Router for T3 Line	$50,000	$0	$0	$0	$0	$0	$0	$0	$0	$0
Subtotal	$180,000	$0	$0	$0	$0	$0	$0	$0	$0	$0
Replacement Items (5Years)										
Equipment Replacement	$0	$0	$0	$0	$0	$23,059	$0	$0	$0	$0
Subtotal	$0	$0	$0	$0	$0	$23,059	$0	$0	$0	$0
Items Not Subject to Replacement										
Installation for T3 Line	$50,000	$0	$0	$0	$0	$0	$0	$0	$0	$0
Subtotal	$50,000	$0	$0	$0	$0	$0	$0	$0	$0	$0
Other										
Working Capital	$9,787	$19,511	$37,725	$46,637	$36,748	$23,282	$13,209	$9,837	$6,170	$1,214
Subtotal	$9,787	$19,511	$37,725	$46,637	$36,748	$23,282	$13,209	$9,837	$6,170	$1,214
=Total Investment Costs	$239,787	$19,511	$37,725	$46,637	$36,748	$46,341	$13,209	$9,837	$6,170	$1,214
=CASH FLOW FROM OPERATIONS	$-342,301	$-32,866	$55,187	$327,166	$511,068	$682,084	$800,047	$829,677	$853,898	$905,151

SHAREHOLDER VALUE

SINGLE SYSTEM FINANCING

Inputs:

Total Number of Cable Subscribers Served by the Company	14,300,000
Debt/Equity Ratio*	1.37
Risk Free Rate of Return (US Treasury 20 Year Bond Yeild 1926-1996)**	6.7%
Beta*	1.0
Average Return on Large Company Stocks (1926-1996)**	14.2%
Cost of Debt (pre-Tax)*	8.8%
Project Risk Premium	2.0%
Number of Years on Loan	10
Number of Shares of Stock Initially*	507,000,000
Current Stock Price	$20.5

Derived Numbers:

Cost of Equity	14.2%
Risk-Adjusted Cost of Equity	17.2%
Weighted Average Cost of Capital (after-Tax)	9.5%
Risk-Adjusted Weighted Average Cost of Capital (after-Tax)	11.5%
Investment Cost (Present Value Plus Continuing Value)	$350,525
Equity Portion	$147,901
Debt Portion	$202,624
Number of Shares of Stock Initially Ascribed to this Cable System	544,582
Number of Shares of Stock to be Issued	7,215
Principal Repayment on Debt per Year	$20,262

Year	1	2	3	4	5	6	7	8	9	10
Earnings Before Interest and Taxes	-$138,515	-$49,355	$56,912	$435,142	$752,672	$1,064,431	$1,189,182	$1,227,799	$1,258,024	$1,326,107
-Interest Payments	$17,831	$16,048	$14,265	$12,482	$10,699	$8,915	$7,132	$5,349	$3,566	$1,783
=Earnings After Interest but Before Taxes	-$156,346	-$65,403	$42,647	$422,660	$741,973	$1,055,516	$1,182,050	$1,222,449	$1,254,458	$1,324,324
Taxes:										
Taxes	-$50,031	-$20,929	$13,647	$135,251	$237,431	$337,765	$378,256	$391,184	$401,427	$423,784
Cumulative Tax Loss Carry Forward (Beginning of Year)	$0	-$50,031	-$70,960	-$57,312	$0	$0	$0	$0	$0	$0
Amount of Tax Loss Carry Forward Applied Against Current Taxes	$0	$0	-$13,647	-$57,312	$0	$0	$0	$0	$0	$0
Cumulative Tax Loss Carry Forward (End of Year)	-$50,031	-$70,960	-$57,312	$0	$0	$0	$0	$0	$0	$0
-Net Taxes	$0	$0	$0	$77,939	$237,431	$337,765	$378,256	$391,184	$401,427	$423,784
=Earnings After Interest and Taxes	-$156,346	-$65,403	$42,647	$344,722	$504,542	$717,751	$803,794	$831,266	$853,031	$900,540
÷Number of Shares of Stock Outstanding	551,797	551,797	551,797	551,797	551,797	551,797	551,797	551,797	551,797	551,797
=Earnings per Share	-$0.28	-$0.12	$0.08	$0.62	$0.91	$1.30	$1.46	$1.51	$1.55	$1.63
-Principal Repayment per Year per Share	$0.04	$0.04	$0.04	$0.04	$0.04	$0.04	$0.04	$0.04	$0.04	$0.04
=Uncommitted Earnings Available to Stockholders per Share	-$0.32	-$0.16	$0.04	$0.59	$0.88	$1.26	$1.42	$1.47	$1.51	$1.60
+Depreciation per Share	$0.07	$0.07	$0.07	$0.07	$0.07	$0.01	$0.01	$0.01	$0.01	$0.01
-Investment Cost per Share (Present Value Plus Continuing Value)	$0.64									
+Capital Raised per Share	$0.64									
=Cash Flow to Stockholders per Share	-$0.25	-$0.09	$0.11	$0.65	$0.94	$1.27	$1.43	$1.48	$1.52	$1.60

MULTIPLE SYSTEM FINANCING

	Value to TCI
Percent of Systems Upgraded to Cable Modem Service	100%
Present Value of Cash Flow to Stockholders per Share	$2.62
Continuing Value of Cash Flow to Stockholders per Share	$1.91
Value to Stockholders per Share	**$4.53**

* *Value Line* (figures as of 9/30/97)

** *Stocks, Bonds, Bills, and Inflation 1997 Yearbook,* Ibbotson Associates

Note: A downloadable file of this spreadsheet is available at www.christophergartner.com

Figure 8.7 *(Continued)*

S-curve is used to derive the annual demand over this period, with the shape parameters chosen using simple judgment. The investment and operating costs are itemized in
Figures 7.2 and 7.4, respectively. Only the incremental
costs for cable modem service are relevant to the analysis.
The most economically significant investment cost is $275
of subscriber premises equipment, and for operating cost it
is $117 for fractional T3 service. There is not much we can
do about the former. For the latter, we will assume 9–10
Mbps of fractional T3 service is installed at a time, which
simulation modeling shows will support 1,670 cable
modem subscribers. This will make the operating costs that
are incurred move in step with demand so that the economics are pay-as-you-go. The annual equipment cost variation and the inflation rate are from Figure 7.5. A 5-year
economic life for the cable modem equipment is appropriate given the historical rate of obsolescence observed in the
computer industry. The financial inputs such as the tax
rate, debt/equity ratio, β, cost of debt, working capital, and
number of shares of stock are from *Value Line*. The risk-free
rate of return and average return on large company stocks
from 1926 to 1996 are from the *Stocks, Bonds, Bills and Inflation 1997 Yearbook*. The project risk premium is based on
judgment. The terms of the loan are similar to other long-
term debt obligations. The cash flows start in Year 1 rather
than Year 0 because it should only take a few months to install the equipment and have cable modem service up and
running.

The cable modem system valuation for TCI shows that
the intrinsic change in the price of TCI shares as a result of
offering cable modem service amounts to $4.53, assuming
100% of its systems are upgraded. To compare this with the
corporate valuation of TCI, we need to account for the dilution of shareholder ownership that occurred with the issuance of new shares of stock to fund the cable modem
project. The analysis on an undiluted basis can be easily
converted to a diluted basis by simply multiplying by the
ratio of old to new shares:

$$\frac{E}{(S+\Delta S)} = \left(\frac{S}{(S+\Delta S)}\right)\frac{E}{S}$$

↑	↑	↑
Diluted Basis	Ratio of Old to New Shares	Undiluted Basis

Applying this gives

$$\begin{aligned}\text{Intrinsic Share Price}\atop\textit{with}\text{ System} &= \frac{E}{(S+\Delta S)} + \frac{\Delta E_{System}}{(S+\Delta S)}\\ &= \frac{S}{(S+\Delta S)}\frac{E}{S} + \frac{\Delta E_{System}}{(S+\Delta S)}\end{aligned}$$

Plugging in the number for TCI using the ratio of old to new shares for a single system (Figure 8.7), since this is identical to that for the company as a whole, gives

$$\begin{aligned}\text{Intrinsic Share Price}\atop\textit{with}\text{ System} &= \left(\frac{544,582}{544,582+7,215}\right)\$25.02 + \$4.53\\ &= \$29.22\end{aligned}$$

We can now determine the *relative* impact of the system on the share price:

$$\begin{aligned}\text{Percentage Change}\atop\text{in Share Price} &= \frac{\text{Intrinsic Share Price }\textit{with}\text{ System}}{\text{Intrinsic Share Price }\textit{without}\text{ System}}\\ &= \frac{\$29.22}{\$25.02}\\ &= 17\%\end{aligned}$$

Comparison of the intrinsic price at which shares of TCI would be expected to trade, after a decision to introduce cable modem service, with the market price of the stock at the time of the analysis provides a more *absolute* measure of the impact of the system on the share price:

$$\text{Change in Share Price} = \begin{array}{c} \text{Intrinsic Share} \\ \text{Price } with \text{ System} \end{array} - \begin{array}{c} \text{Current Market Price} \\ \text{at which Shares Trade} \end{array}$$

$$= \$29.22 - \$20.50$$
$$\uparrow$$

Price at which TCI
shares closed on date
of analysis 9/30/97

$$= \$8.27$$

Both the absolute and relative measures show that offering cable modem service should have a substantial positive impact on the price of TCI shares. Over the 6-month period from 9/30/97 to 3/31/98 TCI shares did indeed tend up, ranging from a low of $19.50 to a high of $33.06. As one would expect, TCI management placed delivering cable modem service high on its list of corporate priorities.

A check of the valuation model was performed by using it to value a deal proposed by @Home Corporation early in 1998 to provide cable modem service to Time Warner[8] (see Figure 8.8). The deal terms were that Time Warner would receive two shares of @Home stock for every household passed by the cable operator. In exchange, @Home would receive 35% of Time Warner's cable modem service revenues and Time Warner would build and operate the local cable modem system. A comparison of the effect of the deal on the value of Time Warner's cable modem business with the value of @Home shares shows agreement to within 5%. Time Warner should have been generally indifferent to the deal under these terms. The deal did indeed fall through.

■ 8.5 RISK ANALYSIS

There are many sources of risk in the analysis of the economics of an information technology system. This is a reflection of the inherent complexity of technology and finance. The risk is that the shareholder value actually

CHECK

Valuation of Proposed @Home Deal With Time Warner

SINGLE SYSTEM OPERATION
Inputs are the same as in TCI Cable Modem System except the tax rate for Time-Warner is 40%

Year	1	2	3	4	5	6	7	8	9	10
Demand Curve (Cumulative %)	4.0%	15.3%	39.0%	68.5%	87.9%	96.0%	98.8%	99.7%	99.9%	100.0%
Cable Modem Penetration of Households	0.7%	2.8%	7.0%	12.3%	15.8%	17.3%	17.8%	17.9%	18.0%	18.0%
Cable Modem Penetration of Cable Subscribers	1.2%	4.6%	11.7%	20.5%	26.4%	28.8%	29.6%	29.9%	30.0%	30.0%
Begin # of Cable Modem Subscribers	0	185	704	1799	3154	4050	4426	4553	4592	4604
End # of Cable Modem Subscribers	185	704	1799	3154	4050	4426	4553	4592	4604	4608
Avg # of Cable Modem Subscribers	92	444	1252	2477	3602	4238	4489	4572	4598	4606
# of Incremental Channels Needed	1	0	0	0	0	0	0	0	0	0
REVENUES										
Subscription Fees	$33,237	$163,171	$468,819	$946,233	$1,403,679	$1,684,427	$1,819,999	$1,890,836	$1,939,558	$1,981,730
Cable Modems	$36,930	$68,876	$96,288	$78,978	$34,614	$9,626	$2,156	$446	$90	$18
Ethernet Connections	$18,465	$34,438	$48,144	$39,489	$17,307	$4,813	$1,078	$223	$45	$9
Installation Charges	$9,233	$26,491	$56,975	$71,896	$48,478	$20,740	$7,146	$2,277	$707	$218
Replacement Cable Modems	$0	$0	$0	$0	$0	$4,731	$5,850	$5,422	$2,949	$857
Replacement Ethernet Connections	$0	$0	$0	$0	$0	$2,365	$2,925	$2,711	$1,474	$428
Replacement Installation Charges	$0	$0	$0	$0	$0	$10,194	$29,833	$65,447	$84,237	$57,936
Total Revenues	$97,866	$292,976	$670,226	$1,136,595	$1,504,079	$1,736,896	$1,868,987	$1,967,361	$2,029,060	$2,041,196
COSTS										
Operating Costs:										
Internet, Bank, PC Telephone Network Connection	$108,000	$108,000	$216,000	$216,000	$324,000	$324,000	$324,000	$324,000	$324,000	$324,000
Cable Modem Service Calls	$2,308	$11,109	$31,293	$61,921	$90,054	$105,947	$112,230	$114,312	$114,958	$115,164
Cable Modem Marketing and Sales	$18,465	$51,943	$109,525	$135,498	$89,572	$30,933	$5,569	$1,207	$1,207	$5,365
Cable Modem Billing	$1,108	$5,332	$15,020	$29,722	$43,226	$50,855	$53,870	$54,870	$55,180	$55,274
Cable Modem Telephone Support	$923	$4,444	$12,517	$24,768	$36,022	$42,379	$44,892	$45,725	$45,983	$46,062
Cable Modem Equipment Maintenance and Software Licensing Fees	$18,000	$18,000	$18,000	$18,000	$18,000	$18,000	$18,000	$18,000	$18,000	$18,000
Cable Modem Hookup and Installation (i.e., churn-related)	$692	$3,333	$9,388	$18,576	$27,016	$31,784	$33,669	$34,293	$34,487	$34,546
Cable Modems	$27,767	$51,786	$72,397	$59,382	$26,026	$7,237	$1,621	$336	$68	$14
Ethernet Connections	$13,884	$25,893	$36,198	$29,691	$13,013	$3,619	$810	$168	$34	$7
Cable Modem Hookup and Installation	$9,233	$26,491	$56,975	$71,896	$48,478	$30,933	$36,979	$67,723	$84,945	$58,154
Replacement Cable Modems	$0	$0	$0	$0	$0	$3,557	$4,398	$4,077	$2,217	$644
Replacement Ethernet Connections	$0	$0	$0	$0	$0	$1,779	$2,199	$2,038	$1,108	$322
Replacement Installation Charges	$0	$0	$0	$0	$0	$10,194	$29,833	$65,447	$84,237	$57,936
=Total Operating Costs	$200,381	$306,331	$577,314	$665,453	$715,407	$667,853	$675,193	$734,951	$766,424	$710,477
-Depreciation	$36,000	$36,000	$36,000	$36,000	$36,000	$4,612	$4,612	$4,612	$4,612	$4,612
=Earnings Before Interest and Taxes	-$138,515	-$49,355	$56,912	$435,142	$752,672	$1,064,431	$1,189,182	$1,227,799	$1,258,024	$1,326,107
Taxes:										
Taxes	-$55,406	$19,742	$22,765	$174,057	$301,069	$425,773	$475,673	$491,119	$503,210	$530,443
Cumulative Tax Loss Carry Forward (Beginning of Year)	$0	-$55,406	-$75,148	-$52,383	$0	$0	$0	$0	$0	$0
Amount of Tax Loss Carry Forward Applied Against Current Taxes	-$55,406	-$49,355	-$22,765	-$52,383	$0	$0	$0	$0	$0	$0
Cumulative Tax Loss Carry Forward (End of Year)	-$55,406	-$75,148	-$52,383	$0	$0	$0	$0	$0	$0	$0
-Net Taxes	$0	$0	$0	$121,674	$301,069	$425,773	$475,673	$491,119	$503,210	$530,443
=Earnings Before Interest but After Taxes	-$138,515	-$49,355	$56,912	$313,468	$451,603	$638,659	$713,509	$736,679	$754,814	$795,664
+Depreciation	$36,000	$36,000	$36,000	$36,000	$36,000	$4,612	$4,612	$4,612	$4,612	$4,612
=Gross Cash Flow	-$102,515	-$13,355	$92,912	$349,468	$487,603	$643,271	$718,121	$741,291	$759,426	$800,276
Investment Costs:										
Items Subject to Replacement (5Years)										
Headend Router Package	$75,000	$0	$0	$0	$0	$0	$0	$0	$0	$0
Local Content Server	$50,000	$0	$0	$0	$0	$0	$0	$0	$0	$0
Cable Network Manager	$5,000	$0	$0	$0	$0	$0	$0	$0	$0	$0
Router for T3 Line	$50,000	$0	$0	$0	$0	$0	$0	$0	$0	$0
Subtotal	$180,000	$0	$0	$0	$0	$0	$0	$0	$0	$0
Replacement Items (5Years)										
Equipment Replacement	$0	$0	$0	$0	$0	$23,059	$0	$0	$0	$0
Subtotal	$0	$0	$0	$0	$0	$23,059	$0	$0	$0	$0
Items Not Subject to Replacement										
Installation for T3 Line	$50,000	$0	$0	$0	$0	$0	$0	$0	$0	$0
Subtotal	$50,000	$0	$0	$0	$0	$0	$0	$0	$0	$0
Other										
Working Capital	$9,787	$19,511	$37,725	$46,637	$36,748	$23,282	$13,209	$9,837	$6,170	$1,214
Subtotal	$9,787	$19,511	$37,725	$46,637	$36,748	$23,282	$13,209	$9,837	$6,170	$1,214
-Total Investment Costs	$239,787	$19,511	$37,725	$46,637	$36,748	$46,341	$13,209	$9,837	$6,170	$1,214
=CASH FLOW FROM OPERATIONS	-$342,301	-$32,866	$55,187	$302,831	$450,855	$596,930	$704,912	$731,454	$753,256	$799,063

Figure 8.8   Check.

237

CHANGE IN VALUE OF OPERATIONS
MULTIPLE SYSTEM OPERATION AND FINANCING BEFORE AND AFTER DEAL
(@Home receives 35% of the Cable Modem Service Monthly Charge per User from Time-Warner)
Inputs:

Total Number of Subscribers Served By Company	12,400,000
Debt/Equity Ratio*	0.40
Risk Free Rate of Return (US Treasury 20 Year Bond Yeild 1926-1996)**	6.7%
Beta*	1.3
Average Return on Large Company Stocks (1926-1996)**	14.2%
Cost of Debt (pre-Tax)*	8.8%
Project Risk Premium	2.0%

Derived Numbers:

Cost of Equity	16.5%
Risk-Adjusted Cost of Equity	18.9%
Weighted Average Cost of Capital (after-Tax)	13.2%
Risk-Adjusted Weighted Average Cost of Capital (after-Tax)	15.2%

Value to Time Warner:

Percent of Systems Upgraded to Cable Modem Service	100%
Present Value of Cash Flow From Operations	$1,018,846,283
Continuing Value of Cash Flow From Operations	$1,023,800,464
Total Value	$2,042,646,747
Value per Cable Subscriber **Before** Deal	$165
Value per Cable Subscriber **After** Deal***	$59
Change in Cable Modem System Value to Time Warner per Cable Subscriber	**$106**

VALUE OF COMPENSATING PAYMENT
GRANT OF @HOME WARRANTS
(Time Warner is granted 2 warrants in @Home per cable household passed where each warrant is a right to buy 1 share of @Home stock for 50 cents)

Number of @Home Warrants per Cable Household Passed	2
Price of @Home Shares at End of Day 2/23/98****	$33.94
Cost per @Home Share	$0.50
Value per Warrant	$33.44
Value of @Home Warrants to Time Warner per Cable Subscriber	**$111**

Percent Difference in Valuations

5%

*   *Value Line* (figures as of 9/30/97)
**   *Stocks, Bonds, Bills, and Inflation 1997 Yearbook*, Ibbotson Associates
***   Must be recalculated manually by subtracting a payment to @Home of 35% of the
         Cable Modem Service Monthly Charge per User
****The story describing the deal broke on 2/23/98 in *Broadcasting and Cable*

Note: A downloadable file of this spreadsheet is available at www.christophergardner.com

Figure 8.8 *(Continued)*

achieved is lower or higher than expected. This risk needs to be understood if it is to be controlled.

The uncertainty in the shareholder value arises from the variables used to calculate it. There are four ways to analyze the risk of an unexpected shareholder value: sensitivity analysis, break-even analysis, scenario analysis, and simulation. They can be applied to any or all of the variables affecting shareholder value. The point of these analytical methods is to provide information on the degree of risk and to suggest steps to reduce it.

Sensitivity analysis involves examining changes in a single variable to see which variables shareholder value is most sensitive to. Steps can be taken to focus on reducing or capitalizing on the sensitivity to these variables.

Break-even analysis involves determining what the maximum amount of change in a variable can be by changing it until the shareholder value becomes zero. This describes how much room there is for error before the system loses money. Areas where there is little room should receive management attention.

Scenario analysis involves letting several variables change simultaneously. An example is a competitor introducing a competing product. This could reduce demand, increase cost, and force a schedule delay (so that a product enhancement can be made). Worrisome scenarios could trigger preventive measures, such as preannouncing a product to neutralize the competitor's action.

Simulation involves examining the combined effects of changes in several variables to find the combined maximum tolerances. The amount of change is usually determined by probability distributions. This directs management to prioritize risk reduction efforts across several critical variables, taking into account how they interact.

Among the variables affecting shareholder value, there are those that management has much control over, such as price, and those that management has little control over, such as inflation. It is worthwhile to separate these in an analysis so that management can concentrate its efforts on the variables it can meaningfully affect and monitor its exposure to the variables beyond its control.

As the number of sources of risk gets to be large, the shareholder value becomes increasingly subject to the central limit theorem of statistics that states that the sum of many random variables always has a simple Gaussian distribution, whatever the distributions of the variables. In the absence of risk reduction efforts, the variance of this distribution will be larger than what is possible, which means an increased level of risk. The benefits of reducing this risk must be weighed against the cost of doing so.

Let's return to our previous illustration and conduct a sensitivity analysis of the TCI valuation. An interesting question to ask here is, what is the risk the valuation is too low?[9] This is the same as asking if there are opportunities to increase shareholder value further. Answering this is important because we might be over- or underestimating the value of the cable modem system project compared with some of the other actions that TCI can take. An underestimate can be just as serious as an overestimate since the outcome is a similar misallocation of company resources to less promising initiatives.

Changing each of the variables in the cable system and cable modem system models for TCI by ± 10% is a straightforward way of conducting the sensitivity analysis. The result of doing this after choosing between ± 10% according to which improved the valuation the most, is shown in Figure 8.9.

For the cable system valuation of TCI—and among the variables management can generally control—increasing the price of cable service by 10% has the largest positive effect on the share price, increasing it by an impressive 50%. However, the second most positive effect of 23% is from increasing the number of subscribers served by the company, which moves inversely with a price increase. One can conclude from this that as long as cable service remains a near-monopoly with price increase only modestly affecting penetration levels, the top priority of TCI will be to continue to raise prices to the extent government regulations will allow. Indeed, this has been the course TCI and other cable operators have taken for a number of years.

The third most important variable is operating cost, with a 10% decline generating a 20% increase in share price. There are many separate components of operating cost. Programming fees are the largest component, but this is itself made up of many individual fees for each of the cable channels carried (e.g., CNN, MTV). An additional complication is that TCI owns many of these cable channels through an affiliated company, Liberty Media. Achieving a 10% reduction in

Sensitivity Analysis

Variable	Percent Change in Variable	Number of Old Shares	Number of New Shares	Ratio of Old to New Plus Old Shares X	Cable System Share Price (undiluted)	Cable System Share Price = (diluted)	Change in Share Price from Cable Modem System + (diluted)	Total = Share Price	Percent Change from Baseline Share Price of $25.02
Cable System Valuation- TCI									
Variables Management Can Generally Control									
Cable Service Average Monthly Charge per Subscriber	10%	N/A	N/A	1	$37.44	N/A	N/A	$37.44	50%
Total Number of Subscribers Served by Company	10%	N/A	N/A	1	$30.75	N/A	N/A	$30.75	23%
Average Annual Operating Cost per Cable Subscriber @60% Penetration	-10%	N/A	N/A	1	$30.14	N/A	N/A	$30.14	20%
Current Cable Subscriber Penetration	-10%	N/A	N/A	1	$29.38	N/A	N/A	$29.38	17%
Peak Penetration in Cable Subscribers	10%	N/A	N/A	1	$28.94	N/A	N/A	$28.94	16%
Cost of Debt	-10%	N/A	N/A	1	$28.57	N/A	N/A	$28.57	14%
Number of Shares of Stock	-10%	N/A	N/A	1	$27.80	N/A	N/A	$27.80	11%
Debt/Equity Ratio	10%	N/A	N/A	1	$26.93	N/A	N/A	$26.93	8%
Average Investment Cost per Cable Subscriber @60% Penetration	-10%	N/A	N/A	1	$26.55	N/A	N/A	$26.55	6%
Number of Years to Peak Penetration	-10%	N/A	N/A	1	$25.51	N/A	N/A	$25.51	2%
Depreciation	10%	N/A	N/A	1	$25.35	N/A	N/A	$25.35	1%
Incremental Investment Cost per Cable Subscriber	-10%	N/A	N/A	1	$25.07	N/A	N/A	$25.07	0%
Incremental Annual Operating Cost per Cable Subscriber	-10%	N/A	N/A	1	$25.04	N/A	N/A	$25.04	0%
Number of Households	10%	N/A	N/A	1	$25.02	N/A	N/A	$25.02	0%
Variables Management Cannot Generally Control									
Average Return on Large Company Stocks	-10%	N/A	N/A	1	$31.37	N/A	N/A	$31.37	25%
Beta	-10%	N/A	N/A	1	$28.26	N/A	N/A	$28.26	13%
Risk Free Rate of Return	-10%	N/A	N/A	1	$27.90	N/A	N/A	$27.90	12%
Inflation Rate	10%	N/A	N/A	1	$27.72	N/A	N/A	$27.72	11%
Tax Rate	-10%	N/A	N/A	1	$26.49	N/A	N/A	$26.49	6%
Base Case	0%	N/A	N/A	1	$25.02	N/A	N/A	$25.02	0%
Cable Modem System Valuation- TCI									
Variables Management Can Generally Control									
Cable Modem Service Average Monthly Charge per Subscriber	10%	544,582	7,488	0.9864	$25.02	$24.68	$5.33	$30.01	20%
Number of Shares of Stock	-10%	490,124	7,215	0.9855	$25.02	$24.66	$5.02	$29.68	19%
Total Operating Cost	-10%	544,582	7,215	0.9869	$25.02	$24.69	$4.94	$29.63	18%
Total Number of Subscribers Served by Company	10%	495,074	7,215	0.9856	$25.02	$24.66	$4.97	$29.63	18%
Peak Penetration in Cable Modem Subscribers	10%	544,582	7,593	0.9862	$25.02	$24.68	$4.81	$29.49	18%
Demand Curve: Parameter b	10%	544,582	7,246	0.9869	$25.02	$24.69	$4.79	$29.48	18%
Demand Curve: Parameter a	10%	544,582	7,195	0.9870	$25.02	$24.69	$4.78	$29.47	18%
Internet, Bank, and PC Telephone Connection	-10%	544,582	7,215	0.9869	$25.02	$24.69	$4.71	$29.40	18%
Project Risk Premium	-10%	544,582	7,247	0.9869	$25.02	$24.69	$4.66	$29.35	17%
Number of Years to Peak Penetration	10%	544,582	7,182	0.9870	$25.02	$24.69	$4.62	$29.31	17%
Number of Cable Modem Subscribers per 6MHz Channel	10%	544,582	7,215	0.9869	$25.02	$24.69	$4.62	$29.31	17%
Total Investment Cost	-10%	544,582	6,493	0.9882	$25.02	$24.73	$4.56	$29.29	17%
Cost of Debt	10%	544,582	7,159	0.9870	$25.02	$24.70	$4.57	$29.27	17%
Installation Charge	-10%	544,582	7,222	0.9869	$25.02	$24.69	$4.56	$29.25	17%
Working Capital	-10%	544,582	6,943	0.9874	$25.02	$24.71	$4.54	$29.25	17%
Debt/Equity Ratio	-10%	544,582	7,621	0.9862	$25.02	$24.67	$4.57	$29.24	17%
Annual Equipment Price or Cost Variation	10%	544,582	7,356	0.9867	$25.02	$24.69	$4.55	$29.24	17%
Markup	10%	544,582	7,215	0.9869	$25.02	$24.69	$4.54	$29.23	17%
Number of Years on Loan	10%	544,582	7,215	0.9869	$25.02	$24.69	$4.54	$29.23	17%
Depreciation	10%	544,582	7,215	0.9869	$25.02	$24.69	$4.53	$29.22	17%
Ethernet Connection Price per Unit	10%	544,582	7,217	0.9869	$25.02	$24.69	$4.53	$29.22	17%
Cable Modem Price per Unit	10%	544,582	7,219	0.9869	$25.02	$24.69	$4.53	$29.22	17%
Economic Life in Years	10%	544,582	7,409	0.9866	$25.02	$24.68	$4.47	$29.15	17%
Number of Households	10%	599,040	7,593	0.9875	$25.02	$24.71	$4.38	$29.09	16%
Current Cable Subscriber Penetration	-10%	490,124	6,943	0.9860	$25.02	$24.67	$4.39	$29.06	16%
Variables Management Cannot Generally Control									
Average Return on Large Company Stocks	-10%	544,582	7,313	0.9867	$25.02	$24.69	$5.28	$29.97	20%
Beta	-10%	544,582	7,266	0.9868	$25.02	$24.69	$4.90	$29.59	18%
Tax Rate	-10%	544,582	7,189	0.9870	$25.02	$24.69	$4.77	$29.46	18%
Inflation Rate	10%	544,582	7,280	0.9868	$25.02	$24.69	$4.63	$29.32	17%
Risk Free Rate of Return	-10%	544,582	7,215	0.9869	$25.02	$24.69	$4.53	$29.22	17%
Base Case	0%	544,582	7,215	0.9869	$25.02	$24.69	$4.53	$29.22	17%

Figure 8.9 Sensitivity Analysis.

operating cost will have to come from many separate cost-cutting initiatives and would likely hurt other parts of TCI's business.

Offering cable modem service ranks about fourth on the list with a 17% base case gain in share price, when benchmarked against the arbitrary choice of a ±10% change in variables. Given the complications associated with trying to reduce operating cost, an argument can be made that cable modem service should be ranked higher, to at least third among management priorities.

For the cable modem system valuation of TCI—and among the variables that management can generally control—increasing the price of cable modem service by 10% increases the impact of cable modem service on the share price the most, raising it slightly from 17% to 20%. However, raising prices will also reduce penetration, which will tend to offset this gain. As for the other variables, little to no effect is observed compared with the base case of a 17% gain. The results cluster between 16% and 19%.

At this point, we should keep in mind that we need to be concerned about not just what variables the valuations are sensitive to, but also *how much* the variables can be changed. Are there any variables that can be readily changed more than 10%? It was pointed out in Figure 7.4 that many cable networks can take advantage of fiber-optic infrastructures used to transport cable television signals from a consolidated headend facility to other headends within a region, which avoids the high cost of leasing high-speed communications services from telephone companies. Where this is the case, the "Internet, Bank, and PC Telephone Connection" cost can be reduced by as much as 100%. The resulting increase in the impact of cable modem service on the share price is substantial, raising it from 17% to 24%. This would place offering cable modem service second among management's top priorities.

For both the cable system and cable modem system valuations, the variables that management cannot generally control turn out to be the same: "Average Return on Large Company Stocks," "Beta," "Tax Rate," "Inflation Rate," and "Risk Free Rate of Return." Though the degree of sensitivity of the valuations to these variables is significant, this is not particularly troubling. In the United States, these variables are on the whole fairly stable.

Overall, the sensitivity analysis shows that TCI management has several opportunities to increase shareholder value. There is a significant risk our valuations are too low. In the context of this broader set of TCI opportunities, the cable modem system project ranks among the top four, and possibly even higher. Committing to provide cable modem service should be viewed as among the most important opportunities that TCI management has to increase shareholder value. It will result in a dramatic gain in TCI's share price.

One final remark. We have not analyzed the reinvestment opportunities created by a cable modem service. Offering telephony, home banking, travel services, interactive advertising, videogames, music distribution, and so on, becomes possible. TCI can be both information service and content provider, with the competitive advantage of having a high-speed network. The option value of these reinvestment opportunities creates additional upside potential for TCI's share price. The value of these options can dominate the economics of information technology. This has happened with Internet companies, for example.

Though this point is made in the context of TCI remaining in the hands of management, a change in ownership can enhance this option value if it results in a greater ability to capitalize on these investment opportunities. If revenue increases and cost reductions in the core business can also be realized, the case for a change in ownership can be compelling. On June 24, 1998, AT&T announced it would acquire TCI and combine its consumer long-distance, wireless, and Internet service units with TCI's cable telecommunications and high-speed Internet businesses. The joint press release cited the following as the primary reasons for the merger:

> *"Today we are beginning to answer a big part of the question about how we will provide local service to U.S. consumers," said Michael Armstrong, chairman and CEO of AT&T.*
>
> *"We are merging with TCI not only for what it is but for what we can become together," Armstrong explained. "Through its own systems and in partnership with affiliates, AT&T Consumer Services will bring to people's homes the first fully integrated package of communications, electronic commerce and video entertainment services. And it will do it with the quality and reliability that people have come to expect from AT&T."*

"This merger is a tremendous growth opportunity for TCI's shareowners and employees," said John C. Malone, chairman and CEO of TCI. "As TCI continues the large-scale deployment of advanced digital set-top devices, AT&T's extraordinary brand and resources are ideal complements to TCI's broadband cable distribution and operations. AT&T Consumer Services will offer consumers a wide variety of entertainment, information and communication products, which thoughtfully address personal tastes, needs, choice, and convenience."

. . . AT&T Consumer Services will own and operate the nation's most extensive, broadband local network platform. Following the merger, the new unit intends to significantly accelerate the upgrading of its cable infrastructure, enabling it to begin providing digital telephony and data services to consumers by the end of 1999, in addition to digital video services.

. . . AT&T and TCI anticipate their merger will result in increased revenue and lower costs, producing synergies of approximately $2 billion per year beginning three years after the merger closes. For example, the merger is expected to improve TCI's cable service penetration and improve customer retention for AT&T's consumer long distance service. It will also help reduce the charges AT&T pays to local telephone companies to handle long-distance calls and allow both companies to reduce their respective customer care, billing, and advertising expenses.

The result of the merger, in Malone's words, is a "supercharged" cable company. TCI shares traded around $40 per share following the announcement.

■ PROBLEMS AND SOLUTIONS

Problem 8.1: Calculate the tax benefit of depreciation. Assume a $100,000 capital expenditure has a 5-year life and is depreciated on a straight-line basis, and the tax rate is 40%.

Solution: The annual depreciation expense is 100,000 ÷ 5 = \$20,000 per year. Therefore, pretax earnings are reduced by this amount, generating a tax benefit of \$8,000 per year.

Problem 8.2: What are some of the difficulties in assuming the rate of return for a system project is the weighted average cost of capital for an enterprise?

Solution: The system project may have a higher or lower level of risk associated with its cash flows than the overall enterprise. Therefore, bad high-risk system projects could be accepted and good low-risk system projects could be rejected. Judgment is required to determine if the level of project risk varies enough from the overall enterprise to merit an adjustment of the cash flows or rate of return. Usually an estimate is made of the project risk premium which is simply added to the *WACC*. Alternatively, the capital asset pricing model can be used,

$$r - r_f = \beta_{project}(r_m - r_f)$$

where r = required rate of return for the system project
r_f = risk-free interest rate
$\beta_{project}$ = proportionality constant relating the expected project risk premium $(r - r_f)$ to the expected market risk premium $(r_m - r_f)$

Unfortunately, this shifts the burden to finding a value for $\beta_{project}$, which is not straightforward. The reader is referred to the literature on the capital asset pricing model for a complete discussion.

Problem 8.3: What are some variables it might be worth examining in performing a sensitivity, break-even, scenario, or simulation analysis?

Solution: Sales, investment costs, operating costs, timing of cash flows, the system lifetime, the rate of return.

Problem 8.4: Is the view that "inflation can be ignored in analyzing cash flows because an inflationary increase in revenues will be offset by a comparable inflationary increase in costs" correct? Why?

Solution: Incorrect. Inflation varies by type of goods or service. To illustrate, the consumer price index (CPI) represents the average change in the costs of a variety of goods and services to the average consumer. A specific good or service used to calculate the CPI can exhibit an inflation rate that is significantly different from the CPI itself. A line-by-line examination of the effect of inflation on cash flows is often worthwhile.

Problem 8.5: Calculate the *NPV* of a personal computer-to-server access system (see facing page). Make the following assumptions. The cost savings generated by the system arise from eliminating the need for 10 one-hour meetings a week, each of which is attended by 10 employees who cost $50 per hour. There are no increased revenues. The investment cost is $500 per user for communications hardware and software (ports, cabling, multiplexers, etc.) and $25,000 for the computer server. The operating cost is $1,000 per month to lease a dedicated telephone line at 1.544 Mbps for five years, $500 per month for system maintenance and repair, and $1,000 per month for system management. The system lifecycle is five years and it takes one year to get everything up and running. Lastly, depreciation is straight-line, the tax rate is 40%, the opportunity cost of capital is 15%, and inflation of 5% will occur only to wage-related items (cost savings, system maintenance and repair, and system management).

Solution: (See facing page)

Problem 8.6a: How can one approach the problem of valuation of an information technology system that acts as a platform for multiple new services, all of which must be provided (they are not separable)? Note: Problems 8.6a, b, and c are often encountered in the high-technology industry.

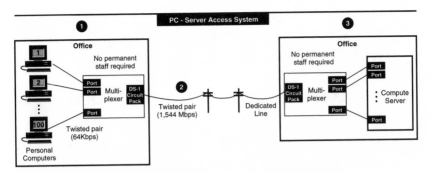

Overview of Operation

Step 1: Messages are transmitted to the multiplexer where they are concentrated and sent out onto a 1,544Mbps circuit
Step 2: Messages are transmitted over a dedicated line to the receiving office
Step 3: Messages are demultiplexed and sent to the compute server

PC-Server Access System Bill of Materials

Item	Quantity	Description
1	100	Personal computers
2	200	Port (multiplexer)
3	2	Multiplexer
4	2	DS-1 circuit pack
5	1	Dedicated line
6	1	Compute server
7	100	Port (computer)
8	1	Communications software and manuals—multiuser package
9	1	Miscellaneous

Solution: ($000's)

Year	0	1	2	3	4	5
Savings	0	273	287	301	316	332
(−) Operating Costs	0	31	32	33	34	35
(−) Depreciation		15	15	15	15	15
(=) Earnings Before Interest but After Taxes	0	227	240	253	267	282
(−) Taxes	0	91	96	101	107	113
(=) Earnings Before Interest, but After Taxes	0	136	144	152	160	164
(+) Depreciation	0	15	15	15	15	15
(=) Gross Cash Flow	0	151	159	167	175	184
(−) Investment Costs	75	0	0	0	0	0
(=) Cash Flow from Operations	(75)	151	159	167	175	184

Net Present Value = 478

Solution: Net present values are additive, so the net present values for each service can be calculated and then summed.

Problem 8.6b: What if one can pick and choose from among the multiple new services in problem 8.6a?

Solution: This allows us to offer only those services that are attractive. From among the alternatives, those with negative *NPV*s can be avoided and the total *NPV* increased by that amount. This has the additional effect of reducing the risk in the total *NPV* (*NPV* is an expected value) because the uncertainty of the cash flows of the avoided services is removed.

Problem 8.6c: What if one can separate out a core service to be provided immediately, then pick and choose *over time* the additional services to provide that are attractive?

Solution: For the core service, the standard approach to NPV applies. To this must be added the value of the options to pursue the additional service opportunities. This requires the use of the Black and Scholes formula for valuing an option that can be exercised at any time before it expires. For a discussion, see R.A. Brealey and S.C. Myers, *Principles of Corporate Finance,* New York: McGraw-Hill, 1988; T.E. Copeland and J.F. Weston, *Financial Theory and Corporate Policy,* Addison-Wesley, 1979; and W.F. Sharpe, *Investments,* Prentice-Hall, 1979.

Problem 8.7: Let's return one more time to our earlier illustration of an office telephone system. What is the net present value of the system? Assume the system life cycle is 5 years, depreciation is straight line, the tax rate is 40%, the opportunity cost of capital is 15%, and maintenance costs will inflate 5% per year. Use the investment and operating costs described in Problem 7.5.

Solution:

Year	0	1	2	3	4	5
Revenues	0	0	0	0	0	0
— Operating Costs	0	(11,000)	(11,150)	(11,308)	(11,473)	(11,647)
— Depreciation	0	4,503	4,503	4,503	4,503	4,503
= Earnings Before Interest and Taxes	0	6,497	6,697	6,805	6,970	7,144
— Taxes	0	2,599	2,659	2,722	2,788	2,858
= Earnings Before Interest but After Taxes	0	3,898	3,988	4,083	4,182	4,286
+ Depreciation	0	4,503	4,503	4,503	4,503	4,503
= Gross Cash Flow	0	8,401	8,491	8,586	8,685	8,789
— Investment Costs	(22,516)	0	0	0	0	0
= Cash Flow from Operations	(22,516)	8,401	8,491	8,586	8,685	8,789

Net Present Value = $6,190

From this result, we can state the following: (1) the system should be installed because the net present value is positive; (2) the degree of impact on wealth is small; (3) the system can be justified on cost savings alone, but no new services are likely to be provided; therefore, it is important our cost estimates be accurate. (Since we have not considered the value of the cost benefits of the additional call handling capabilities of the PBX, we have some margin for error.)

■ NOTES

1. There is a large body of evidence that strongly supports the reliability of this approach to measuring shareholder value and, for this reason, it is adopted here. See *Valuation: Measuring and Managing the Value of Companies;* T. Copeland, T. Koller, and J. Murrin; New York: John Wiley & Sons, 1990; and G. Bennet Stewart III, *The Quest for Value,* New York: HarperCollins, 1991.

2. Gross cash flow from operations less investment costs is also called "free cash flow."

3. This treats depreciation as an accounting matter and not as an actual cost. Though this is standard practice, Warren Buffett has pointed out that depreciation is an economic cost "every bit as real as wages, materials, or taxes." If you are in the business of valuing going concerns, as Buffett is, there is a tendency to overlook early investments in the business that will need to be replenished later. We have chosen to follow the conventional approach, while alerting the reader to this criticism, which is essentially a warning to make sure ongoing investment costs have been fully accounted for. See *Berkshire Hathaway, Inc. Annual Report 1996,* p. 66.

4. J. Poterba and L. Summers, "A CEO Survey of U.S. Companies' Time Horizons and Hurdle Rates," *Sloan Management Review,* Fall, 1995.

5. T. Copeland, T. Koller, and J. Murrin. *Valuation: Measuring and Managing the Value of Companies,* New York: John Wiley & Sons, 1990.

6. See Erich A. Helfert, *Techniques of Financial Analysis,* Chicago: Irwin, 1997, 172–185.

7. The book value of debt can sometimes be nearly the same as the market value of debt. This was true of TCI in 1997 and often holds for debt with floating rates.

8. *Broadcasting and Cable,* February 23, 1998, p. 21.

9. The opposite question—what is the risk the valuations are too high—could also be asked. This is best answered with a break-even analysis, which would show how easily shareholder value could become zero.

Epilogue

In The South Seas there is a cargo cult of people. During the war they saw airplanes land with lots of good materials, and they want the same thing to happen now. So they've arranged to make things like runways, to put fires along the sides of the runways, to make a wooden hut for a man to sit in, with two wooden pieces on his head like headphones and bars of bamboo sticking out like antennas—he's the controller—and they wait for the airplanes to land. They're doing everything right. The form is perfect. It looks exactly the way it looked before. But it doesn't work. No airplanes land. . . . (It is) difficult to explain to the South Sea Islanders how they have to arrange things so that they get some wealth in their system. . . . But there is *one* feature I notice that is generally missing. . . . It's a kind of scientific integrity . . . that corresponds to a kind of utter honesty—a kind of leaning over backwards . . . the first principle is that you must not fool yourself—and you are the easiest person to fool.

—Richard P. Feynman *Surely You're Joking, Mr. Feynman*
(taken from the CalTech commencement
address of 1974)

Do the math.

—Anonymous

There is no doubt that analyzing the economics of information technology systems is hard and complex. This is why the alternative—an intuitive approach—is much more commonly practiced. The track record for the intuitive approach, however, is what you would expect: spotty. It is exacerbated by the human tendency to be overly optimistic, the exaggerated claims of some exponents of the high-tech industry, and management's desire for quick results. Everyone is keenly interested in receiving the rewards that can come with a system design that resonates with the market, and wishful thinking is rampant. The conditions are nearly perfect for lightning to strike.

In this book, we have attempted to describe an analytical approach that lays bare the essentials that management must consider in assessing whether the economics of an information technology system are attractive. This should make decision making more rational, with greater awareness of the rewards and the risks involved in a system investment. The long-term result should be fewer investment mistakes, with capital, labor, and management employed productively. Fundamentally, this book is a tool to solve a class of complex business problems that are being encountered with greater frequency and whose solutions have substantial impact. We hope that in its writing it inspires others to push this work even further. There are several areas where further research is warranted.

Here are six problems in the economic analysis of information technology systems whose solution will advance understanding for the field.

1. How can the accuracy of demand forecasts be improved?

2. What are the mathematical expressions that fully describe the behavior of chained systems where the information rate becomes correlated with the information length?

3. How can the optimal system design be more closely approximated, without having to analyze all possible designs?

4. What cost functions are followed by system components?

5. How can the error limits in the valuation of a system be made more transparent?

6. How can the option value of a system be more easily calculated?

The solutions to these problems require a capacity for sustained effort on the part of the researchers who choose to focus their energies on them. The sole judge of the correctness of their work will be how well they are borne out in practice. I hope the reader will join me in wishing them great success.

Appendix A
Market Research Methods

Step	1. Describe Information Product	2. Select Interviewees	3. Plan Discussion	4. Organize Logistics	5. Conduct Interviews	6. Derive Product Requirements and Demand Levels
Primary Objective	Clearly describe the information product to be assessed.	Identify who will be interviewed.	Determine what questions to ask and how to go about it.	Create a smooth research process.	Obtain the customer's input.	Determine product requirements and estimate demand.
Key Activities	Pick information product. Generate hypothesis on segments, value of features, price, and likelihood to purchase. Write up service description. Create product demonstration, e.g., videotape, prototype/ sample, actual product.	Determine whether to focus on typical customer or to obtain a wide spectrum of views. Lay out profile and number of interviewees desired. Obtain list of candidates. Select interview candidates and summarize in a contact list.	Define information needed and format (phone, face-to-face). Conduct preliminary research to avoid asking unnecessary questions. Write interview guide: – purpose of interview – background questions – feature, price, and likelihood to purchase questions. Conduct dry run. Determine position on matters of confidentiality, sharing of information, etc.	Decide who should conduct interviews, timing/phases. Arrange facilities for phone or face-to-face interviews. Schedule interviews using contact list. Take steps to show appreciation of interviewees' cooperation: – confirm discussion in advance – arrange for any honorariums – write thank-you letter.	Make introductions and explain purpose. Use the interview guide to structure the discussion. Pursue interesting lines of discussion as warranted. End the interview when discussion is no longer productive or if interviewee gives signals. Write up notes from each interview. Send thank-you letter/honorarium.	Lay out the number of interviews completed. Summarize research findings: – focus on how each customer type responded to the issues of features, price, and likelihood to purchase – Illustrate with representative quotations – make additional observations. Develop profile of target segment sizes and scale findings. Correct for service awareness/ penetration levels. Calculate level of demand.
End Result	Product concept description. Hypothesis on segments, features, price, and likelihood to purchase.	Sample designed. Contact list of interview candidates developed.	Interview materials written. Strategy for discussion developed.	Actions, responsibilities, resources, and timing determined.	Data obtained and recorded.	Product description of most promising opportunities. Demand levels determined.

Figure A.1 Interview Methodology.

Step	1. Describe Information Product	2. Retain Market Research Firm	3. Select Interviewees	4. Plan Discussion	5. Organize Logistics	6. Conduct Focus Groups	7. Derive Product Requirements and Demand Levels
Primary Objective		Retain a suitable market research firm.					
Key Activities	See Step 1, Figure A.1.	Draw up list of possible firms. Develop criteria for choosing. Obtain information on suitability through references and proposals submitted. Choose preferred firm. Draw up and sign contract.	See Step 2, Figure A.1 and substitute for the second item: Layout profile and number of groups desired.	See Step 3, Figure A.1 and substitute for the third item: Write moderator guide: – purpose of focus group – background on subject matter and participants – agenda and rules for discussion – feature, price, and likelihood to purchase questions – thought starters to elicit opinions – juxtapositions to avoid premature formation of consensus.	See Step 4, Figure A.1 and substitute for the first item: Decide who should act as moderator. See Step 4, Figure A.1 and add the fifth item: Determine which sessions will be videotaped or observed first-hand.	See Step 5, Figure A.1 and substitute for the second item: Use moderator guide to structure the discussion.	See Step 6, Figure A.1 and substitute for the second item: Illustrate findings with videotape clips, if available.
End Result		Market research firm under contract.					

Figure A.2 Focus Group Methodology.

257

Step	1. Describe Information Product	2. Retain Market Research Firm	3. Select Participants	4. Design Survey	5. Organize Logistics	6. Conduct Survey	7. Derive Product Requirements and Demand Levels
Primary Objective			Identify who will be surveyed			Obtain the customer's input	Determine product requirements and estimate demand.
Key Activities	See Step 1, Figure A.1.	See Step 2, Figure A.2.	Define population of customers to sample from. Lay out profile and number of customer participants desired.	See Step 3, Figure A.1 and substitute fthe word "survey" for "interview."	See Step 4, Figure A.1 and substitute for the second item: Arrange facilities for phone survey or distribution and collection mechanism for written survey. See Step 4, Figure A.1 and substitute for the third item: Schedule administration of survey.	Make written/oral introduction and explain purpose. Instruct participant to complete survey. Provide clarification where necessary. Collect surveys. Deal with errors in responses. Send thank-you letter/honorarium.	Lay out the number of surveys completed. Tabulate, classify and cross-classify the responses. Summarize findings: – focus on how each customer type responded to the issues of features, price, and likelihood to purchase. Develop profile of target segment sizes and scale findings. Correct for service awareness and penetration levels. Calculate level of demand.
End Result			Sample designed. Contact list of survey candidates developed.			Database of results created.	Product description of most promising opportunities. Demand levels determined.

Figure A.3 Survey Methodology.

Step	1. Describe Information Product	2. Retain Market Research Firm	3. Select Participants	4. Design Conjoint	5. Organize Logistics	6. Conduct Conjoint Fieldwork	7. Derive Product Requirements	8. Derive Demand Levels
Primary Objective				Identify the features to be measured and their values.			Determine product requirements.	Develop an estimate of demand.
Key Activities	See Step 1, Figure A.1.	See Step 2, Figure A.2.	See Step 2, Figure A.1.	Specify the product features (e.g., content, format, frequency correctness). Specify values for each feature (e.g., frequency can be hourly, daily, weekly, monthly). Write instruction booklet and questionnaire. Conduct dry run test.	See Step 4, Figure A.1	See Step 5, Figure A.1	Apply heuristics to identify promising feature/value combinations. Calculate regression coefficients and y-intercept. Iterate between above to find the product with the highest likelihood to purchase. Model case where existing products are offered simultaneously with the new product to determine degree of cannibalization. Describe corresponding customer segments.	Lay out the number of conjoint responses completed. Tabulate, classify, and cross-classify the results. Develop profile of target segment sizes and scale findings. Correct for service awareness and penetration. Calculate level of demand: Segment size × Likelihood to purchase × Price paid × Correction factors − Cannibalization = Level of demand
End Result				Conjoint designed.			Product description of most promising opportunity. Customer segments identified. Likelihood to purchase calculated. Degree of cannibalization determined.	Demand levels determined

Figure A.4 Conjoint Analysis Methodology.

Step	1. Develop Sample of Information Product	2. Retain Market Research Firm	3. Select Test Subjects/ Locations	4. Plan Measurements	5. Organize Logistics	6. Conduct Market Test	7. Derive Product Requirements and Demand Levels
Primary Objective	Create physical version of product in sample quantity.		Identify who will participate and where.	Determine what observations to make and how to go about it.	Create a smooth research process.	Obtain data on customer behavior.	
Key Activities	Determine product requirements. Develop detailed design. Build protype. Qualify and test. Manufacture sample quantity. Establish service capability.	Optional. See Step 2, Figure A.2.	Define population of customers to sample from. Lay out profile and number of customers/locations desired. Obtain list of candidates. Select participants and sites and summarize in a contact list.	Define information needed: – profile of participants – reaction to features – purchase intention – price paid. Decide best mechanism for making measurements: – observations – interviews – duration of test. Lay out observation process and write interview guide. Conduct dry run test. Determine position on matters of confidentiality, sharing of information, etc.	Decide who should be responsible for what; timing. Develop distribution mechanism for responding to orders and delivery. Establish working production process. Create measurement tracking and reporting system. Debug.	Explain test to participants as needed. Follow the observation process and interview guide. Vary parameters of test such as features, price, to gauge effect on purchase behavior. Monitor progress and end test as appropriate. Build database.	See Step 6, Figure A.1, substituting "market tests" for "interviews."
End Result	Sample of product manufactured and supported		Test subjects/ locations chosen Contact list of market test candidates developed	Observation process described with interview materials written Strategy for measurements developed	Actions, responsibilities, resources, and timing determined. Distribution, production, and tracking mechanisms in place.	Data obtained and recorded.	

Figure A.5   Market Test Methodology.

Step	1. Develop Sample of Information Product	2. Retain Market Research Firm	3. Select Target Market	4. Plan Measurements	5. Organize Logistics	6. Launch Product	7. Derive Product Requirements and Demand Levels
Primary Objective			Identify the target customers and locations.			Obtain data on customer behavior.	
Key Activities	See Step 1, Figure A.5, replacing "sample" with "production quantity."	Optional. See Step 2, Figure A.2.	Define population of customers to target. Lay out profile of most attractive customers/ locations. Obtain list of prospects. Select target customers and locations and summarize in a contact list for sales force. Describe adjacent markets that may also show interest to sales.	See Step 4, Figure A.5.	See Step 5, Figure A.5, and add: Develop plan for withdrawal of product from market if introduction is unsuccessful.	Prepare for introduction: – manufacturing – distribution – marketing – sales – service. Follow the observation process and interview guide. Vary parameters of test such as features, price to gauge effect on purchase behavior. Monitor progress and end test as appropriate. Build database.	See Step 6, Figure A.1, focusing on prospects reached.
End Result			Target customers/ locations chosen. Contact list for sales developed.			Data obtained and recorded.	

Figure A.6 Product Introduction Methodology.

Appendix B

Selected Probability Distributions

Continuous Distributions

Uniform [min, max]: Uniform distribution on the interval [min, max]. Used as a first approximation for a random variable when only its range is known.

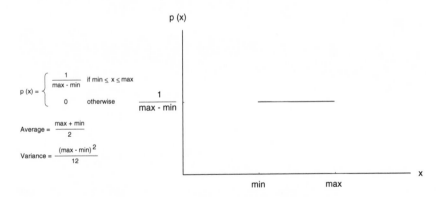

$$p(x) = \begin{cases} \dfrac{1}{max - min} & \text{if } min \leq x \leq max \\ 0 & \text{otherwise} \end{cases}$$

$$\text{Average} = \frac{max + min}{2}$$

$$\text{Variance} = \frac{(max - min)^2}{12}$$

Negative Exponential [μ]: Negative exponential distribution with scale parameter μ. Used for service times where the probability of completion during a small time interval is directly proportional to the length of the interval and independent of all other intervals.

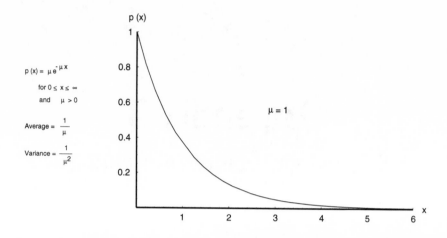

$$p(x) = \mu e^{-\mu x}$$

for $0 \le x \le \infty$
and $\mu > 0$

Average $= \dfrac{1}{\mu}$

Variance $= \dfrac{1}{\mu^2}$

Normal Distribution [μ, σ]: Normal distribution with average μ and standard deviation σ. Describes the distribution of the mean of a large number of random variables that follow any distribution with bounded variance, according to the Central Limit Theorem.

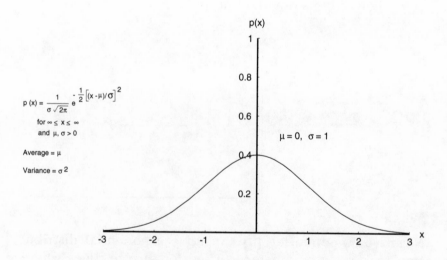

$$p(x) = \frac{1}{\sigma \sqrt{2\pi}} e^{-\frac{1}{2}\left[(x - \mu)/\sigma\right]^2}$$

for $\infty \le x \le \infty$
and $\mu, \sigma > 0$

Average $= \mu$

Variance $= \sigma^2$

Erlang - M ([μ, M]: Erlang - M distribution with parameters μ, M. Used to describe the service time for a system with M stages where the time taken for each stage is exponentially distributed, with the same average value, and service begins only after all stages have been cleared.

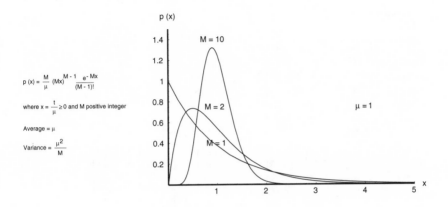

Triangular Distribution [min, max, mode]: Triangular distribution on the interval [min, max] with mode the location of the center of the data, specifically the value that occurs most often. Used as a first approximation for a random variable when only its range and mode are known.

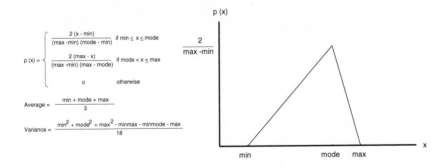

Note: p(x) is a probability density function, with $p(x)\Delta x$ the probability that x falls in the interval Δx.

Discrete Distributions

Discrete Uniform [j, k]: Discrete uniform distribution among the integer values between j and k. Used as a first approximation for a random variable that can assume integer values between j, k.

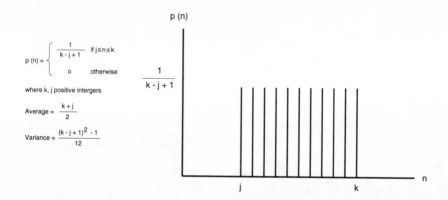

$$p(n) = \begin{cases} \dfrac{1}{k-j+1} & \text{if } j \le n \le k \\ 0 & \text{otherwise} \end{cases}$$

where k, j positive intergers

$$\text{Average} = \frac{k+j}{2}$$

$$\text{Variance} = \frac{(k-j+1)^2 - 1}{12}$$

Geometric [p]: Geometric distribution with parameter p. Similar to the negative exponential distribution.

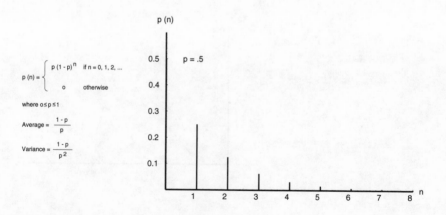

$$p(n) = \begin{cases} p(1-p)^n & \text{if } n = 0, 1, 2, \dots \\ 0 & \text{otherwise} \end{cases}$$

where $0 \le p \le 1$

$$\text{Average} = \frac{1-p}{p}$$

$$\text{Variance} = \frac{1-p}{p^2}$$

Poisson [λ,t]: Poisson distribution with rate parameter λ. Used when independent events occur at a constant rate.

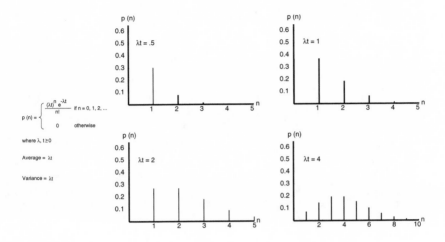

$$p(n) = \begin{cases} \dfrac{(\lambda t)^n e^{-\lambda t}}{n!} & \text{if } n = 0, 1, 2, \dots \\ 0 & \text{otherwise} \end{cases}$$

where $\lambda, t \geq 0$

Average $= \lambda t$

Variance $= \lambda t$

Appendix C
Selected Queuing System Results

The equations describing the utilization, throughput, and time spent in a system are often very complicated and hard to use. Systems and formulas shown have been selected based on a subjective assessment of the insight gained per unit effort.

Utilization (ρ): The server utilization is the ratio of the actual load on the server to its capacity.

Throughput (γ): The throughput of a system with an infinite queue is equal to the information arrival rate, $\gamma_{avg} = \lambda_{avg}$, since no blocking can occur. For systems with finite queues, the throughput is equal to the number of arrivals minus the number blocked, per unit time, or $\gamma_{avg} = \lambda_{avg} (1 - P_B)$, where P_B is the probability of blocking.

Time Spent Waiting for Service (T_{wait}): The time spent waiting for service in the queue, T_{wait}, plus the service time, $1/\mu$, equals the total time spent in the system. The final objective in the investigation of systems with delay is always the probability distribution of the time spent in the system. The expressions for the probability distribution of the time spent in the system are complex, so we focus here instead on the time spent waiting for service that provides much insight and expressions of greater simplicity.

Kendall Notation:

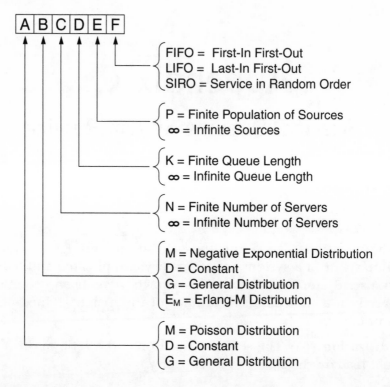

A B C D E F

FIFO = First-In First-Out
LIFO = Last-In First-Out
SIRO = Service in Random Order

P = Finite Population of Sources
∞ = Infinite Sources

K = Finite Queue Length
∞ = Infinite Queue Length

N = Finite Number of Servers
∞ = Infinite Number of Servers

M = Negative Exponential Distribution
D = Constant
G = General Distribution
E_M = Erlang-M Distribution

M = Poisson Distribution
D = Constant
G = General Distribution

References

Kleinrock, L. *Queueing Systems Volume I: Theory,* New York: John Wiley & Sons, 1975.

Tanner, M. *Practical Queueing, Analysis,* New York: McGraw-Hill, 1995.

Gross, D. and Harris, C. *Fundamentals of Queueing Theory,* 2nd ed. New York: John Wiley & Sons, 1985.

Bellamy, J. *Digital Telephony.* New York: John Wiley & Sons, 1991.

M/D/1:

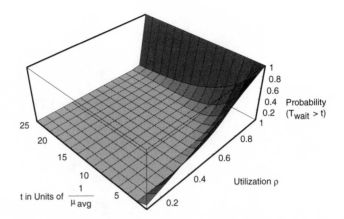

$$\rho = \frac{\lambda_{avg}}{\mu_{avg}}$$

$$\gamma_{avg} = \lambda_{avg}$$

$$\text{Probability } (T_{wait} > t) = 1 - (1 - \rho) \sum_{k=0}^{n} \frac{(k - \mu_{avg}t)^k \rho^k e^{-\rho(k - \mu_{avg}t)}}{k!}$$

where n is defined as the integer part of $\mu_{avg} t$

$$\text{Average Value } (T_{wait}) = \frac{\rho}{2\mu_{avg}(1 - \rho)}$$

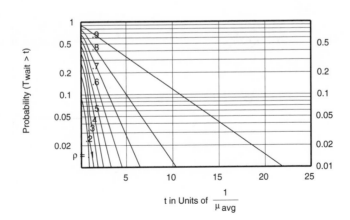

M/M/1:

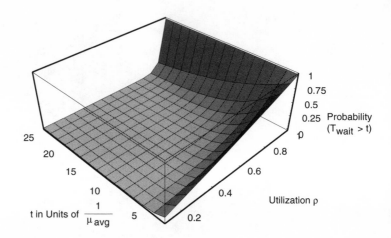

$$\rho = \frac{\lambda_{avg}}{\mu_{avg}}$$

$$\gamma_{avg} = \lambda_{avg}$$

Probability $(T_{wait} > t) = \rho e^{-\mu_{avg}(1-\rho)t}$

Average Value $(T_{wait}) = \dfrac{\rho}{\mu_{avg}(1-\rho)}$

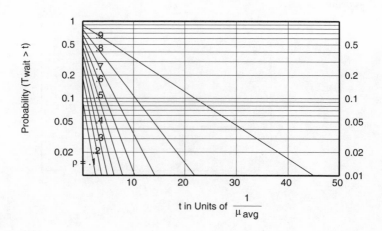

M/M/N:

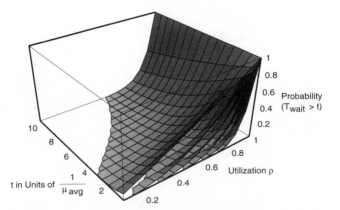

$$\rho = \frac{\lambda_{avg}}{N\mu_{avg}}$$

$$\gamma_{avg} = \lambda_{avg}$$

Probability $(T_{wait} > t) = E_{2,N}(N\rho)\, e^{-N(1-\rho)\mu_{avg}t}$

where $E_{2,N}(r)$ is Erlang - C formula which is defined as

$$E_{2,N}(r) = \frac{\dfrac{r^N}{N!}}{\dfrac{r^N}{N!} + (1 - \dfrac{r}{N}) \displaystyle\sum_{k=0}^{N-1} \dfrac{r^k}{k!}}$$

Average Value $(T_{wait}) = \dfrac{E_{2,N}(N\rho)}{N\mu_{avg}(1-\rho)}$

Curves shown correspond to ρ = .1, ..., .9 in the following plots.

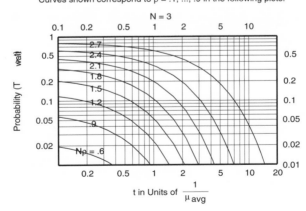

Curves shown correspond to ρ = .1, ..., .9 in the following plots.

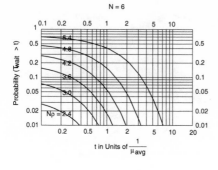

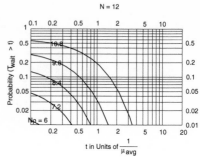

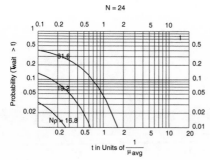

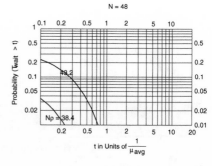

Glossary of Notation

Symbol	Definition
English	
M	Negative exponential distribution
D	Constant value
G	General distribution
E_M	Erlang-M distribution
N	Number of servers
K	Queue length
P	Number of sources
C,c	Capacity of device (continuous)
T_{wait}	Time spent waiting for service in the queue
P_B	Probability of blocking
t	Time
$E_{2,N}(r)$	Erlang-C formula
BSBH	Busy season, busy hour
K	Number of time intervals
t_f	Final time
t_m	Midpoint time
n_a	Number of arrivals
n_d	Number of departures
N_a	Cumulative number of arrivals
N_d	Cumulative number of departures
N_b	Cumulative number backed up
T_{backup}	Backup time
t_0	Initial time
L	Information length

Symbol	*Definition*
CCS	Hundred call seconds
bps	Bits per second
M	Million
k	Thousand
G	Billion
Hz	Hertz, same as cycles per second
tps	Transactions per second
MIPS	Millions of instructions per second
cps	Characters per second
V_f	Number of possible values of feature f
V_p	Number of possible prices
f	A feature
F	Total number of features

Greek

λ_{avg}	Average information arrival rate
μ_{avg}	Average information service rate, same as average server capacity
λ	Information arrival rate
μ	Information service rate, same as server capacity
γ_{avg}	Average throughput
γ	Throughput
ϕ	Information flux
ϕ_{in}	Incoming information flux
ϕ_{out}	Outgoing information flux
ρ	Server utilization
κ	Total number of time intervals
ψ	Information structure
Σ	Sum

Bibliography

Chapter 1

Hall, P. *Great Planning Disasters.* Berkeley: University of California Press, 1980.

Chapter 2

Porter, M.E. *Competitive Strategy.* New York: Free Press, 1980.

Porter, M.E. *Competitive Advantage.* New York: Free Press, 1985.

Vogel, H.L. *Entertainment Industry Economics.* Cambridge, England: Cambridge University Press, 1988.

Chapter 3

Albaum, G., Green, P., and Tull, D. *Research for Marketing Decisions.* Englewood Cliffs, NJ: Prentice Hall, 1988.

Arthur, B.W. *Increasing Returns and Path Dependence in the Economy.* Ann Arbor: University of Michigan Press, 1994.

Day, G.S., Reibstein, D.J., and Gunther, R.E., Eds. *Wharton on Dynamic Competitive Strategy.* New York: John Wiley & Sons, Inc., 1997.

Foster, D. *Innovation.* New York: Summit Books, 1986.

Rogers, E.M. *Diffusion of Innovations.* New York: Free Press, 1962.

Tufte, E. *The Visual Display of Quantitative Information.* Cheshire, CT: Graphics Press, 1983.

Whiteley, R. *The Customer Driven Company.* Reading, MA: Addison-Wesley, 1991.

Chapter 4

Gates, B. *Customer-Driven Companies: First Systems, Then Instincts.* Microsoft Corporation, August 13, 1996.

Kotler, P. *Marketing Management.* Englewood Cliffs, NJ: Prentice Hall, 1980.

Moore, G.A. *Crossing the Chasm.* New York: HarperBusiness, 1991.

Schnaars, S. *Megamistakes: Forecasting and the Myth of Rapid Technological Change.* New York: Free Press, 1989.

von Hippel, E. *The Sources of Innovation.* New York: Oxford University Press, 1988.

Chapter 5

Armstrong, A., and Hagel, J. *Net Gain.* Boston: HBS Press, 1997.

Bellamy, J. *Digital Telephony.* New York: John Wiley & Sons, Inc., 1991.

Bertsekas, D., and Gallager, R. *Data Networks.* Englewood Cliffs, NJ: Prentice Hall, 1992.

Comnet III User's Manual, La Jolla, CA: CACI Products Company, 1997.

Gross, D., and Harris, C. *Fundamentals of Queueing Theory,* 2nd ed. New York: John Wiley & Sons, Inc., 1985.

Harnett, D.L. *Introduction to Statistical Methods.* Reading, MA: Addison-Wesley, 1975.

Kelton, W., and Law, A. *Simulation Modeling and Analysis.* New York: McGraw-Hill, 1991.

Khintchine, A.Y. *Mathematical Methods in the Theory of Queueing.* Hafner, 1969.

Kleinrock, L. *Queueing Systems, Volumes 1, 2.* New York: John Wiley & Sons, Inc., 1975, 1976.

McComas, M., and Law, A. "Simulation Software for Communications Networks: The State of the Art." *IEEE Communications Magazine,* March 1994.

Meijer, A., and Peeters, P. *Computer Network Architectures.* London: Pitman, 1982.

Rayport, J.F., and Sviokla, J. "Exploiting the Virtual Value Chain." *Harvard Business Review,* November–December 1995.

Rey, R.F. *Engineering and Operations in the Bell System.* Murray Hill, NJ: AT&T Bell Laboratories, 1989.

Schwartz, M. *Telecommunications Networks.* Reading, MA: Addison-Wesley, 1987.

Tanner, M. *Practical Queueing Analysis.* New York: McGraw-Hill, 1995.

Wolfram, S. *The Mathematica Book,* 3rd ed. Cambridge, England: Wolfram Media/Cambridge University Press, 1996.

Wurman, R.S. *Information Architects.* New York: Graphics Inc., 1997.

Chapter 6

Bell, C.G., McNamara, J.E., and Mudge, J.C. *Computer Engineering.* Bedford, MA: Digital Press, 1978.

Boehm, B. *Software Engineering Economics.* Englewood Cliffs, NJ: Prentice Hall, 1981.

Chiddix, J.A., and Pangrac, D.M. *Fiber Backbone: A Proposal for an Evolutionary CATV Network Architecture.* 1988 NCTA Technical Papers.

Conway, L., and Mead, C. *Introduction to VLSI Systems.* Reading, MA: Addison-Wesley, 1980.

Feynman, R.P. *The Feynman Lectures on Computation.* Reading, MA: Addison-Wesley, 1996.

Harnett, D.L. *The Computer Glossary.* Reading, MA: Addison-Wesley, 1995.

Haskell, B., and Netravali, A. *Digital Pictures.* New York: Plenum, 1988.

Lorin, H. *Aspects of Distributed Computer Systems.* New York: John Wiley & Sons, Inc., 1988.

Patterson, D., and Hennessy, J. *Computer Architecture: A Quantitative Approach,* 2nd ed. San Mateo, CA: Morgan Kauffmann, 1996.

Chapter 7

Brooks, F.P., Jr. *The Mythical Man Month.* Reading, MA: Addison-Wesley, 1975.

Horngren, C.T. *Cost Accounting.* Englewood Cliffs, NJ: Prentice Hall, 1977.

Chapter 8

Amram, M., and Kulatilaka, N. *Real Options: Managing Strategic Investment in an Uncertain World.* Boston: HBS Press, 1998.

Bennett, S.G., III. *The Quest for Value.* New York: HarperBusiness, 1991.

Brealey, R.A., and Myers, S.C. *Principles of Corporate Finance.* New York: McGraw-Hill, 1988.

Copeland, T.E., Murrin, J., and Koller, T. *Valuation.* New York: John Wiley & Sons, Inc., 1991.

Copeland, T.E., and Weston, J.P. *Financial Theory and Corporate Policy.* Reading, MA: Addison-Wesley, 1979.

Helfert, E.A. *Techniques of Financial Analysis.* Chicago: Irwin, 1997.

Jensen, M.C. "Agency Costs of Free Cost Flow, Corporate Finance, and Takeovers." *AEA Papers and Proceedings,* Vol. 76, No. 2, May 1986.

Jordan, B.D., Ross, S., and Westerfield, R.W. *Fundamentals of Corporate Finance,* 4th ed. Chicago: Irwin McGraw-Hill, 1998.

Kishimoto, N. "Pricing Contingent Claims under Interest Rate and Asset Price Risk." *Journal of Finance,* Vol. XLIV, No. 3, July 1989.

Schaefer, S.M. "Immunization and Duration: A Review of Theory, Performance, and Applications." *Midland Corporate Finance Journal,* Vol. 2, No. 3, Fall 1984.

Shareholder Value Management, Boston: The Boston Consulting Group, 1996, 1997.

Sharpe, W.F. *Investments.* Englewood Cliffs, NJ: Prentice Hall, 1978.

Van Horne, C. *Financial Management and Policy.* Englewood Cliffs, NJ: Prentice Hall, 1977.

Epilogue

Kauffman, S. *At Home in the Universe.* New York: Oxford University Press, 1995.

Townsend, R. *Up the Organization.* New York: Fawcett Crest, 1970.

Index

About the Author

Christopher Gardner is a management consultant. Born in Los Angeles in 1957, he was educated at the Bronx High School of Science and the University of Chicago where he received his BS in Physics in 1979 and an MBA in Finance a year later in 1980. He spent his summers working at Fermilab and at the Enrico Fermi Institute. After graduation, he joined the Digital Equipment Corporation where he worked as a manager in the semiconductor, office workstation, and VAX computer system development groups, from 1980 to 1988. With the support of Digital, he cofounded The Software Agency in 1984, a company engaged in the business of representing software authors to software publishers. He became a management consultant first for McKinsey & Company from 1989–1992 where he was an information technology specialist. He continued consulting at A.T. Kearney from 1992–1995 where he was elected principal by the board of directors, and moved from there to Bain & Company from 1996–1997 where he was a vice president. He is currently a partner at PricewaterhouseCoopers LLP, where he leads the Information Technology Strategy Group in the New York office. He can be reached at christophergardner.com.